The Role of the Military Professional in U. S. Foreign Policy

Donald F. Bletz

The Praeger Special Studies program—utilizing the most modern and efficient book production techniques and a selective worldwide distribution network—makes available to the academic, government, and business communities significant, timely research in U.S. and international economic, social, and political development.

The Role of the Military Professional in U. S. Foreign Policy

PRAEGER SPECIAL STUDIES IN U.S. ECONOMIC AND SOCIAL DEVELOPMENT

Praeger Publishers   New York   Washington   London

PRAEGER PUBLISHERS
111 Fourth Avenue, New York, N.Y. 10003, U.S.A.
5, Cromwell Place, London S.W.7, England

Published in the United States of America in 1972
by Praeger Publishers, Inc.

Library of Congress Catalog Card Number: 71-170468

Printed in the United States of America

This study is respectfully dedicated
to my colleagues in the American
military profession

And is anything more important
than that the work of the
soldier should be done well?

Plato, <u>The Republic</u>

Through the years, the role of the military
professional in the United States has been a changing one. During World War II--and especially since
then--the American military officer has become more
intimately associated with the formulation of foreign policy while continuing in his role as implementer of that policy when his particular expertise
is required. The cold war, which came closely on
the heels of the termination of hostilities in 1945,
placed new and unfamiliar responsibilities on the
professional officer. Now a "new era" in international affairs is dawning, and even greater demands
are being made on the nation's military profession.

The purpose of this study is to identify the
extent to which the professional military officer
has entered into the field of foreign affairs, to
evaluate the effect of this changing role on the
military profession, and to conceptualize some potential broad courses of action for the military
profession. The task is approached by examining
American military professionalism as it existed from
the nation's early history through World War II and
the cold war to the present. The complex politico-
military bureaucracy and its associated bureaucratic
machinery is examined. The proliferation of staff
agencies both in the Departments of State and Defense and in the White House, whose stated purpose
is to balance the politico-military equation, is reviewed in the context of the fact that the term
politico-military has become very much a part of
the Washington lexicon and can be expected to continue as an area of grave concern.

In an effort to identify further what has come
to pass as a result of the politico-military revolution, the vast military educational system is

examined from the point of view of its preparation
of the professional officer in the field of politico-
military affairs. The need for constantly increased
politico-military expertise on the part of the professional officer is noted as is the conflicting requirement for ever-increasing technical knowledge
by the same professional. A conceptual approach
that identifies "levels of professionalism" is developed in association with the review of military
education.

Militarism and the military mind are used as
vehicles for studying how the American body politic
thinks about military matters and how military men
think about international political matters. Militarism in a democracy is a real possibility and is
a threat to the democracy itself. The very socio-
political nature of American democracy contributes
to the possibility. There is, for example, a
military-industrial complex in the United States.
It is inherent in a highly democratic, highly technically developed society. To passionately decry
its existence or to coldly dismiss it as only a nonexistent fabrication are equally foolish. If it
can be understood, it can be controlled and a reasonable politico-military balance in the United
States depends on this sort of understanding.

The essential differences between the international environment that "was," that "is" now, and
that likely "will be," develop from an examination
of the elusive concept of victory. Clearly identifying what needs to be done--stating the objective--
has become an extremely critical issue. Unconditional surrender of the enemy is no longer, by itself, a meaningful objective, but if military force
is used and no clear political objective is assigned,
military victory will become an end in itself. The
politico-military equation constructed in the ab-
sence of a political objective will become excessive-
ly weighted with military consideration. It is suggested that the professional military officer must
understand these distinctions and conduct himself
accordingly. It is not enough for the military

professional to be able to recommend the intelligent application of military force--he must be equally prepared to recommend its nonuse when he sees an imbalance in the politico-military equation developing.

This study has been something over five years in preparation during which time the author, a professional military officer, spent two years on duty in the Pentagon and a year and a half in Vietnam. While those three and one half years were not conducive to preparation of an academic study, they do represent a spectrum of experience in politico-military affairs that has proven invaluable. The rest of the five years was spent at The National War College in Washington and at the Center for International Affairs at Harvard University. These latter experiences were most conducive to academic endeavors and the bulk of the actual writing was done during these periods.

The author has been a soldier since 1943 and has served in grades from private soldier to colonel. He accepts second place to none in pride of his chosen profession and at the same time admits to being one of its sharpest critics. In this study, especially in the final chapter, there are some rather severe criticisms of the American military profession. They are made in a constructive sense and it is hoped they will be received in that light.

The increasing role of the American professional military officer in the foreign policy process has presented unique problems for the foreign policy planner and for the professional military officer as well. The effects of this phenomenon on the nation's foreign policy, on its military policy, and on its very security is of vital concern to all Americans. Particularly in light of the wave of antimilitary feeling now sweeping the country, it is sincerely hoped that this study will, in some small way, contribute to a better understanding of this vital segment of American life by interesting others to further investigate the problem areas identified.

In the final analysis it is the United States Army, which made possible a period of graduate study in the mid-1960's and an additional period in academe in the early 1970's, that provided the incentive and the time to undertake the effort. To the army and the Department of Defense must also go the credit for permitting the open publication of this study despite its sometimes critical content. The views of the author do not purport to reflect the position of the Department of the Army or the Department of Defense. For the errors and omissions, the author, of course, assumes full responsibility.

ACKNOWLEDGMENTS

Above all, I wish to express my sincere appreciation to Durward V. Sandifer, Professor Emeritus of International Relations at The American University, for his stimulating seminar on national security policy that provided the initial inspiration for this study some years ago. I am also indebted to Professor Sandifer for his patience, understanding, and encouragement over the subsequent years, which eventually led to this publication.

A sincere thanks is also offered to my colleagues at The American University School of International Service and the Harvard University Center for International Affairs for their many comments and suggestions on various parts of this effort.

A brief word of acknowledgment is inadequate to express my appreciation to countless officials, both civilian and military, of the Departments of State and Defense who somehow found time in their busy schedules to discuss various aspects of the study with me. A sincere thanks is also offered to those many military colleagues who took the time to reply to written questionnaires distributed at various stages of research.

For many hours of reading, checking, correcting, and suggesting on the final manuscript, and for taking on the unpleasant but essential chore of preparing an index I am indebted to my daughter, Susan D. Bletz.

CONTENTS

The Role of the Military Professional in U. S. Foreign Policy

1

INTRODUCTION

Shortly after the close of World War II, the military profession of the United States found itself engaged in a role for which it had not been prepared by experience, education, or temperament. For a brief moment, at the end of the war, it appeared that the military profession would fade into the background as it had following other wars in which American military might had been mobilized. The trend in this direction was actually under way in the form of massive demobilization and general dismemberment of the mightiest military machine the world had ever known. The rather general consensus of American opinion seemed to be that the military profession had accomplished its assigned mission-- the winning of the war--and it was now time for civilian leadership again to assume control and maintain the "peace" that had been won.

Suddenly, or so it seemed to most Americans, it was evident that the peace they sought was not to become a reality and that a continued strong military posture would be a necessity. The existence of a large military establishment, in times other than war, presented new and challenging problems to the civilian officials of the government as well as to the professional military officers. This

was something new; the nation had no experience in
it; the United States was unsure of the ground on
which it was treading; and no one knew where it
would all lead. Although it was probably recognized
by only a few of the more astute thinkers at the
time, the entire American concept of politico-
military relationships in general and military professionalism in particular was no longer completely
valid. The basic problem, then, was that the old
and familiar conceptual foundations that had historically dictated the role of the military profession in the national policy-making procedure had
been suddenly swept away by the cold war.

If the historic underpinnings had been removed
and the old concepts were no longer capable of fulfilling the requirement, what then was to take their
place? Since the close of World War II, and more so
since President Eisenhower's farewell address in
which he warned of the presence of "an immense military establishment and a large arms industry," there
has been much ink spilled over the subject. Most of
the writing, although expressing widely divergent
views, has been sincere and responsible and has contributed significantly to mutual understanding.
Some, however, has been dangerously irresponsible
and has succeeded only in creating mutual distrust
between civilian and military authority and between
the government and elements of American society.
The prolonged U.S. military involvement in Vietnam
has significantly aggravated the situation.

In order to develop intelligently the problem
suggested by the title of this study it is perhaps
wise to define the terms used.

Responsible writers do not agree on the specifics of the term military professionalism. However, there seems to be enough general agreement so
that a working definition can be constructed without great difficulty.

Webster defines military as: "Of or pertaining to soldiers, arms, or war;..." The same source

defines <u>profession</u> as: "The occupation, if not commercial, mechanical, agricultural, or the like, to
which one devotes oneself; a calling; as the profession of arms,..."

The fall 1963 issue of <u>Daedalus</u> was entitled
"The Professions," and in one of the articles the
following observation was made: "Professionals
<u>profess</u>. They profess to know better than others
the nature of certain matters, and to know better
than their clients what ails them and their affairs."[1]

Samuel P. Huntington devotes a full chapter in
<u>The Soldier and the State</u> to "Officership as a Pro-
fession." He says "the modern officer corps is a
professional body and the modern military officer
is a professional man." He further states that
"the distinguishing characteristics of a profession
as a special style of vocation are its expertise,
responsibility, and corporateness."[2] Morris Janowitz offers the following definition of the military professional: "In broadest terms, the professional soldier can be defined as a person who has
made the military establishment the locus of his
career."[3] The expression <u>professional soldier</u> as
used by Janowitz is generic and includes the professional officer of all the armed services. It is
used in the same sense throughout this study.

In an article published several years after
<u>The Soldier and the State</u>, Huntington expressed the
following view of the military profession:

> Not all officers are professional mili-
> tary officers. The professional mili-
> tary officer is distinguished from
> other officers by his skill and by his
> commitment.... Many officers are spe-
> cialists--albeit relatively primitive
> ones--in the management of violence, but
> they have no commitment to officership
> as a career. Others make a career out
> of officership but specialize in skills
> not directly related to the management

of violence. Some officers possess
neither military skill nor career
commitment. Quite obviously all four
types of officers are essential to
the modern officer corps....[4]

Huntington's expression "the management of violence"
is borrowed from Harold D. Lasswell who coined the
term some years ago. Lasswell used the expression
to describe some of the methods that could be used
by the ruling elites of the garrison state in managing the affairs of the state. To the military
establishment he assigned the role of management of
"violence."[5] More recently a British soldier, Sir
John Hackett, defined the function of the profession
of arms in a democratic society as "the ordered application of force in the resolution of a social
problem."[6] While Hackett's definition is certainly
more palatable it is also considerably more descriptive.

Huntington's comment emphasizes the complex
composition of the contemporary officer corps and
illustrates the difficulty of attempting to draw a
hard, clear line between the professional officer
and his brother in uniform who does not so qualify.
In the article from which the above quotation is
taken, Huntington asserts that just under one half
of the officer corps in the United States comprise
the military profession.

By combining the thoughts expressed in the preceding paragraphs an initial working definition can
be constructed. For the purpose of this study then,
the military professional is defined simply as the
career officer who devotes himself to the expertise,
responsibility, and corporateness of the profession
of arms. Of particular importance is the fact that
the definition of the military professional excludes
the civilian official of the defense establishment.
It is interesting to note, however, that the United
States has developed a group of highly competent
civilians who have made a career, or at least a partial career, of national defense. It would be

difficult indeed to find many flag or general officers* who have as much experience in national-level
defense planning as have many of the civilians in
high places in the Department of Defense. At the
national level it would be equally difficult to find
the depth of experience in an officer in uniform
that is found in many career civil servants in the
military establishment. Many of these civilians
are true professionals to whom the nation and the
armed forces owe a debt of gratitude. The role of
the professional military "civilian" in the shaping
of the nation's military and foreign policy is an
area that deserves research in depth. For the purpose of this study, however, it suffices to recognize the existence of this group while limiting the
effort to consideration of the professional military officer.

     The adjective <u>politico-military</u>, or variations
of it, is very much a part of the lexicon of the
contemporary American policy maker. It is virtually impossible to find a dissertation on contemporary
U.S. foreign policy in which some variation of the
term is not used. All too often it is used without
a clear understanding of what it is all about. In
this study the expression denotes <u>the coming together of the purely political and the purely military points of view with the ultimate aim of effect-
ing the integration of the nation's foreign policy
and its military policy</u>.

     The expression <u>politico-military equation</u> ap-
pears throughout the study. It suggests the appropriate insertion of political and military considerations into the thought processes in a given situation in light of <u>all</u> factors relevant to that situation. A properly balanced politico-military equation may, for example, be weighted heavily with
political considerations in one situation, with

---

     *This refers to officers who have attained the
rank of admiral or general in their respective service.

military considerations in another, and possibly be
equally weighted in yet another.

Through the years the role of the military professional in the United States has been a changing
one. Especially since World War II the professional
military officer has become more intimately associated with the dynamics of formulation and constant
reevaluation of the nation's foreign policy as well
as continuing in his more traditional role as implementer of that policy when his particular expertise
was required for that purpose. The so-called cold
war, which came closely on the heels of the end of
hostilities in 1945, placed new and unfamiliar responsibilities on the professional military officer
and on the civilian official as well. For the most
part, neither was adequately prepared to assume
those responsibilities.

The increasing role of the military officer in
the foreign policy areas has essentially added a
new dimension to military professionalism in the
United States. Current literature on the subject
suggests conflicting conclusions as to the requirement for the military professional to become involved in this new dimension. It further suggests
differing views on the effect of this involvement
on the military profession itself.

There is one school of thought that argues
that a return to a more traditional form of military professionalism is in the national interest
because the military establishment is becoming diluted and is less capable of performing its basic
"fighting" mission as a consequence. In a sense,
the argument is that a broad professional base is
being sought at the expense of military technical
proficiency. Another school of thought suggests
that the realities of the current and anticipated
international environment make this new dimension
an absolute necessity. Without it, it is argued,
the nation will be ill served.

It is the overall objective of this study to examine in detail the extent to which the requirements

of this new dimension have impacted on the military
profession in order to make a valid judgment on the
degree to which the national interest is being
served and to recommend courses of action for the
future.

In order to place American politico-military
conceptual thinking, at the outset of the cold war,
in a common perspective, a brief historical review
of the period from the turn of the century through
World War II is provided in Chapter 2. Chapter 3
examines the quarter century from the initiation of
the cold war to the present in greater detail to
identify the major trends in the integration of U.S.
military and foreign policies, and to identify the
sources of much of our contemporary politico-
military thinking. In Chapters 4 and 5 the contemporary politico-military balance is examined
from the point of view of certain institutionalized
manifestations of the currently accepted concepts.
In this, primary emphasis is placed on organizational and educational developments which are especially
applicable to the role of the professional military
officer in the national security policy-making process. Two emotionally charged concepts, "militarism" and the "military mind," are examined in Chapter 6 in an effort to evaluate how Americans think
about things military and how American military professionals think about the nation. The relation of
both to the politico-military equation is suggested.
The meaning of "win" in the contemporary international environment and its application in politico-
military matters is addressed in Chapter 7. Chapter
8 serves the threefold purpose of summarizing the
many factors touched on in the study, of venturing
a look into the future, and of making some rather
general recommendations for the nation's military
profession in the decade ahead.

                          NOTES

     1. Everett C. Hughes, "Professions," Daedalus,
Fall, 1963, p. 565.

10 THE ROLE OF THE MILITARY PROFESSIONAL

2. Samuel P. Huntington, The Soldier and the State (Cambridge, Mass.: The Belknap Press, 1959), pp. 7-8.

3. Morris Janowitz, The Professional Soldier (New York: The Free Press of Glencoe, 1960), p. 54.

4. Samuel P. Huntington, "Power, Expertise and the Military Profession," Daedalus, Fall, 1963, pp. 785-86.

5. Harold D. Lasswell, The Analysis of Political Behavior (New York: Oxford University Press, 1949), p. 152.

6. Sir John Hackett, The Profession of Arms (London: Times Publishing Company, 1962), p. 3.

Military professionalism was late in developing in the United States. Late at least in comparison with most of the Western European nations. Most writers seem to agree that this was due primarily to the basic political philosophy of Americans from colonial times to the present. For that matter, to this day many Americans are thoroughly convinced that there is something inherently sinister about the military and that the more "professional" the military happens to be, the more sinister it is.

William G. Carleton, Professor Emeritus of History and Political Science at the University of Florida, expressed it as follows:

> Pre-twentieth-century Americans had
> strong feelings against military pro-
> fessionalism. Their regular army was
> little more than a token force. They
> despised conscription, and until the
> Civil War they rejected it. Even in
> the Civil War the draftees were sec-
> ondary to the volunteers. In fight-
> ing their wars, Americans traditional-
> ly relied on voluntary and temporary
> military service.[1]

PRE-TWENTIETH CENTURY

Before the Revolutionary War, each of the thirteen colonies had its own militia. While universal military service was poorly enforced, all males from sixteen to sixty were, theoretically at least, subject to service in the militia. The militia turned in a respectable performance in quelling disturbances and fighting local Indians, but when it came to operating against the more sophisticated Spanish and French forces in the late seventeenth and eighteenth centuries the need for a more reliable military establishment became apparent. Although it may be somewhat disconcerting to the avid patron of the rugged American colonial, it must be admitted that the remarkable British victories in the new world in 1759, which climaxed in the taking of Quebec, were largely the result of the efforts of British regular troops.

Americans, however, tended to forget their relatively poor record in the colonial wars and eagerly came to accept two major events that gave weight to their conviction that nonprofessionalism was superior to professionalism. According to Professor Carleton the events were

> the improvised New England Expedition
> of a fleet of fishing smacks and 4,000
> volunteers which in 1745, captured
> Louisbourg, in Nova Scotia, the mighti-
> est fort in North America . . . [and]
> the spectacular defeat, in 1755, at the
> fork of the Ohio, of Edward Braddock's
> crack British regulars by a handful of
> Frenchmen and their Indian allies.[2]

Certainly in the colonial period there were many other examples of events of more local significance which tended to reinforce the feeling of the superiority of rugged individualism over formalized regimentation. The exaltation of the nonprofessional was reinforced by the American Revolutionary War and has by no means disappeared from the

American philosophy of warfare to this day. Although it is beyond the scope of this study to examine in detail the impact of this philosophy on the confrontation in Vietnam, it is suggested that some Americans have found it natural to identify with the "irregulars" in their struggle against the "professionals."

Generally speaking it can be argued that the United States did not experience true military professionalism until early in the twentieth century. This is not to say that the nation has not been well served by excellent military leadership prior to that time. Certainly the United States has been fortunate in that sound military leadership appeared when the need arose. There is nothing particularly sacred about this time. Some writers vary it considerably either way. It is used here because it identifies the general time frame of the Spanish-American War.

Sir John Hackett takes a broader approach to the emergence of the American military profession. He sees the profession emerging over a period of nearly sixty years:

> The years between 1860 and World War I saw the emergence of a distinctive American professional military ethic, with the American officer regarding himself as a member no longer of a fighting profession only, to which anybody might belong, but as a member of a learned profession whose students are students for life.[3]

The United States had no regular army at the time of the Revolutionary War but was compelled to rely on improvisation and a very inadequate and undependable volunteer system. Since that war was "won" even though most of the battles were "lost," the American tradition of nonprofessionalism, carried over from the colonial period, was confirmed.

The Continental army, commanded by General George Washington, was composed of contingents from the several states with varying terms of enlistment along with militiamen from some states. Many militia units fought somewhat independently of the Continental army and bands of minutemen and other irregulars frequently conducted guerrilla operations throughout the country, especially in the more remote backwoods areas.

As the nation's first great military leader, Washington was himself not a military professional within the context of the definition given in Chapter 1. He was a gentleman farmer, with some military experience, who agreed to command the fledgling army so that he, and others like him, could return to being gentlemen farmers at the earliest opportunity. Neither Washington nor most of the military officers of the infant nation made the military the "locus of his career." Their military service was rather an interruption of another chosen career.

As the United States moved from the position of what we would now call an "emerging" or "developing" nation to great power status, a slow but nonetheless perceptible movement toward the existence of a military profession was noticeable. As the infant nation moved from the Revolution, through the War of 1812 and the Mexican War, into the Civil War, it was apparent that it had come to possess some officers who met the requirements of the definition of military professional. To say for example, that General Winfield Scott and many of his officers were not military professionals would be a distortion of the truth. However, to conclude that because of the existence of some officers with highly professional qualifications the nation was possessed of a true military profession would equally distort the facts. To comment similarly about many of the officers on both sides in the Civil War would also be unjust as well as incorrect. The semantics of whether an individual officer deserved the name of professional, or even if the military system of

the nation at a given time should be credited with
professionalism, can be argued either way. In this
study it is held that the United States did not possess a true military profession until the turn of
the century and that the Spanish-American War clearly pointed up this lack of professional status as a
major weakness of the American military system.

President McKinley's "splendid little war"
with Spain, just before the turn of the century,
clearly illustrated the need for a truly professional military establishment in the United States. The
navy actually conducted itself quite admirably, but
the army found itself without many of the fundamental
plans and procedures that a professional establishment should have possessed. The history of the
United States Army in the war with Spain reveals
many creditable actions on the part of individuals
and small units, but as an example of acceptable
military professionalism at the highest levels, it
must go to the bottom of the list.

One explanation of this phenomenon is that the
navy, at the close of the Civil War, was old and
thoroughly worn out. It was part sail and part
steam and the administration in 1883 was virtually
forced into the position of commencing a rebuilding
program or having no navy at all. This rebuilding
decision preceded the "navalism" of Theodore Roosevelt and, it can be argued, without it Assistant
Secretary of the Navy Roosevelt would have had no
navy with which to express his philosophies. By
1890 the United States Navy, which Secretary Tracy
described to President Harrison in his annual report
of November 26, 1890, was "a motley collection of 33
wooden, iron, or steel vessels in commission, some
of them having smooth bore guns and dating from pre-
Civil War days."[4] The close of the decade, however,
saw a truly respectable navy. The army, unfortunately, experienced no such revitalization during the
period and continued at a low level of efficiency
until, and regrettably through, most of the Spanish-
American War.

The Spanish-American War was perhaps the first of the "modern" wars fought by the United States. While there was no lack of tactical skill on the field of battle, the army found it almost imposssible to transport and sustain an expeditionary force of 20,000 men only ninety miles from American shores. Comparing this with the subsequent deployment of forces overseas in the twentieth century, the limitation is all the more apparent. Some costly lessons were learned in this war and, although corrective action was slow in being implemented, it does represent a significant turning point in the development of a true military profession in the United States.

EARLY TWENTIETH CENTURY

In the mid-nineteenth century Denis Hart Mahan defined the relationship of the military profession to war and the distinction between the military spirit and the bellicose one. He said: "The trouble with the United States as a country was that we are perhaps the least military, but not behind the foremost as a warlike one."[5] In this statement is to be found the virtual heart and soul of politico-military thinking in the United States as the new century dawned. Historically, Americans have seldom been reluctant to support a foreign policy that would lead to war but the nation has been consistently timid about supporting a military policy that would prepare the nation for that war. In other words, there was little or no appreciation of the relationship between the military and foreign policies of the nation. The development of the military profession in the United States is closely related to the growth of politico-military awareness on the part of the American body politic. For this reason the remainder of this historical sketch attempts to trace, in broad terms, the parallel development of politico-military philosophy and military professionalism in the United States through the first half of the twentieth century.

The emergence of the United States as a world
power following the Spanish-American War placed new
stresses and strains on the generally accepted American concepts of military professionalism and the
role of military power in world affairs. For perhaps the first time in American history the basic
philosophical differences between, what for lack of
a more descriptive term will simply be referred to
as, idealism and realism in international affairs
were sharpened and national and international issues were widely debated. If one was willing to
argue that military power had a place in international politics then he could easily accept the
fact that there might be some practical relationship between the foreign and military policies of
the United States. If, on the other hand, he was
more prone to contend that power was a poor substitute for morality, he could find it difficult indeed to accept the thesis that there was a meaningful relationship between the nation's foreign policy
and its military policy. The attendant polemics had
a distinct bearing on the development of the fledgling American military profession.

A developing awareness of the relationships between the policies of the several services and between the nation's overall military and "national"
policies is found in a comment initially made in
1901 in relation to the Philippines.

> The defense of the Philippines belongs,
> not alone to an army or navy or forti-
> fied harbors, but to an intelligent
> combination of them all. This defense
> cannot be relegated to those expedi-
> ents that are alone consequent upon
> sudden war, but must be inherent in
> the national policy of the Republic
> and the military preparations of prior
> years. It cannot be left to the
> shifts of unforeseen combat, but must
> be predetermined by existent condi-
> tions and such works as knowledge and

labor of man may evolve out of the
science of war.[6]

Certainly a degree of national sophistication
can be seen in the above comment to include the
rudiments of understanding of the role of military
power and a military profession in national and international affairs.

Between 1900 and World War I, the military
policy of the United States provided only forces
for the limited protection and administration of
the newly acquired overseas possessions. The possibility of American involvement in a major war was
far from the minds of the nation's citizens and its
leaders. Actually, it can be argued that there was
nothing especially unsound about such a policy in
the years immediately after the turn of the century.
As the international situation began to deteriorate,
however, American military policy did not adjust
and it was soon very much out of line with the realities of the international, especially the European,
milieu.

Before moving on to the years immediately preceding World War I, recognition must be given to a
series of developments that greatly contributed to
the growth of the military profession in the United
States. The accomplishments of Elihu Root upon his
accession to the War Department are now well known.
They centered primarily on the creation of a general
staff headed by a chief of staff; the establishment
of an Army War College, which could direct the intellectual exercise of the army, acquire information, and also devise plans and advise the commander in chief; and the creation of a viable regular
army structure. During the otherwise lean years,
from a professional point of view, the Root reforms
served the army, the military profession, and the
nation well. Lord Haldans summarized Root's contribution clearly when he said:

Really, you know, I do not need to know
anything about armies and their organization, for the five reports of Elihu

> Root, made as Secretary of War in the
> United States, are the very last word
> concerning the organization and place
> of an army in a democracy.[7]

The army was well on its way to developing a level
of professionalism enjoyed only by the navy in previous years.[8]

By the time war clouds were gathering in Europe
in the years preceding World War I, the United
States had progressed to the point where the military establishment had taken on some of the more
promising characteristics of a profession. Even
though some military officers, and civilians closely associated with the military, had come to appreciate the merits of professionalism and politico-
military integration, this appreciation was not in
evidence throughout the government. The lack of understanding by the commander in chief of the role
his military advisors were expected to fulfill is
well illustrated by the following example:

> In the autumn of 1915, the Acting Sec-
> retary of War, Henry Breckinridge, was
> summoned to the presence of Woodrow
> Wilson. He found the President trem-
> bling and white with passion, holding
> in his hand a copy of the Baltimore
> Sun. The President pointed to a
> story in the paper reporting that the
> General Staff was preparing plans for
> the eventuality of war with Germany.
> When the President then directed him
> to investigate, and if he found that
> it was true, to relieve every officer
> on the General Staff and order him
> out of Washington.[9]

This example is a classic in illustrating the difficulty in the United States of achieving a true appreciation for the role of the military professional
in the national policy-making process. This example
is particularly interesting in light of the president's rather "hawkish" comment a year earlier when

Admiral Mayo caused an international incident by
making demands on the Mexican government as a result of the U.S.S. <u>Dolphin</u> incident. When the report of the incident reached Washington, President
Wilson is reported to have commented, "I do not see
how Mayo could have done otherwise."[10]

In the period between the Spanish-American War
and World War I, many influential individuals in
the United States found it difficult to accept the
fact that power shared a place with morality in
foreign affairs. This was to be expected of the
European nations, they conceded, but somehow the
United States was felt to be above it all. In support of Mahan's comment at the beginning of this
section, it is interesting to note that while the
American nation generally agreed on the immorality
of the use of military power in international relations it could see nothing wrong with punishing a
nation that was not conducting its affairs in a
"moral" manner, and if necessary, using military
force to do the punishing.

As the European nations became involved in
what was to become World War I, the United States
let it be known that it expected to stay out of the
conflict. This again raised the basic question of
military and foreign policy relationships. If it
was the national goal of the United States to stay
out of the war in Europe how could this best be accomplished? By a statement of neutrality based on
military strength that would make the warring nations think carefully before violating U.S. neutrality? Or could it best be done from a position of
relative military weakness? The strength in the
latter case came from the nation's stand on the issues of international law and morality.

Strong appeals to morality and adherence to international law did not deter Germany from declaring
unrestricted submarine warfare. Would a strong
antisubmarine capability on the part of the U.S.
navy have done it? The answer is conjecture and
need not be pursued here. The fact is that the

United States chose to follow a foreign policy that
was based on moral strength without regard to military strength.

In the minds of most Americans in 1914, peace
and preparedness were incompatible. The moral ra-
tionalization for this is commented on above. There
was also the deep-seated conviction of the invulner-
ability of the United States. In December, 1914,
Secretary of State William Jennings Bryan told an
audience in Baltimore that "the President knows that
if this country needed a million men, and needed
them in a day, the call would go out at sunrise and
the sun would set on a million men in arms."[11]
Such a comment by a small-town Independence Day ora-
tor may be excused, but for the secretary of state
of the United States to make such a statement publicly is today almost beyond belief. The secretary was
in truth, speaking not only for himself, but for a
significant segment of the nation as well. Less
than two and one half years later the United States
was at war. A foreign policy that now called for
war was hampered because the military policy to support it was deficient.

When isolation ended and the United States
faced entry into a world war, American liberalism
could justify participation in the war only in
terms of defending its ethos. Bryan is quoted by
The New York Times as saying in February, 1917:
"This country should fight till the last man was
killed if it were invaded, but . . . we should
settle all other matters by arbitration."[12]

Even after the nation became fully committed
in the war, the president continued to express his
deep doubt and distrust of the military profession,
a view shared by many other Americans according to
Elting E. Morison. With reference to the recommendations of senior naval officers concerning convoy
techniques for the protection of allied shipping
against the submarine threat, Wilson is reported to
have remarked that "this war, being completely unprecedented, was therefore, in a sense, a war for

amateurs."[13] The age-old colonial heritage of preference for the irregular over the professional was
still a strong factor in American thinking.

On September 4, 1918, an Allied force under
British command, including 4,500 American soldiers,
went ashore at Archangel in the north of Russia in
one of the most unusual military operations in the
nation's history. In a sense the historic American
politico-military roles were if not reversed at
least badly distorted with the president approving
a military operation for purely political reasons
against the recommendation of the army chief of
staff. Of this strange event George Kennan comments:

> The senior officials in the War Depart-
> ment remained, throughout, of the same
> opinion as Bliss. General March and I,
> Baker had stated in his cable of July 8,
> . . . have been in conference with the
> President about the Murmansk expedition
> . . . none of us can see the military
> value of the proposal. . . .[14]

Compared with President Wilson's very antimilitary,
and at times ultra-idealistic, comments of earlier
years the employment of American military forces in
pursuit of a clearly political objective is most interesting. In this respect the president was far
ahead of his military advisors in understanding the
role of military force in international relations.

When the year 1919 dawned, it was already apparent that the U.S. foreign and military policies
would be subjected to thorough examination. The
elections of November, 1918, had resulted in significant gains for the opponents of the administration, and the armistice in Europe opened the door
to the forces of pacifism and antimilitarism. The
war to save the world for democracy having been won,
there was obviously no more requirement for large
military formations, so the United States quickly
reduced its forces to the barest essentials. The
small forces that remained in being virtually

retreated to the naval bases and the army posts
throughout the country and literally withdrew from
the remainder of American society. The civilian
population had little or nothing to do with the
military and the military had even less interest in
the civilians. It was in this cloistered atmos-
phere that professional military officers studied
the art of war in the military school systems and
practiced that art to the limited degree permitted
by virtually nonexistent military budgets. While
this social isolation is sometimes exaggerated it
is normally credited with contributing to the
strengthening of military professionalism during
this period of disuse.[15]

In the general area of politico-military affairs, the war colleges of both services stressed
the views of Clausewitz as the accepted doctrine.
In addition, "American officers of both services referred to the armed forces as the 'instruments' of
the government and constantly reiterated the dictum
that national policy dictated military policy."[16]
The major complaint of officers at that time was
that the government was remiss in its duty of enunciating a clear national policy so that the military
professionals could prepare a meaningful military
policy.

It has been suggested that "the First World
War reiterated the necessity of making the Nation's
foreign and naval policies one and the same"--and
this view is but another manifestation of a growing
awareness in the United States of the relationship
between foreign and military policy.[17] Yet the 1928
Democratic vice presidential candidate, Senator
Joseph T. Robinson, in commenting on the Kellogg-
Briand Pact, told a London audience that U.S. support of the outlawry of war was motivated by "the
twin desire to keep clear of foreign involvements
and to assume no burdens in enforcing the peace."[18]
The road to national maturity in the affairs of
states was not without its roadblocks.

That there was, however, a developing awareness
of the nation's role in the international community

and of practical politico-military relationships in
the United States cannot be discounted because of
the anachronistic utterances of a few. An excellent
example of this maturation, particularly in the
realm of politico-military relationships in the
1930's, is illustrated by an article authored by a
flag officer and published in <u>Foreign Affairs</u>. The
article addressed the dichotomy created by the need
for modernization of the fleet and the threat to international stability.

> The technical problems which I have in-
> dicated here may present difficulties
> at the coming naval conference. But
> after all, the main question is politi-
> cal. It must be this: will the good
> beginning in the establishment of se-
> curity and the preservation of peace
> made at the Washington Conference be
> allowed to pass into the limbo of for-
> gotten things?[19]

Still another example of the realization of politico-
military relationships at this time is found in a
comment by the assistant secretary of war in 1937.
In a memorandum to the president he said:

> I find that this action of the State
> Department, in ignoring military ad-
> vice, has been characteristic of its
> attitude for many years past. My in-
> vestigation discloses that this is an
> attitude not assumed by the foreign
> office of any other nation. On the
> contrary, none embarks upon foreign
> policy having any military implica-
> tions without giving the fullest con-
> siderations to the advice of the re-
> sponsible military authorities. May
> I respectfully ask that you consider
> directing the Secretary of State to
> afford an opportunity to the War De-
> partment to express its views upon
> all matters having a military implica-
> tion, immediate or remote.[20]

For many reasons, for which the professional
military officer and the civilian policy maker must
share responsibility, there still was not a really
workable politico-military balance in the years preceding World War II. One military writer comments
that "World War II was a watershed in relations between the American public and the military services."[21] Once the crest had been reached, the way
was opened to the acceptance of a new type of civil-
military relations, a new approach to politico-
military affairs, and a changing military professionalism. Prior to World War II, however, the concept of politico-military integration was still on
the long climb up the far side of the ridge from
the post-World War I period.

Actually the foreign policy debates in the
United States following World War I were not, as
often depicted, simply between the forces of isola-
tionism and collective security, or between absten-
tion from and participation in world affairs. According to one historian, "The real clash was between two groups, each eager to aid in preventing
war but disagreeing on how far the United States
should commit itself in advance."[22]

When, on March 19, 1920, the Senate failed to
approve the Versailles Treaty, it did not vote the
United States out of the international community.
Even if this had been the intent of the Senate, it
could not have succeeded. Like it or not, the
United States emerged from the war as the most po-
tent nation on earth and it thereby inherited certain international responsibilities. The military
policy to be adopted by the nation would have a significant bearing on the courses of action open to it
in the area of foreign policy.

The national debates dealing with military
policy took a somewhat different turn. The natural
reaction to the termination of the war was to de-
mobilize as quickly as possible and this was accomplished with remarkable speed and efficiency. Military leaders warned of the dangers of such complete
destruction of the nation's military strength, but

for the most part their warnings went unheeded.
Public sentiment was clearly opposed to a large
military establishment. Pacifism and antimilitary
sentiment carried the day and the voices of such
stalwarts as Jane Addams and Lillian Wald were
heard in the Congress over those of the nation's
military leaders. The virtual withdrawal of the
professional military officer from the American
mainstream was noted earlier.

In the years following the war, the United
States assumed many international obligations and
responsibilities that should have called for a corresponding modification in the nation's military
policy. A rather vigorous foreign policy in the
Far East and rumblings of unrest in Europe should
have at least made Americans realize the necessity
for maintaining some reasonable military strength.

The United States still had its Pacific possessions to protect so there was less inclination to
cut too deeply into the strength of the naval forces.
For practical purposes, the army had been reduced to
a position from which it could scarcely be considered an instrument of national policy. It had virtually no capability to perform any mission outside
the United States, other than limited defense of
the Pacific possessions. During this period the
military policy of the United States was in effect
its naval policy. The term naval policy is frequently seen in the literature of the period in lieu
of military policy. An indication that there was
not a complete lack of appreciation for the complementary positions of the foreign and military policies of the nation is found in the fact that the
term political-naval affairs appeared from time to
time in commentaries on the situation in the Pacific.

From the point of view of politico-military affairs, one of the major effects of the depression
was the further reduction of the already dangerously low military budgets. Unfortunately, they were
not accompanied by similar reductions in American
foreign policy commitments in the Pacific. This

tended to bring the nation's military policy even
further out of balance with its foreign policy.

According to one historian, the nation's military policy was clearly stated by President Hoover
in a Navy Day address of October, 1931. The president said: "The first necessity of our government
is the maintenance of a navy so efficient and so
strong that, in conjunction with our army, no enemy
may ever invade our country."[23] The author of the
article, Charles Beard, takes the pacifists and the
militarists equally to task. He uses President
Hoover's remarks as a statement of a good middle-of-
the-road military policy. In a book published some
fourteen years later, the same author again emphasized that "foreign policy and preparations are in-
separably linked in any wise and efficient administration."[24]

The president's comment was apparently intended
as justification for the reductions in military, especially naval, expenditures. There can be no argument that a smaller navy would be required to defend
the shores of the United States than would be required to maintain our position in the Pacific. As
indicated above, however, the military policy was
not accompanied by a modified foreign policy.

Viewed in overall perspective, the American
military policy of the 1920's and early 1930's was
actually not in complete disharmony with the nation's foreign policy, but neither was it in true
harmony with the realities of the international
situation. Military policy, instead of providing a
means for furthering the national interest, imposed
serious limitations on the foreign policy makers.
It was, in fact, the military professionals who, in
the early 1930's "urged the statesmen to tread cau-
tiously warning them of American military weakness."[25]

While the United States was given a sound lesson
in the value of politico-military considerations in
and before World War I, the lesson was apparently
not learned. Although there was an occasional spark

of recognition in the period between the wars,
America was not yet psychologically prepared to accept power as an instrument of international relations.   Somehow, Americans, as a whole, still were
convinced that military strength was immoral.

The coming of the Roosevelt administration did
not bring any significant change in this area.   In
fact there was great concern among the New Dealers
that anything that carried a military connotation
ran counter to the principles of the New Deal.   It
was not until the international situation had completely deteriorated that America began to face the
realities of the situation.   Even then, the administration was compelled to take actions short of
what it would have desired until the American public
had been fully aroused.   When war again threatened
Europe in the late 1930's, one American commented
that there was "no hope for Europe.   There is, however, an escape for us.   It is to refuse, under any
circumstances, to get involved in that tangle."[26]
Of the same period Julius Pratt commented as follows:

> Thus, when in 1940 the United States
> found itself facing another grave cri-
> sis, it was not much better prepared
> than it had been in 1917. . . . Ameri-
> can diplomacy vis-à-vis Germany, Italy,
> and Japan (1936-1941) was handicapped
> by a wholly inadequate Army and Air
> Force, a Navy designed for one ocean
> when two were at stake, and a neutral-
> ity policy that told the world the
> United States would have no part in
> other people's wars.[27]

WORLD WAR II

One of the most remarkable documents of World
War II was actually prepared a few months before
the United States became officially involved in the
war.   The search by the nation's military leadership for some specific statement of national objec-

tives upon which a solid military policy could be constructed was not productive. The closest thing to a national objective that could be identified was the statement of broad principles found in the Atlantic Charter. In the view of military men, these policy statements were "more or less nebulous" and consequently led to the enunciation of national objectives by the military staff. This statement of objectives is found in the "Joint Board Estimate of United States Over-all Production Requirements" dated September 11, 1941. In the words of William Langer and Everett Gleason it was "utterly devoid of false hope or self-delusion." It defined the "major national objectives of the United States" as

> preservation of the territorial, eco-
> nomic and ideological integrity of
> the United States and of the remainder
> of the Western Hemisphere; prevention
> of the disruption of the British Em-
> pire; prevention of the further exten-
> sion of Japanese territorial dominion;
> eventual establishment in Europe and
> Asia of balances of power which will
> most nearly ensure political stability
> in those regions and the future secur-
> ity of the United States; and, so far
> as practicable, the establishment of
> regimes favorable to economic freedom
> and individual liberty.[28]

Of significance here is the fact that the na-
tion's military leadership was not provided with a meaningful statement of national objectives even when directed to prepare an "Estimate of Over-all Production Requirements" to support military operations should they become a reality. Such an esti-
mate, to be meaningful, must of necessity be based on some goal. Because no objective was provided, one was constructed. The realistic terms in which the national objective was stated by the military staff is all the more remarkable in contrast with the necessarily idealistic and ambiguous wording of the Atlantic Charter.

The above statement is an excellent example of
the type of national objective an accomplished
politico-military team should produce. Historically, of course, it is now known that the war was not
fought within the context of this objective, but
rather within a much narrower framework that can be
simply stated in the words of the then secretary of
war: "The only important goal of the war was victory, and the only proper test of wartime action was
whether it would help to win."[29]

The Joint Board's statement of a national objective, which so well incorporated the essential
elements of a pragmatic foreign and military policy,
was an anachronism in the summer of 1941. Unfortunately, it did not represent the prevailing views
of the national policy makers, or for that matter,
of the military profession as a whole. Rather,
when the United States entered World War II, the
more typical American approach to foreign policy
and military professionalism prevailed. It would
be difficult to find a better example of the antith-
esis of the views of Clausewitz than in the comment
of Secretary of State Cordell Hull to Secretary of
War Henry Stimson when it became apparent that diplomacy had run its course and war was inevitable.
"I have washed my hands of it," Hull told Stimson a
few days before Pearl Harbor, "and it is now in the
hands of you and Knox--the Army and Navy."[30] This
statement by the secretary of state was symbolic of
the abdication of power by civilian authorities to
the military establishment. It was completely in
keeping with the accepted concept of politico-
military affairs at that time.

As the war progressed, the military hierarchy
became increasingly involved in the making of foreign policy decisions. One school of thought argues
that this transition from purely military areas of
concern was actually forced on a reluctant military
profession because the responsible civilian authorities failed to fulfill their rightful obligation.
Another school argues that this was bland usurpa-
tion of civil authority by military men and that it

was not forced at all, but rather was actively sought by the Pentagon. There is no intent to argue the case of either school of thought here, but simply to recognize the fact that the military did become heavily involved in matters that were traditionally outside the sphere of the American professional military officer.

President Roosevelt is frequently criticized for not providing the political guidance that was necessary in the war. William R. Emerson does not subscribe to this thesis. He writes that

> Roosevelt was far more sensitive than was generally realized to the political aspects of the war; he performed truly the function of the American commander in chief, which is to bind together the varied political and military strands which make up war, keeping each in its proper relation to the whole.[31]

The above view would indicate that there was a proper politico-military balance in the United States during the war. There is little room for argument that the president, as the civilian commander in chief, was the final decision maker. There is, however, a valid question as to the relative weight the president gave to the recommendations of his military and civilian advisors. The secondary position to which the secretary of state had been relegated, even in matters of great political significance, cannot be overlooked.

For example, Robert Sherwood has argued that President Roosevelt overruled the opinions of his military chiefs on only two occasions during the entire war--in July, 1942, on the North African invasion and in December, 1943, on the question of a projected operation in Burma and the Bay of Bengal. There were, of course, other occasions on which the Joint Chiefs of Staff did not present a unanimous recommendation to the president and he was compelled

to select one choice among several.[32] Samuel Huntington suggests that there was something lacking in
that relationship. He expressed it as follows:

> Too much harmony is just as much a
> symptom of bad organization as too
> much conflict. On the face of it,
> something is wrong with a system in
> which, during the course of a four-
> year war, the political Chief Execu-
> tive only twice overrules his profes-
> sional military advisors. This can
> only mean that one of them was neglect-
> ing his proper function and duplicating
> the work of the other.[33]

If in actuality, something was wrong with the system, and the military professionals had become less
professional, what had happened? Huntington further
explains:

> The acquiescence of the military was
> in part the result of daily contact
> with the President and his appealing
> persuasiveness. But it was even more
> due to the fact that as the Joint
> Chiefs became the alter egos of the
> President in the conduct of the war
> it was only natural that similar re-
> sponsibilities and similar perspec-
> tive should produce similar policies.

The above comment suggests that the military
simply acquiesced to external pressures and for the
sake of the prosecution of the war diluted its professionalism, reluctantly perhaps, but nonetheless
effectively. As was indicated earlier, there is by
no means complete acceptance of this thesis. There
are those who are convinced that the military moved
into the arena of international politics intentionally, anxiously, and with eyes wide open.

As the war progressed, the line between purely
military and purely political matters became less

well defined. This was especially true at the highest levels of government. Within the military establishment, however, below the level of the Joint
Chiefs of Staff and the military theatre commanders,
the lack of understanding of the relationship between military and political policies rather generally persisted. In his dealings with the military
in North Africa, Robert Murphy found that there was
something less than an adequate appreciation of the
role of the State Department in time of war. He reports that his dealings at the top level left no
cause for complaint; however, a typical military
outlook is expressed in the following exchange:

> One day an American major general
> asked me: "Will you please tell me
> what in hell the State Department is
> doing in an active theatre of war?"
> He was asking for information, so
> this is in effect what I told him.
>   War is a projection of policy
> when other means fail. The State De-
> partment is responsible to the Presi-
> dent for foreign policy. . . .   The
> State Department had direct responsi-
> bility in the preparatory stage lead-
> ing to the invasion. It was directly
> concerned in the political decisions,
> and it will have to deal with the
> postwar political effects of this
> campaign.[34]

Of significance is the fact that a major general in
the army found it necessary to ask such a question,
and that a representative of the State Department
found it necessary to answer in such basic and fundamental terms. The general was most probably expressing the accepted professional military view as
he learned his trade before the war. He was willing to accept the fact that military action was an
extension of political policy, and he was probably
just as willing to agree that when the military had
achieved its purpose in North Africa, the State Department should properly assume responsibility for

the area. The idea that the military and political
establishment should, or even could, effectively
work side by side was apparently foreign to him.
Although this example uses a military officer as
the vehicle for illustrating lack of understanding,
the same thing may well be said of many of our civilian officials at the time.

THE DIPLOMAT IN UNIFORM

It is clear from this brief historical survey
that the nation's foreign and military policies
have not always been viewed as parts of one integrated national policy. Even through World War II,
the basic concept of a close relationship between
the two policies was not generally accepted.

The above comment notwithstanding, to say that
the military, until relatively recently, was not involved in U.S. foreign policy would be to distort
the facts. Throughout the nation's history, from
the time of the Revolution to the present, military
officers have been used in many capacities in the
formulation and implementation of foreign policy.
In a paper prepared at Harvard University in the
summer of 1964, a naval officer wrote on the role
of "The Military Diplomat."[35] He illustrated the
great extent to which military officers have been
used in many diplomatic capacities. In our earlier
history these were primarily naval officers. In
later years officers of the other services were used
also.

The use of military officers was not limited
to wartime diplomacy, but was practiced in peacetime as well. Nor was the use of the military diplomat limited to military negotiations, but it also
involved many other areas of national interest.
For example, the use of naval officers to arrive at
commercial and trade agreements with foreign governments in our early history was not uncommon.[36]

For the most part, the basic decision that the
nation would seek a commercial agreement with a

given foreign nation, or that the nation would associate itself with a foreign power or powers for whatever the reason may be, was not a politico-military
decision as we would use the term today. There was
not normally a conscious effort at the national
level to integrate the military considerations with
the economic, political, and other aspects of a
given situation. The military officer was involved
many times, not because military expertise was required, but because he was available to perform the
assignment. In those instances where the military
officer initiated action that had significant political implications, the action was normally taken
either because no instructions were given from Washington, or because authority for such decisions had
been delegated to the military officer.

An example of the first type of situation can
be found in General Andrew Jackson's invasion of
Florida in 1818. Operating under vague orders, he
captured two Spanish posts, executed two British
subjects who were accused of aiding the Indians,
and before returning to the United States, appointed
one of his subordinates as military governor of
Florida. These bold actions brought a sharp and immediate protest from Spain and precipitated a Cabinet crisis in Washington.[37]

The decision to halt at the Elbe, 123 years
later, serves as an example of the other type of
situation. In this instance, the political leadership specifically delegated the decision-making authority to the military commander. Critics of the
decision argue that General Eisenhower should have
given more weight to the international political
aspects of the problem. Defenders of the decision
say that he had no choice but to place maximum emphasis on the military factors.[38]

The "right" or "wrong" of these two decisions
can be argued at great length, but it is simply
pointed out that both had a significant bearing on
the nation's foreign policy, and both were undertaken presumably without the benefit of a thorough

evaluation of the politico-military ramifications
at the national level.

In Jackson's time the United States didn't
possess a national military profession, but by
Eisenhower's time it had progressed to a high state
of military professionalism. In Jackson's time the
administration apparently did not appreciate the relationship between foreign and military policy, and
in Eisenhower's time, policy makers apparently still
had not learned that lesson adequately. The development of a military profession in the United States
did not automatically bring with it an evolution in
politico-military understanding. The nation had,
during certain times in its history, military officers involved in foreign affairs, but it never really had true politico-military integration.

Whether the military liked it or not and whether the civil authorities like it or not, as World
War II came to a close, the military profession was
deeply involved in international political affairs.
Immediately after the war, it appeared that the military would withdraw to its prewar status. However,
as events have proved, the military did not revert
to its prewar position in politico-military affairs.
The role of the military in general and military
professionalism in particular had taken on a new
dimension. It soon became apparent that the military profession was a thing to be recognized and
accepted in the national policy formulation circles.
Both the military professional and the civilian
leadership found the new relationship awkward. Both
found it necessary to reexamine old values and old
concepts. This then was the status of politico-
military relationships in the United States as the
nation moved into a new form of conflict: the cold
war.

NOTES

1. William G. Carlton, "Raising Armies Before the Civil War," Current History, June, 1968, p. 327. This issue of Current History, which is devoted entirely to a review of "U.S. Military Service in Perspective," provided excellent background material for this section of the chapter.

2. Ibid.

3. Sir John Hackett, The Profession of Arms (London: Times Publishing Company, 1962), p. 25.

4. Quoted in Kenneth Bourne and Carl Boyde, "Captain Mahan's 'War' with Great Britain," United States Naval Institute Proceedings, July, 1968, pp. 71-78.

5. Quoted in Samuel P. Huntington, The Soldier and the State (Cambridge, Mass.:   The Belknap Press, 1959), p. 221.

6. Homer Lea, The Valor of Ignorance (New York: Harper, 1909), p. 254.

7. Philip C. Jessup, Elihu Root, Vol. I (New York: Dodd, Mead and Company, 1938), p. 240.

8. See Russell F. Weigley, History of the United States Army (New York: The Macmillan Company, 1967), pp. 313-27, for a brief summary of the Root "reforms."

9. Quoted in Huntington, op. cit., p. 144.

10. Quoted in Samuel Flagg Bemis, ed., The American Secretaries of State and their Diplomacy, Vol. X (New York: Alfred A. Knopf, 1929), p. 16.

11. Quoted in Robert E. Osgood, Ideals and Self-interest in America's Foreign Relations (Chicago: The University of Chicago Press, 1953), p. 204.

12. The New York Times, February 11, 1917,
p. 11.

13. Elting E. Morison, Admiral Sims and the
Modern American Navy (Boston: Houghton Mifflin
Company, 1942), pp. 359-361.

14. George F. Kennan, The Decision to Intervene (Princeton, N.J.: Princeton University Press,
1958), p. 378.

15. See Morris Janowitz, The Professional
Soldier (New York: The Free Press of Glencoe,
1960), p. 4.

16. Huntington, op. cit., p. 307.

17. Brook E. Lee, Jr., The Politics of Our
National Defense (Senior thesis submitted to the
Department of Politics, Princeton University, April
1940. Reprinted as U.S. Senate Document No. 274,
76th Cong., 3d sess. Washington; U.S. Government
Printing Office, 1941), p. 5.

18. Selig Adler, The Isolationist Impulse
(New York: Abelard-Schuman, 1957), p. 237.

19. William V. Pratt, "Pending Naval Questions,"
Foreign Affairs, April, 1935, p. 419.

20. Louis Johnson, Assistant Secretary of War,
in a memorandum to President Roosevelt, 1937.
Quoted in U.S., Congress, Senate, Committee on Government Operations, Hearings before the Subcommittee
on National Security Staffing and Operations, 88th
Cong., 2d sess., June 25, 1964 (Washington: U.S.
Government Printing Office, 1964), p. 553.

21. Martin Blumenson, "Some Thoughts on Professionalism," Military Review, September, 1964,
p. 13.

22. Richard W. Leopold, The Growth of American
Foreign Policy (New York: Alfred A. Knopf, 1962),
p. 396.

23.   Charles A. Beard, "Our Confusion Over National Defense," Harpers Magazine, February, 1932, p. 267.

24.   Charles A. Beard, American Foreign Policy in the Making: 1932-1940 (New Haven, Conn.:   Yale University Press, 1946), p. 36.

25.   Huntington, op. cit., p. 306.

26.   John T. Flynn, "The War Boom Begins," Harpers Magazine, July, 1937, p. 122.

27.   Julius W. Pratt, A History of United States Foreign Policy (Englewood Cliffs, N.J.: Prentice-Hall, 1955), pp. 29, 37.

28.   William L. Langer and S. Everett Gleason, The Undeclared War, 1940-1941 (New York: Harper and Brothers, 1953), pp. 739-40; also see Robert E. Sherwood, Roosevelt and Hopkins (New York: The Universal Library, 1950), pp. 410-18.

29.   Henry L. Stimson and McGeorge Bundy, On Active Duty in Peace and War (New York: Harper and Brothers, 1948), pp. 472, 565-66.

30.   Quoted in Huntington, op. cit., p. 317.

31.   William R. Emerson, "F.D.R. (1941-1945)," in The Ultimate Decision, ed. Ernest R. May (New York: George Braziller, 1960), p. 176.

32.   Sherwood, op. cit., pp. 446, 615.

33.   Huntington, op. cit., pp. 329, 333.

34.   Robert Murphy, Diplomat Among Warriors (Garden City, N.Y.:   Doubleday and Company, 1964), p. 156.

35.   William R. Westlake, "The Military Diplomat." Unpublished seminar paper prepared for Professor William Y. Elliot, Harvard University, August 17, 1964; also see Huntington, op. cit., p. 306.

36. Ibid.

37. See Marquis James, Andrew Jackson: The
Border Captain (Indianapolis, Ind.: The Bobbs-
Merrill Company, 1923), especially Chapter XVIII,
"The Florida Adventure," pp. 308-24.

38. See Forrest C. Pogue, "The Decision to
Halt at the Elbe (1945)," in Command Decisions,
prepared by the Office of Military History, ed.
Kent Roberts Greenfield (New York: Harcourt, Brace
and Company, 1959), pp. 374-87.

3

THE

COLD

WAR

At the outset of this chapter it is perhaps
wise to define the term cold war to insure a common
understanding of the phenomenon that is being addressed. There are a number of definitions that
might be used. For the purpose of this study two
of them will be considered. The first is found in
a study prepared at Georgetown University. It defines a cold war as a war that involves

> forcible, semi-forcible, and non-
> forcible techniques. It includes
> propaganda, economic warfare, sabo-
> tage, espionage, subversion, the fo-
> mentation of strikes, civil distur-
> bances, terrorism, psycho-political
> attack (in the form, for example, of
> threats of nuclear obliteration), dip-
> lomatic pressures, guerrilla warfare,
> and limited, conventional, "undeclared"
> war.[1]

Another more recent and perhaps more workable
definition is provided by the Joint Chiefs of Staff.
Cold war is defined as

> a state of international tension,
> wherein political, economic, techno-
> logical, sociological, psychological,
> paramilitary, and military measures
> short of overt armed conflict involv-
> ing regular military forces are em-
> ployed to achieve national objectives.[2]

Of particular interest is the fact that these
two definitions, one from a civilian and one from a
military source, both emphasize the many-sided nature of the cold war.   Inherent in both definitions
is the concept that the military contribution is
short of overt armed action by regular forces, and
that even then it is but one of several means by
which the national objective may be achieved.   While
by no means rejecting the first definition, the
second one will be used.   It is also desirable to
devote a few words to how the United States came to
be involved in this particular cold war.

There are a number of opinions as to exactly
how and when it all started.   Those opinions vary
to the extent of a few months to many years in the
"when" category, and from specific instances to
broad abstracts for the "how."   The view of Thomas
Wilson will be used here.   "It takes two to make a
fight," he commented.   His thinking is related to
the U.S. reaction to continued occupation of Iran
by Soviet forces.   In March, 1946, President Truman
gave the Soviet Union an ultimatum in which he made
it quite clear that either the Soviet troops would
be withdrawn from that country or the United States
would take action to insure that it was done.   It
was then, according to Wilson, when the United
States indicated its intention to use force, if
necessary, that the cold war was "declared."[3]   For
practical purposes, however, we need only accept
the thought that the cold war was the direct outgrowth of the international environment created by
World War II and that it began shortly after that
war, in the 1945-47 time frame.

If there is one characteristic of the cold war
that has persisted throughout, it is that it has

been dynamic in nature. Changes in the international milieu have in turn brought about changes in the nature of the confrontation itself. The dynamism of the conflict is most important here because as the nature of the cold war itself changed, there were of necessity corresponding alterations in the role of the American military profession. Each of these alterations brought new stresses and strains to bear on the existing concept of politico-military affairs and military professionalism.

Authors writing on the cold war have seen fit to divide it into parts for the purposes of making it a mechanically manageable project. There is nothing particularly sacred about any of the formats, so in this study the period will be divided by the U.S. political administrations. This categorization fits reasonably well with a discussion of the military profession and the politico-military equation in the cold war.

THE TRUMAN ADMINISTRATION

This portion of the discussion covers the period from the initiation of the cold war through the bulk of the Korean War. This is not intended to be a detailed account of the history of the period, but rather a brief overview to emphasize those matters that most affected politico-military affairs.

At the root of the problem in the few years immediately following World War II was the time-honored peacetime tension between military necessity and American liberalism. In the words of Samuel Huntington: "The basic issue raised was: how can a liberal society provide for its military security when this requires the maintenance of professional military forces and institutions fundamentally at odds with liberalism."[4]

The first major conflict, and perhaps the most bitter, between the military professionals and the "liberals" came over the question of universal

military training. The administration, upon the
recommendation of the Joint Chiefs of Staff, proposed the program to the Congress and to the public.
The reaction was violent to say the least. Isolationists and liberals alike took bitter exception
to the proposal. Henry A. Wallace, one-time vice
president, bitterly attacked the concept in an article entitled "Militarization in the United States."
He said: "After Roosevelt's death the military
promptly moved in to take over complete control of
the government and the nation."[5]

A similar view was expressed about sixteen
years later by Fred Cook when he commented on the
administration proposal for universal military
training:

> In all this, the military took the
> lofty view that it was acting strict-
> ly from patriotic motives, strictly
> for the safety and good of the coun-
> try. This, of course, has been the
> justification of the military in every
> era and every nation in which it has
> arrogated to itself supreme power.[6]

Then following appropriate comments on Napoleon,
Mussolini, and Hitler, Cook continued: "Such naked
military grabs for power can always be rationalized
on the loftiest plain, though their results almost
always are tragic."

The arguments for or against universal military training are irrelevant here. What is quite
relevant, however, is the effect of the debate on
military professionalism in the United States.
Assume, for the sake of discussion, that the professional military recommendation for universal
military training was not a "naked military grab
for power" but was rather a sincere recommendation
of a national security requirement as viewed by the
military leadership. The failure of this recommendation to be enacted into law can be looked upon as
the unwillingness of the American body politic,

expressing its views through the Congress, to accept a type of military structure in peacetime that
would touch upon its private lives and that it
thought was unnecessary. For the military, who had
virtually unlimited power during the war, and who
had come to accept a concept of military professionalism that was quite different from that of the
1920's and 1930's, this came as a not-too-subtle
hint that the American public expected a return to
the unrecoverable past. The basic problem was that
the nation had placed new and untested requirements
on its military profession but still expected that
profession to conduct itself as it had in the past.

An underlying desire, even on the part of the
military itself, to return to the prewar concept
of politico-military affairs is also evident during
this period. General Eisenhower, when testifying
as the army chief of staff before the Senate Subcommittee on Appropriations in June, 1947, said:

> I appear before you only as a profes-
> sional soldier, to give you a soldier's
> advice regarding the national defense.
> I am not qualified to proceed beyond
> that field; and I do not intend to do
> so. It is my duty as Chief of Staff
> to tell you gentlemen, what I believe
> to be necessary for national security.[7]

In the latter part of this period, the American
military profession found itself in a most uncom-
fortable position--one toward which it had been
slowly edging since 1938. The military leadership
became closely associated with the administration
in power. Furthermore, military officers were frequently called upon to make public statements in
support of the administration's national security
policy. This concept was carried through into the
Eisenhower years also.

Perhaps the most prominent example of this during the Truman tenure is found in the criticism
directed against General Omar Bradley, chairman of

the Joint Chiefs of Staff. General Bradley made a
number of public addresses in which he openly defended the defense policies of the administration,
and by so doing publicly argued against the policies
of the opposition party.

This sort of conduct on the part of a high-
ranking military officer caused a rather violent
reaction. Among those commenting was Justice William
O. Douglas who warned that "the increasing influence
of the military in our thinking and in our affairs
is the most ominous aspect of our modern history."[8]
General Bradley assured the nation that the military
had no intention of assuming improper powers. He
said: "There is no military clique . . . civilians
are in charge."[9]

Assuming that both men were sincere in what
they were attempting to do, there is a certain rele-
vancy of this controversy from the point of view of
politico-military affairs. General Bradley, apparently feeling that the decisions made by the administration were necessary for national defense, saw
nothing out of order in speaking out publicly in
support of them. The fact that his comments were
related to an existing domestic political issue did
not carry as much weight with him as did his belief
that his position was correct from the point of view
of the national security. Justice Douglas, on the
other hand, presumably viewed the general's comments
as primarily of a domestic political nature and
therefore well outside the area of military professionalism.

The role of the professional military officer
when national security policy becomes a domestic
political issue is indeed difficult. If he, as the
commander in chief's professional military advisor,
assists the president by publicly supporting a controversial policy is he guilty of nonprofessional
conduct? On the other hand, if he simply recommends
the policy to the president but then does not support it publicly, is he fulfilling his professional
obligation? The answers to these questions are

still wanting in the United States. They epitomize, however, a dilemma of the military professional.

The Truman administration presented several interesting problems in civil-military relations but certainly none so interesting or so perplexing as the Korean War.* Historically this nation has gone to war as a great crusade, with the military establishment being called upon to use its professional skill to lead the crusade on the battlefield. This was not the case in the Korean War. It was fought simply as a pragmatic extension of national policy. For practical purposes the American people did not go to war, only the U.S. government went to war.

In the wars of this century the basic concept that "in war there is no substitute for victory" was accepted by military officers, civilian authorities, and the public as well. It was never really questioned. Actually, universal acceptance of this concept in the United States made the task of the military professional relatively simple. Simple, that is, from the intellectual point of view. The professional military officer had no great problem in fixing on his objective. It was quite simply victory over the armed forces of the enemy. Once this victory had been achieved, the civilian authorities would again take over and determine what was to be done.

In the Korean War it soon became apparent that, in this particular war, there would be a substitute for victory. What this substitute would be was not

---

*The expression civil-military relations as used in this study refers essentially to the relationship of the military profession with the civilian leadership of our government. Politico-military relations refers to the interaction of the nation's foreign and military policies in the affairs of state. The first is namely domestic, the latter namely international. The two are, of necessity, closely related.

immediately clear but it was apparent that the U.S. government, as the agent of the United Nations, would be willing to accept something less than complete military victory. The military leadership in the Korean War was provided by officers who had gained their experience in World War II. In that war there was never any question that complete military victory was the ultimate goal, and after January, 1943, this concept was even further strengthened by the declaration of "unconditional surrender."

Considering the experience of the professional military officers who provided the leadership in Korea, it is perhaps possible to appreciate the frustrations they endured in the prosecution of that war. Those who had learned their trade in a general war had now to adjust themselves to a new concept of warfare: limited war. In certain respects, the Korean War was the most truly professional war the U.S. military establishment had been called upon to fight at that point in time.

From the point of view of a study in military professionalism and the politico-military equation, the high point of the Korean War was the relief of General MacArthur by President Truman. Basically, the conflict was simply a difference of opinion on the role of the military professional under the American form of government.

An interesting insight into General MacArthur's view of civil-military relations is suggested by S. E. Finer. In addressing himself to the basic question of to whom or to what the professional officer owes allegiance he says:

> General MacArthur was to make the distinction explicit when he said in 1952: "I find in existence a new and heretofore unknown and dangerous concept that the members of the armed forces owe primary allegiance or loyalty to those who temporarily exercise the authority of the Executive

Branch of Government rather than to
the country and its constitution
which they are sworn to defend."

"No proposition," added General
MacArthur, "could be more dangerous." On the contrary it is General
MacArthur's view which opens Pandora's
box. The moment the military draw
this fine distinction between nation
and the government in power, they be-
gin to invent their own private notion
of national interest, and from this it
is only a skip to the constrained sub-
stitution of this view for that of the
civilian government; . . .[10]

Certainly an officer of General MacArthur's experience was also aware that while members of the
armed forces are sworn to defend the country and
its constitution they are also expected to obey the
lawful orders of those above them, including, of
course, the president as the commander in chief.
Assuming that Finer's presentation of the general's
view is even reasonably accurate, the conclusion
that he draws is most valid. If each professional
military officer were to defend the constitution as
he interpreted it individually, without reference
to the administration in power, the American democratic system would be unworkable. It would be the
same thing if every officer in the chain of command
were free to question every order from above in
light of his own interpretation of the constitution.
Neither General MacArthur nor any military professional worthy of the name would subscribe to such a
thesis.[11]

Whatever General MacArthur may have said or
not have said, it is apparent that his views of
military professionalism conflicted with those of
President Truman. Wilber W. Hoare presents the
president's views as follows:

A disagreement over strategy between
the commander-in-chief and a subor-

dinate of MacArthur's stature was
not out of place in Truman's conception of military relationships, as
he himself acknowledged in his memoirs. What angered the President and
led to his decision to relieve the
general was the fact that, as he saw
it, MacArthur appealed over his head
to the public and, in addition, injected issues of foreign policy that
were not in his domain.

The career of MacArthur had been
a brilliant one. This very brilliance,
however, led to its end, for because
of it he was permitted, during the
1940's, to become more than a soldier.
When, in 1950, Truman tried, in a not
unkindly way, to lay him in the Pro-
crustean bed of a mere theatre commander he could no longer fit, and
the President attributing this to
contumaciousness, lopped him off.[12]

Whether General MacArthur or President Truman
had the better politico-military solution to the
problem of the Korean War is completely beside the
point. The fact is that a military professional
had exceeded the accepted bounds of military professionalism and was properly relieved. It is suggested that had President Truman not taken the position he did in the MacArthur case, military professionalism in the United States may well have suf-
fered a serious blow, and the concept of politico-
military integration could have been set back many
years.

The first seven years of the cold war brought
about a distinct change in the position of the military in the United States, and a consequent change
in the accepted concept of politico-military affairs. The military had become an accepted, if not
welcomed, peacetime fixture in the American society.
The very same conditions that brought acceptance of
a large peacetime military establishment brought

problems in the area of military professionalism, civil-military relations, and politico-military affairs. The dominent role played by the military in World War II was not to be accepted in the cold-war era. In an effort to safeguard the nation against the dangers, real or imagined, of excessive militarism more and more civilian control was injected into the system. The overall trend in this period was to increase the peacetime responsibilities of the military professional to an unprecedented degree, while at the same time to decrease military influence in the decision-making process. Politico-military thinking, as it had come to be accepted during World War II, was rejected and tended toward the prewar concept. Clemenceau's time-worn phrase that "war is too serious a matter to be left to the generals" had considerably greater acceptance in the United States in 1952 than it did in 1945.

THE EISENHOWER ADMINISTRATION

The basic trend toward greater civilian control of the military continued in this administration. It was this emphasis on civil control that presented the most perplexing problems in the area of politico-military affairs.

With the election of General Eisenhower, many military officers looked forward to a better day for the military professional. After all, here was a man who understood the military problem and who would set things right. As it turned out, President Eisenhower was to demonstrate a very "civilian" attitude toward the military. This was the era of the cold war in which massive retaliation became the overriding thesis of American national security policy, economy was stressed with emphasis on the "more bang for the buck" approach, and "brinkmanship" characterized U.S. foreign policy.

The three services enjoyed very different positions of favor with the administration. At the risk of oversimplification it may be said that the

air force was fully committed to the concept of massive retaliation and therefore was in general agreement with the administration's policy; the navy was
reasonably content to maintain the status quo and,
although not in full agreement with the administration, was not prone to oppose it openly. The army,
on the other hand, was relegated to a very minor
role in the defense structure and took the sharpest
blows from the economy axe. It was not completely
unexpected, therefore, that most of the serious differences with the administration on defense policy
came from the army.

The professional military officer who is in accord with the policies of the administration in
power really has no problem with his professional
conscience. On the other hand, the officer who
feels that the national policy is not adequately
providing for the defense of the nation is faced
with the dilemma of silently supporting a policy
that he feels is inadequate or speaking out
against it.

Upon departing the office of chief of staff of
the army, General Matthew B. Ridgeway expressed his
view of the role of military professional:

> I view the advisory role of a member
> of the Joint Chiefs of Staff as fol-
> lows: He should give his competent
> professional advice on the military
> aspects of the problems referred to
> him, based on his fearless, honest,
> objective estimate of the national in-
> terest, and regardless of administra-
> tion policy at any particular time.
> He should confine his advice to the
> essentially military aspects. . . .
>   However, in my opinion, the mil-
> itary advisor should be neither ex-
> pected nor required to give public
> indorsement to military courses of
> action against which he has previous-
> ly recommended. His responsibility

should be solely that of loyal vigorous execution of decisions by proper
authority.

This aspect is perhaps the most
difficult one for the military advisor,
particularly as he strives to keep
himself detached from domestic politics at the time domestic political
forces attempt to use him for their
own purpose. In his role as advisor,
he gives his best advice. In his
role as a commander, he implements decisions. Both roles must be respected
by civilian officials, as he must respect theirs. In this regard, as the
political climate shifts and changes,
different assessments will be made of
his proper role; but whatever the
situation, he must remain outside the
field of partisan politics. It is
incumbent upon civilian officials to
see that he stays outside, and to protect him from becoming involved.[13]

This rather lengthy quotation is taken from a
letter written by General Ridgeway to Secretary of
Defense Charles Wilson. It is most significant
here because it clearly points up the problem of
the military professional who is not in agreement
with the administration. This was the time during
which President Eisenhower was emphasizing the
"team" concept in the defense establishment. The
view was that once a decision had been made, all
members of the team would fully support the decision publicly and before Congress whether they
agreed with it or not.

Considering President Eisenhower's own military
experience this is an interesting concept. Within
the military structure itself, that is at the operational level, this concept is unquestioned. Any
military professional, from the highest ranking general or flag officer to the most junior lieutenant
or ensign, is fully aware that it is his duty to

recommend as he sees fit, to argue his case to the
limits of his ability, but then to execute the decision whether or not it was in accord with his recommendation. The issue, however, is that at the level
of the Joint Chiefs of Staff the military professional is expected to provide military advice to the
president and to the Congress as well. When the
president, as commander in chief, makes a decision,
is the military professional then obliged to <u>support</u>
this decision before the Congress? If this question
were put in a slightly different context by asking
whether the military professional is obliged to
<u>execute</u> the decisions of the president, the answer
is clearly yes. However, in the area of subordi-
nating his recommendations to the Congress to an administration decision the answer must be no, and is
no by law and by direction of the secretary of defense.

In his letter, General Ridgeway emphasized the
two roles of the members of the Joint Chiefs of
Staff, the role of the staff officer as an advisor,
and the role of the commander as the implementer of
decisions. He then placed the responsibility on the
civilian authorities to respect both these roles and
to see to it that the military professional is not
drawn into partisan politics.

The basic concept of civilian control of the
military in the United States has never been seriously questioned. The true military professional
accepts it and welcomes it. The point of contention was, and for that matter still is, not whether
there should be civilian control, but rather at
what levels it should be exercised. Being out of
step with the military policy of the Eisenhower administration, the army had by far the most to say
about this aspect of politico-military affairs.

General James Gavin commented as follows:

> Civilian control means civilian
> decision-making. It does not mean
> decisions that are made by the

> Chairman of the Joint Chiefs of Staff,
> then confirmed by the Secretary of De-
> fense. If the Secretary of Defense
> is going to make the decisions, he
> needs the best possible professional
> military advice upon which to base
> them.[14]

General Gavin then goes on to make the point
that civilian control of the military had progressed
to the point where the military professional had
been moved so far down in the defense structure
that truly professional advice seldom found its way
through the several levels of civilian officials to
the secretary of defense. In fact then, he felt,
the secretary was compelled to make military decisions without the benefit of military advice.

General Maxwell Taylor, sharing generally the
same views as those expressed by Generals Ridgeway
and Gavin above, took his argument to the public
when he left the service upon completion of his appointment as army chief of staff. In the foreword
to his well-known book, General Taylor summed up
his objections as follows: "I have undertaken to
write this book because of my conviction that the
defense of the United States is presently controlled
largely by nonmilitary factors or by military factors which have become outmoded."[15] There are many
arguments in favor of the administration's military
policy, just as there are many arguments in support
of the views expressed by the military professionals
quoted above. This period of the cold war, be it
right or wrong, good or bad, saw the continued
growth of civilian control over the military at increasingly lower levels and the insistence that the
military professional actively support the policies
of the administration before Congress. This trend
tended to identify more closely the professional
military officer with the administration and therefore tended to make him a domestic political being.

Of particular significance to the study of
politico-military affairs is the ever-increasing

civilian control of the military in the Eisenhower
administration. The great danger lay, not in the
fact that the military was subject to civil control;
this was a concept fully accepted by the professional military officer. The danger rather was in the
many layers of civilians placed between the military professional and the decision maker. It was
becoming increasingly difficult for the military
professional to gain a hearing in the national
policy-making councils at any meaningful level.
The overall effect was the gradual dilution of military professionalism and a weakening of the military
contribution to the politico-military equation.

    It is interesting to note that during the Eisen-
hower administration it was a professional military
officer, in disagreement with some of his military
colleagues and the president's highest civilian advisors who advised the president that the United
States should not militarily intervene in Indo-China
in 1954 unless the nation was willing to pay "the
tremendous cost in men and money that such an inter-
vention would have required." General Ridgeway, in
writing after the fact has said: "It was incredible
to me that we had forgotten that bitter lesson
[Korea] so soon--that we were on the verge of making
the same tragic error."[16]

    One author, not unreasonably, summarized the
period from the end of World War II through the
Eisenhower administration as an era that from the
politico-military viewpoint

> was dominated by a monopoly of the
> United States in nuclear weapons and
> strategic air power, and the success-
> ful containment of Soviet and Chinese
> expansionist tendencies within the
> boundaries loosely defined at Yalta
> and Potsdam.[17]

THE KENNEDY/JOHNSON ADMINISTRATION

    Although proponents and opponents of Presidents
Kennedy and Johnson may prefer to separate the

administrations for a number of reasons, none of
which have much to do with politico-military affairs, they do represent a common political philosophy and will best serve the purpose of this study
by being combined. During this period of the nation's history the cold war itself had taken on a
new complexion and the old concepts of military professionalism and politico-military affairs had been
reevaluated.

About a year after the Kennedy administration
took the reins in Washington there was considerable
feeling that the détente between the United States
and the Soviet Union had reached the point where it
could be considered that the cold war was a thing
of the past. It was pointed out, however, that
while the outlook might have been brighter, and the
possibility of nuclear war might have been less,
the nation still felt that the Soviet Union had not
changed its fundamental objectives and that the
United States had a requirement to remain militarily strong and alert. Whether or not the cold war
had actually come to an end and there was instead
some sort of suspension between normalcy and cold
war is really beside the point. The name is not
important. The change in the international environment is important. For the purpose of this study
the expression <u>cold war</u> will continue to be used to
refer to the environment in which the Kennedy/
Johnson administration operated--this with the full
realization that the semantics could be argued in
some detail.

A good review of President Kennedy's philosophy, as it applies to the role of the military
profession, is found in excerpts from an article by
McGeorge Bundy, special assistant for national security affairs:

> Yet the Kennedy years show again, as
> the terms of strong Presidents have
> shown before, that harmony, not con-
> flict, is the normal relation between
> the Armed Forces and the Presidency.
> The maintenance of clear Presidential

control over the military policy and
over public statements gave rise to
some criticism, and intermittently
there were assertions that this or
that military need was being over-
ridden--this or that viewpoint
silenced.

The American tradition of civilian control is strong and the tradition of loyalty among professional
officers high; the services are eager
for a strong Commander-in-Chief. The
armed strength of the United States,
if handled with firmness and prudence,
is a great force for peace.[18]

The broad concept will be commented on briefly in
terms of civil-military relations, and in more detail in terms of expanded military professionalism
and politico-military affairs.

The basic concept of civilian control of the
military did not change during these administrations. There was, however, a continuation of the
trend that had been evident since the end of World
War II to increase this control. The introduction
of the so-called Whiz Kids into the Pentagon
decision-making apparatus caused considerable re-
sentment on the part of many military professionals.
The military officer again had been effectively
moved further down the line in the decision-making
process. The concern of the true professional officer in this area was much more than a jealous reaction to his further loss of status to the young
civilian. There was a genuine and deep-felt concern that the military point of view had not received adequate emphasis in the making of decisions
directly dealing with the national security. In
the words of one professional air force officer:

Although the American military have
not always been submissive to civilian controllers, they have never seriously challenged the right or the

tradition of civil control. They
have recognized that the ultimate decision maker must balance military
recommendations against other considerations. It is not too difficult
for a military man to accept an adverse decision based on non-military
considerations. It becomes extremely
difficult, however, for him to recon-
cile himself to an adverse decision
by his civilian superiors based on
military considerations. This strikes
at the very raison d'etre of the military man. It challenges his military
professionalism.[19]

In the early 1960's, if this country really
had a military structure composed of truly professional officers, was the administration not dangerously toying with the national security by placing
too many layers of civilian officials between the
military professionals and the decision makers? Or
is it possible that the military, by virtue of its
conception of professionalism, possessed adequate
expertise in only one, or at best some, of an increased number of growingly complex aspects of national security and it was therefore necessary to
sift military recommendations through the several
layers of civilian officials in order to place the
recommendations in a usable perspective before they
reached the decision maker?

Any discussion generated by these two questions was, and to a degree still is, frequently
bitter, usually long, seldom productive, and not
always unemotional. Within the military profession
itself, extreme positions were taken by more conservative military officers on the one hand and the
other extreme was argued just as passionately by
their more liberal colleagues. As is most usually
the case when a dichotomy of this sort exists, the
workable solution was to be found somewhere between
the two extremes. During this period a discernable
trend toward a workable balance was continued.

The trend did not start with the Kennedy administration.   In actuality, it started with the
cold war itself and has become more pronounced
through the years.   The most evident appearance,
however, of a new concept dates from the time of
the Kennedy administration and the appointment of
General Taylor as chairman of the Joint Chiefs of
Staff.

Earlier in this study Generals Eisenhower and
Ridgeway were quoted in support of the argument
that the military professional should be called
upon to provide purely military advice and that the
responsibility rests with someone else to place
this advice in proper perspective.   In a speech
made in February, 1964, General Taylor presented
another view:

> I do not share the view that each ad-
> visor should be a specialist bringing
> to the table a narrow specialized
> view of the problem derived from the
> interests of the agency of government
> which he represents.   President
> Kennedy solved any doubt in the minds
> of the Joint Chiefs of Staff as to
> his views on the subject when in
> April 1961 he wrote to them as fol-
> lows: "While I look to the Chiefs to
> present the military factors without
> reserve or hesitation, I regard them
> to be more than military men and ex-
> pect their help in fitting military
> requirements into the over-all con-
> text of any situation, recognizing
> that the most difficult problem in
> Government is to combine all assets
> in a unified, effective pattern."[20]

It is quite apparent from the above statement that
military professionalism had taken on a new dimension in the Kennedy administration, and there is no
evidence to lead this writer to conclude that President Johnson saw fit to revise that concept subsequently.

On the surface this new concept had considerable merit. It did, however, present a most difficult challenge for the military profession.   In
this concept the military profession was expected
to provide officers who possessed the necessary expertise in the technical aspects of the profession
to successfully conduct large- or small-scale military operations as required. At the same time the
profession was expected to provide officers who
were capable of intelligently integrating the political, economic, and other aspects of national security into their military advice.

While the trend in other professions in our
society was, and continues to be, toward more and
more specialization, the professional military officer was now expected to be, if not an expert, at
least very well informed in many fields. Is there
not a danger in this concept of diluting the military profession to the point that the professional
officer is versed in a variety of areas but expert
in none? While the concept could possibly have
some merit in the cold war, would it prepare the
military profession to fight a hot war if the occasion arose?

President Kennedy's commitment to South Vietnam
in 1961 and President Johnson's subsequent dispatch
of combat troops to that country in 1965 in response
to the commitment did, in fact, test the ability of
the military profession to fight a hot war, albeit
a most unusual one, within the overall context of
the cold war. The wisdom of the commitments and
the subsequent escalation of the conflict in Vietnam
has been argued, is now being argued, and will continue to be argued for years to come. It will not
be argued further here. The purpose of these paragraphs is to examine the politico-military equation
in the latter half of the Kennedy/Johnson administration.

Having been determined that it was in the national interest to preserve the state of South
Vietnam and that the application of American

military force was necessary to achieve that interest, it needed only to be decided how much and what
sort of military force would be required to see it
through. In other words, how should the politico-
military equation be constructed initially and then
kept in balance?

A gradual increase of military pressure, in order to force the "other side" to desist in its efforts to achieve a decision in its favor by force,
and at the same time preclude an enlargement of the
war, was decided upon. Most senior military professionals saw this as a poor use of military power
and warned of the consequences. They argued instead
for a more decisive use of the nation's military
power to achieve the political objective in the
shortest reasonable time. The author must admit
that the "graduated response" concept seemed sound
to him at the time. The fact that over six years
after the deployment of combat forces the United
States is still involved in the same contest is evidence that the selected approach did not work as it
was expected to work. While the lack of success
gives some comfort to the "I told you so" group, the
outcome, had more military power been applied at the
outset, is conjecture at best. In terms of the
politico-military equation a concept that was designed to provide maximum flexibility for the political side of the equation was used.

Up to this point in the Vietnam adventure it
can be said that the actual conduct of military operations by the military professionals was, on the
whole, reasonably well done. The balancing of the
politico-military equation to achieve the national
objective was considerably less successful.

The politico-military dilemma of Vietnam is
probably best stated by Sir Robert Thompson. Essentially he felt that the "war" in Vietnam was viewed
either as an external invasion supported by internal
insurgency, or as an internal insurgency supported
by an external invasion.[21] Depending upon which
view of the war one chose to accept, his approach

to resolving it would differ. As evidenced by the
State Department's explanations at the time, the administration presented the war to the public in the
context of the first view.[22] Had it been viewed
differently, the politico-military equation would
have been constructed differently.

For many reasons--the war dragged on despite
the bombing halt in the fall of 1968 and the subsequent initiation of talks in Paris, and frustrations
on the part of the American body politic--the military profession, and the administration grew. This
collective frustration, a preview of which had begun
to manifest itself in the latter stages of the
Korean War, is responsible, at least in part, for
the administration's increasing emphasis on the military side of the politico-military equation. This
weighting is explained by one author:

> The legacy that Johnson inherited
> from Kennedy in Vietnam strongly dis-
> posed him toward greater military in-
> volvement there, but it did not pre-
> determine his decisions to increase
> our military commitments or his per-
> sistent preference for military means
> over other strategies. These deci-
> sions were more the product of the
> domestic politics of protracted wars,
> so clear since the Korean War.[23]

Nobody of consequence seemed to disagree that the
United States sought a "political" objective in
Southeast Asia but how to achieve it remained elusive. This thought is developed further in a later
chapter entitled, "The Elusive Concept of Victory."

Victory remained elusive, frustrations at home
grew, and President Johnson was virtually forced
out of the 1968 presidential race. The Kennedy/
Johnson administration came to a close with the nation deeply involved in an unpopular "hot war" being
fought in a peacetime environment within the overall
context of the cold war. The American political

objective in Vietnam still had to be achieved and there were public complaints that the military had too many political constraints placed on it to "win" the war. As was suggested above, these same complaints were heard at the time of the Korean War, but an eventual political settlement resolved the issue before the public became too involved.

Conceptually there had been no significant change in the line of politico-military thinking that had been evolving since World War II. Practically, however, some underlying differences did exist. Essentially it continued to be agreed by civilian officials and military professionals that there were no purely political or purely military problems but that a complete integration of the nation's foreign and military policies was essential. There were rumblings, probably inherent in the growing frustrations of the time, that the nation's foreign and military policies were inhibiting, rather than complementing one another. Critics of the administration spoke of the "militarization" of the foreign policy or of the "politicization" of the military policy, depending upon their personal persuasion.

As suggested above, the Truman and Eisenhower administrations were dominated by a politico-military philosophy centered on American military superiority and a policy of containment. This line of thinking was criticized as being too rigid and without the necessary amount of politico-military flexibility. The Kennedy/Johnson administration was dominated by a "flexible response" philosophy that, in theory at least, provided the maximum politico-military flexibility, but that apparently lost the confidence, or at least the patience, of the American people when put to the test of protracted war. The administration that was to take office in January, 1969, was not unaware of the problems associated with each of the philosophies identified above.

THE NIXON ADMINISTRATION

This portion of the discussion of the cold-war
period represents both the shortest and the most recent period in time. The time considerations coupled with the fact that the administration is currently in power makes a truly objective evaluation
of this period extremely hazardous. At least a
tentative evaluation is extremely important, however, for several reasons. First, the cold war itself has taken on a new complexion and second, the
concepts of military professionalism and politico-
military affairs carried over from the previous administration face new stresses.

The new administration undertook two basic pro-
cedural changes that had a direct impact on the
military profession and the role of the professional
in the decision-making processes. The first was an
internal adjustment within the Department of Defense
that restored greater responsibility to the military
professionals in the budget processes within the defense establishment. This move had the direct effect of somewhat lessening the civilian involvement
in affairs that many military professionals felt
were exclusively military matters. The second
change was a restructuring of the National Security
Council machinery to provide for more farmalized integration of the political, military, and other aspects of national security planning. It is emphasized that neither of these efforts represented any
significant conceptual change from the previous administration. The changes were a matter of emphasis and technique, not substance.

Although the President did not specifically
state that the cold war had come to an end, he said
essentially the same thing in declaring a "new era"
of international relations. He pointed out that
"the whole pattern of international politics was
changing." He commented further that "the postwar
period in international relations has ended."[24]
This expression may not have been as precise as a
positive declaration of the end of the cold war,

but it clearly recognized a changed environment and pointed the way from an era of confrontation manifested primarily in the conflict in Vietnam.

The fact that the President saw this new era as "an era of negotiation" by no means resolved the many deep differences between the United States and the Soviet Union, but it did, by its emphasis on negotiation, tend to soften the lines of confrontation and provide the conceptual framework for shifting attention to the political side of the politico-military equation.

Critics of the administration rather generally failed to accept the government's "rhetoric" in light of the facts as they saw them in Southeast Asia. They seized upon the Cambodian operation of May-June, 1970, as proof that the politico-military equation had come wholly out of balance. The president was accused of "selling out to the military" by failing to take into account the international political implications of the decision to enter Cambodia. This line of thinking was illustrated by Joseph Kraft's column of June 21, 1970, to which he assigned the title, "Mr. Nixon's Win Policy," and the subtitle "Gap Between Rhetoric and Fact Makes Clear U.S. Policy is to Beat Enemy on Ground."[25] Another example of expressed concern referred to the President's

> failure to include any top-level State Department officials in his weekend meeting at San Clemente, Calif., underscores what diplomatic sources believe to be an indifference to the political implications of his moves in Southeast Asia. . . .
> It is assumed that the President wanted a "progress report" from Gen. Abrams. . . . But diplomatic officials regard the military and political factors as so closely linked as to require concerted attention.[26]

The other thought of significance to the balancing of the politico-military equation is the apparent gentle shift in emphasis from a philosophy
of gradual response to one with greater emphasis on
strategic deterrence. This line of thought is inherent in the "Nixon Doctrine" and in the President's
report to the Congress of February, 1970. While, as
suggested above, there were those critics who felt
the administration was not implementing its own policies, it is by no means clear what future implementation will be and certainly it is even less clear
how it will all turn out. It is quite clear, however, that there will be the ever-present strains on
the politico-military equation and that American
military professionalism will continue to be challenged by the dynamics of the international and domestic political environments.

CONFLICTING CONCEPTS OF MILITARY
PROFESSIONALISM

In the preceding pages two divergent concepts
of military professionalism can be identified   For
purposes of identification they are here called
traditional professionalism and new professionalism
respectively. Traditional professionalism is that
which existed prior to World War II. It continued,
with some significant modification, through the war
years and extended on into the period of the cold
war in a somewhat diluted form. The basic tenet of
this concept was the separation of the military and
political function. Further, it demanded purely
military advice and recommendations from the military professional, leaving to the civilian superiors
the task of integrating the raw military recommendation into the broader framework of the national
security policy.

New professionalism, as a distinct concept,
has appeared primarily in the decade of the 1960's.
The appearance of the new concept, however, was not
especially abrupt. It had been evolving through
the years in the form of modification to the

traditional concept. The requirement that President
Kennedy placed on the Joint Chiefs of Staff to "help
in fitting military requirements into the overall
context of any situation" was simply the formal
recognition of this new approach.

Devoted and sincere military and civilian leaders and scholars are divided in their opinions as to
the relative merits of these two basic concepts.
Considering then the task of the military professional and the international environments of the
cold war, which of these concepts will best contribute to a meaningful politico-military balance
in U.S. national policy councils? In an attempt to
answer this question there is a temptation to construct great lists of the advantages and disadvantages of each concept and then to engage in a la-
borious and painful comparison and analysis of each.
It is felt, however, that a more general and admittedly less precise summary of the major advantages
and disadvantages of each, from the viewpoint of
national security, will be more meaningful.

Advantages: In the traditional concept the advice and recommendations sent forward to the decision maker by the military professional represents
the pure military viewpoint. This viewpoint is in
no way diluted by political, economic, or other considerations, therefore offering to the decision
maker a clear picture of the military requirement.
The expertise of the military professional, which
is the result of many years of service and experience, comes through most clearly. Further, it permits the military officer to confine his thinking
to a relatively narrow area in which he can be a
true expert. To use an old cliché, he will not become a "jack of all trades and a master of none"
but will rather be a true master of his trade. Finally, this concept, by limiting military participation to purely military matters, enhances the time-
honored concept of civilian control of the military.

Disadvantages: The primary disadvantage of
this concept is that the purely military recommendation that goes forward to the decision maker is

frequently incompatible with the overall national
policy. By placing the responsibility for modification of the military recommendation on a civilian
authority, these modifications are too often arbi-
trary and not in keeping with sound military judgment. Within this concept the military view is not
completely represented in the modification process
and frequently results in very "unprofessional" decisions. While this concept advances the cherished
American adherence to civilian control of the military it also encourages a degree of involvement
that is the basis of complaint of many professional
military and civilian officials. Finally, the military professional is essentially removed from the
process of balancing the politico-military equation.

When considering the advantages of two conflicting concepts it is obvious that many of the advantages of one will be the converse of the disadvantages of the other. An argument could be made,
therefore, for simply recognizing this dichotomy
and not commenting on the concept of new professionalism any further. For the sake of emphasis, however, the major advantages and disadvantages of the
newer concept will be indicated.

Advantages: The decision maker who has received a recommendation from his military advisors
that has already taken into account the political,
economic, and other aspects of the given situation
is not faced with the problem of making major alterations to fit the recommendation into the overall national policy. The military viewpoint, which
is expressed under this concept, will seldom be the
ideal one from the purely military point of view
but will already have included in it those com-
promises the military feels to be acceptable if not
ideal. This approach will not destroy the concept
of civilian control of the military but could assist
in reducing to an acceptable level the overinvolve-
ment that too frequently results in militarily unacceptable decisions. In essence it will reduce the
probability that the military viewpoint is read out
of a given problem even before it reaches the
decision-making level.

   Disadvantages: The most apparent disadvantage
is the real possibility of generating diluted military professionalism. It places a great requirement
on the military to be versed in the nonmilitary aspects of the national policy while still retaining
a very high level of purely military expertise.
This approach tends to broaden the base of military
professionalism at the possible expense of in-depth
expertise in a growingly complex technological military environment. There are many other officials
in the policy-making machinery who are expected to
advise on the political, economic, and other aspects
of a given problem, but only the military professional has the necessary training and experience to
bring the military view into proper focus.

COLD WAR TRENDS

   In the years from the end of World War II to
the present, several related trends in the area of
military professionalism, civil-military relations,
and politico-military affairs can be identified.
The nature of the cold war itself has strengthened
general acceptance of the thesis, which resulted
from the experiences of World War II, that the political and military viewpoints must be thoroughly
integrated into any meaningful national security
policy. Acceptance of this basic thesis seems to
be essentially universal. However, there is by no
means universal agreement as to exactly how the
politico-military equation should be constructed
and then kept in balance.

   For the purpose of this evaluation of the cold
war years there are three trends that should be identified. The first is the trend toward increasing
civilian control of the military, including increased
involvement in the technical aspects of the formulation of military advice before it reaches the decision maker. The second is the trend from what earlier has been called "traditional" to the "new" professionalism. The third is the trend from politico-
military policies, which in fact provided little

flexibility in balancing the politico-military equation, to considerably more flexible, but of necessity, less-precise policies. These three trends
were parallel developments that, while not necessarily mutually interdependent, were very closely related. Broadly speaking, "traditional" professionalism has been more comfortable with the somewhat
less flexible politico-military policies and with
less-civilian involvement in the details of military matters. The "new" professionalism, on the
other hand, is more at home with the more flexible
views of the decade of the 1960's and finds it less
frustrating to live with increased civilian involvement.

The apparent shift at the outset of the 1970's
from "flexible response" thinking toward emphasis
on strategic deterrence does indicate an adjustment
in the politico-military equation and will certainly
impact to some degree on military professionalism in
the United States. The proverbial pendulum continues to swing and when its current movement will come
to its furthest point remains to be seen.

This chapter on the cold war would not be complete without mention of the so-called Pentagon
Papers that were released by the press in the early
summer of 1971, and the effect they may have on
American military professionalism and the politico-
military equation. This chapter was initially written well before the papers were made public and the
author finds it difficult to identify anything he
would have said differently had they been available.
Clearly, the revelations support the argument for a
properly balanced politico-military equation and
for an ever-greater mutual understanding by the
civilian government officials of the military professional and by the military professional of his
civilian colleague. The American public, probably
expressing itself through the Congress, can be expected to demand an ever-higher level of professionalism of its civilian and military leadership.

One might hazard a guess that the operative effects of the papers on immediate policy decisions

will probably be small. The reflective effect on
overall American thinking about the role of the
United States in world affairs may well prove to be
the most lasting and meaningful effect. In the
short run it would appear that the papers have so
far primarily succeeded in providing documentation
for the proponents of virtually every school of
thought about Vietnam to support already preconceived and fixed prejudices.

NOTES

1.   James D. Atkinson, "An Approach to National
Security," in National Security, ed. David M.
Abshire and Richard V. Allen (New York: Frederick
A. Praeger, 1963), p. 569.

2.   U.S., Department of Defense, Joint Chiefs
of Staff Publication No. 1; Dictionary of United
States Military Terms for Joint Usage (Washington:
U.S. Government Printing Office, August 1, 1968),
p. 47.

3.   Thomas W. Wilson, Cold War and Common Sense
(Greenwich, Conn.:   New York Graphic Society, 1962),
p. 211; also see John Lukacs, A History of the Cold
War (Garden City, N.Y.:   Doubleday and Company,
1961), pp. 1-37.

4.   Samuel P. Huntington, The Soldier and the
State (Cambridge, Mass.:   The Belknap Press, 1959),
p. 346.

5.   Henry A. Wallace, "Militarization in the
United States," The New Republic, January 26, 1948,
p. 22.

6.   Fred J. Cook, The Warfare State (New York:
The Macmillan Company, 1962), p. 101; for more of
this type of comment see John M. Swomley, Jr., The
Military Establishment (Boston: Beacon Press, 1964),
especially Chapter 12, pp. 139-76.

7. Dwight D. Eisenhower, Testimony before the Subcommittee on Appropriations, U.S. Senate, June 28, 1947.

8. "Should We Fear the Military?" Look, March 11, 1952, p. 34.

9. Ibid., p. 35. For the situation prevailing in the United States between the military and civilian authorities at this time see Walter Millis, et al., Arms and the State (New York: The Twentieth Century Fund, 1958), pp. 141-44.

10. S. E. Finer, The Man on Horseback (New York: Frederick A. Praeger, 1962), p. 26.

11. See Thomas H. Reese, "Divided Loyalty for the Military Officer," Military Review, October, 1964, p. 17.

12. Wilber W. Hoare, Jr., "Truman (1945-1953)," in The Ultimate Decision, ed. Ernest R. May (New York: George Braziller, 1960), p. 207.

13. Matthew B. Ridgeway, "Text of a Letter Addressed to Secretary of Defense Charles E. Wilson," June 27, 1955; U.S. News and World Report, July 29, 1955.

14. James M. Gavin, War and Peace in the Space Age (New York: Harper and Brothers, 1958), p. 258.

15. Maxwell D. Taylor, The Uncertain Trumpet (New York: Harper and Brothers, 1960), p. x.

16. Matthew B. Ridgeway, Soldier (New York: Harper and Brothers, 1956), pp. 274-80.

17. Charles Maechling, Jr., "The Next Decade in American Foreign Policy," The Virginia Quarterly Review, Summer, 1969, p. 370.

18. McGeorge Bundy, "The President and the Peace," Foreign Affairs, April, 1964, pp. 354-65.

    19.   Robert N. Ginsburgh, "Challenge to Mili-
tary Professionalism," Foreign Affairs, January,
1964, p. 255.

    20.   Maxwell D. Taylor, "Military Advice--Its
Use in Government," Vital Speeches, March 15, 1964.

    21.   Sir Robert Thompson, No Exit from Vietnam
(New York: David McKay Company, 1969).

    22.   U.S., Department of State, "Aggression
from the North: The Record of North Viet-Nam's
Campaign to Conquer South Viet-Nam," Department of
State Publication 7839, Bureau of Public Affairs
(Washington: U.S. Government Printing Office, 1965).

    23.   Paul Y. Hammond, The Cold War Years:
American Foreign Policy Since 1945 (New York:
Harcourt, Brace and World, 1969).

    24.   Richard Nixon, U.S. Foreign Policy for the
1970's: A New Strategy for Peace.   A Report to the
Congress by the President of the United States, February 18, 1970 (Washington: U.S. Government Printing Office, 1970), pp. 1, 2.

    25.   Joseph Kraft, "Mr. Nixon's Win Policy,"
The Washington Post, June 21, 1970, p. B7.

    26.   Peter Lisagor, "State Feels Left Out on
War," The Evening Star (Washington, D.C.), June 2,
1970, p. A2.

4

POLITICO-
MILITARY
ORGANIZATION

"Military and political institutions are inseparable; in a certain sense they are mutually
dependent variables. A change in the character of
one produces a corresponding change in the other."[1]
As is pointed out in the preceding chapters, the
basic philosophy expressed above is rather universally accepted today. There is little argument
that it is indeed difficult to distinguish between
the purely military and the purely political aspects of a given national security problem. There
is also little argument that the solution to any
significant national security problem with other
than a very narrow domestic connotation, is to be
found within the framework of a proper balance to
politico-military equation. The determination of
where or what that proper balance is, however,
presents a continuing and dynamic challenge to the
nation's civilian and military policy makers.

Early in the cold war, Harold D. Lasswell and
Abraham Kaplin attempted to identify the point at
which a problem is primarily military or primarily
civil. While their effort was addressed specifically to civil-military relations it is perhaps
equally relevant to politico-military terminology

as well. When is a problem more military than political and when is it more political than military?
They said: "An arena is <u>military</u> when the expectation of violence is high; <u>civic</u> [political] when
the expectation is low."2 This relationship to
violence may serve to indicate a direction in which
to look, but the determination of the line between
"high" and "low" expectations of violence is yet to
be accomplished. The fact is that it is virtually
impossible to clearly identify a purely political
or a purely military environment regardless of the
direction from which the question is approached.
In its relations with the other members of the international community the nation does not, for
practical purposes, have political or military
problems--it has politico-military problems.

It is not impossible to identify a situation
in which the military side of the politico-military
equation is clearly and heavily weighted. Nor is
it impossible to find a situation in which the political side of the equation is similarly weighted.
Situations of this type, however, would be compara-
tively rare and represent the exception rather than
the rule. Between these two extremes is to be
found the great proverbial grey area in which a
clear determination is impossible. It is within
this grey area that most of our national security
problems fall. It is within this grey area that
the practical problems of politico-military affairs
are most perplexing.

The implication of a great overlap of the political and military areas of interest certainly
points up the requirement for a mutual understanding between the professional military officer and
the foreign policy maker. In this regard, Senator
J. W. Fulbright commented in the early 1960's:

> The military professional is now in-
> volved intimately in national policy
> processes. This involvement is not
> the result of any conscious quest for
> political power on the part of the

> military but rather the inevitable
> product of the new world-wide commit-
> ments of the United States and of the
> revolution in military technology.
> Power in a democracy is inseparable
> from responsibility. Accordingly,
> the Military Establishment is under
> the most compelling obligation to
> exercise the power which has been
> thrust upon it with wisdom and re-
> straint.[3]

Senator Fulbright's observation is still sound
and it is unlikely that strong exception would be
taken to it. The comment was made in a speech to
an audience consisting primarily of selected military officers, so the emphasis on the responsibility of the military to use its power wisely was most
appropriate. Presented in another context, however,
the speech may well have emphasized the responsibility of civilian officials in exercising the
powers they hold over the military. It is a two-
way proposition in which the civil and military
policy makers must accept their responsibilities
fully and conduct their incursions into the domain
of the other prudently and wisely.

Accepting the basic premise that the military
professional has certain interests and responsibilities in the field of international politics, and
that the international political professional (foreign service officer and others) has certain interests and responsibilities in the field of military affairs, this study will now examine one of
the ways in which the achievement of a proper balance to the politico-military equation is sought
through organization. A text prepared for use by
the Industrial College of the Armed Forces commented on the requirement for this sort of organization
as follows:

> A nation's security rests on many re-
> sources: human, natural, technological,
> political, to name but a few. Among

the most important assets is the
ability to organize these resources,
to arrange and focus them into a co-
herent, intelligent pattern. This
organizational capability is a prime
factor in the management of national
security. It depends primarily on
individuals, the nation's leaders,
for, in the words of Richard E.
Neustadt, "Men are of the essence:
what they carry in their heads, and
how they use their minds, and where
they look for information." Yet no
less important are the means these
men employ to achieve national goals,
the institutions and processes involved in the formulation and implementation of national security policy.[4]

The formulation and implementation of the
foreign policy of the United States through the
Department of State is a highly demanding and complex task. Likewise, the formulation and implementation of the military policy of the United
States through the Department of Defense is a size-
able undertaking. The integration and coordination
of the efforts of these two departments into one
realistic national security policy is indeed a mon-
umental charge. To assist in this integration and
coordination, the nation is served by the National
Security Council at the highest level, and by a
complex politico-military structure within the Departments of State and Defense and at lower levels.

In midsummer, 1789, George Washington
complained that he had no leisure to
read and answer the dispatches that
were pouring in upon him from all
quarters. A year later he confided
to his friend, David Stuart, "The
public meetings . . . with the references to and from the different departments of state . . . is as much,
if not more, than I am able to

undergo. . . ." Yet Washington pre-
sided over only six executive departments, employing only about 2,000
public officials, and he had Alexander
Hamilton to do his work for him.[5]

From the above it would appear that the complexity of managing the affairs of the United
States has been a practical problem from the very
beginning. While the requirement for coordination
was apparent from the beginning, the machinery for
achieving that coordination is of more recent vintage. In a recent article, Rocco M. Paone, an
associate professor of international relations at
the United States Naval Academy, commented: "The
idea that foreign policy and military power are
closely interrelated is not new to basic U.S. doctrine, although the machinery for political-military
coordination in foreign affairs is of relatively
recent origin."[6]

The vast machinery that exists today for the
coordination of the political and the military
policies of the United States is relatively new.
It came about primarily as a result of the lessons
learned in World War II and in the early years of
the cold war. There has been a proliferation of
politico-military offices and staff agencies of
varying descriptions whose coming into existence
was directly attributable to the desire of official
Washington to keep the politico-military equation
in balance. To be sure, much of the politico-
Military machinery was constructed with the primary
intent of insuring full and complete integration of
political and military factors into national security planning. Some was constructed with the more
negative intent of insuring that the private domain
of some particular sector of the bureaucratic construct was not violated. For whatever reason, it
is a fact that the expression politico-military
appears frequently on the organization charts in
the Executive Office of the President, the Department of Defense, the Department of State, and in
the field, just as the expression has become part

of the lexicon of the national security community
at all levels. Whatever the motive, growth of the
politico-military machinery is generally considered
to be a positive contribution to the overall planning procedure.

In a survey conducted by the author of the
National War College classes of 1968 and 1970, the
following question pertaining to politico-military
machinery was asked: "In your view does adequate
governmental machinery exist for the integration of
the nation's foreign and military policies?"
Seventy percent of the respondents felt that the
machinery was adequate. There was no significant
difference between the responses from the classes
of 1968 and 1970. It was interesting, but not
really surprising, that the military officers who
felt the machinery was inadequate believed that it
provided undue recourse to the proponents of the
politicial point of view. The civilian respondents
who explained their negative response felt exactly
the opposite. It is worthy of note that the percentage of military and civilian respondents who
replied in the positive and the negative was essentially the same.

Prior to 1939 the closest thing the United
States had to a politico-military coordinating
agency was the Joint Board consisting of four high-
ranking officers from each of the services. This
was a purely military agency that was subordinate
to the secretaries of the two military departments.
In 1939 the Joint Board was placed directly under
the president and its responsibilities quickly expanded. In the words of William Emerson:

> The Military Order of 1939 had the
> effect of raising the Joint Board
> above the departmental level. By
> placing the chiefs in a special re-
> lationship to the President, it made
> them in some way independent of their
> immediate civilian superiors. In
> their new circumstances, the chiefs

extended the range and scope of their
interests. Increasingly after 1939
the Joint Board, under the control of
the President, concerned itself with
questions of national rather than
service strategy. In prewar studies
it produced basic plans that were to
have great influence later.[7]

At the Arcadia Conference of December, 1941-
January, 1942, the Combined Chiefs of Staff, consisting of the American Chiefs and the British
Chiefs of Staff Committee, was born. In order to
coordinate the American view, the Joint Board, with
some modifications, became the Joint Chiefs of
Staff. The members of the Joint Chiefs of Staff
had the dual function of formulating American policy and also representing the United States on the
Combined Chiefs of Staff.

Of particular importance is the fact that both
the expansion of the Joint Board in 1939 and the
organization of the Joint Chiefs of Staff in 1942
were the direct results of military necessity. In
theory, both the Joint Board and the Joint Chiefs
of Staff were purely military agencies that should
have been the providers of professional military
advice to the government. This, however, was not
to be the case. Samuel Huntington says:

> Although created in response to func-
> tional military imperatives, however,
> both organs were drawn by organiza-
> tional and political pulls into oper-
> ating as political as well as mili-
> tary bodies. The Joint Chiefs of
> Staff became, next to the President,
> the single most important force in
> the overall conduct of the war, the
> level and the scope of their activ-
> ities far transcending those of a
> purely professional body. As a
> result, the Joint Chiefs ended the
> war with no experience in functioning

simply as a military organization.
Four years of war had given them a
political tradition and role.[8]

The Joint Chiefs of Staff organization was,
for all practical purposes, the national coordinating agency for World War II. The United States
did not have a politico-military body such as the
British War Cabinet or our present National Security Council. Actually several agencies that easily could have evolved into a "war council" did
exist in the immediate prewar years, but they
either ceased to operate or played a very minor
role during the war. It was not until December,
1944, that a politico-military body was created.
It was the State-War-Navy Coordinating Committee
(SWNCC), composed of assistant secretaries of the
represented departments. Its initial concern was
with surrender terms and occupation policy. It
was the direct ancestor of the National Security
Council.[9]

During the war, major emphasis was placed on
the military side of the politico-military equation, and the use of the Joint Chiefs of Staff as
the national planning agency reflected that emphasis. Toward the end of the war, when it came time
to consider problems of surrender and occupation,
the emphasis commenced to shift toward the political side of the equation. The creation of SWNCC
reflected this shift. It can be said that the
creation, in the United States, of a formal organization for the coordination of political and
military policy directly reflected the basis dynamics of American politico-military philosophy of
the time.

As the United States entered the era of the
cold war, the shift in the political-military balance toward the political side of the equation
continued. This was the result of a number of
factors that ranged from the changing international environment to the historic antimilitary sentiment in the United States following the war. It

was within this setting that the National Security
Council emerged as the "war council" of the United
States.

EXECUTIVE OFFICE OF THE PRESIDENT

The president, as an individual, occupies the
central position in the formulation, direction, and
execution of national security policy. In the final analysis it is the president who constructs the
politico-military equation and keeps it in balance
in accordance with his personal evaluation of the
many conflicting determinations in any given situation. The president derives his powers in the
field of national security from the constitutional
grant of responsibility for carrying on the nation's international relations and from his role as
commander in chief of the armed forces.

It goes without saying that the president cannot fulfill his national security responsibilities
without assistance. While there are many functions
performed in the Executive Office of the President
that contribute, in greater or lesser degree, to
the construction and balancing of the politico-
military equation, the National Security Council
and the special assistant to the president for national security affairs will be specifically addressed. The two, as will be seen, are institution-
ally separate but functionally inseparable.

The National Security Council (NSC) was created by Public Law 253 in 1947 as one of the answers to the frustrations met by World War II
policy makers in trying to coordinate military and
foreign policy. As was indicated above, it was the
direct descendent of the SWNCC. The Council was
assigned by the National Security Act of 1947 (Public Law 253) the mission of advising the President.

> With respect to the integration of
> domestic, foreign, and military poli-
> cies relating to the national security

so as to enable the military services
and other departments and agencies of
the Government to cooperate more effectively in matters involving the
national security.

Even though the NSC was created by statute,
each president has seen fit to determine how it
would best serve him. Debate as to the best manner in which the NSC might be employed by a president will be a continuing thing. Likewise, the
debate as to the necessity or the desirability of
the Planning Board and the Operations Coordinating
Board will also continue. These are essentially
matters of value judgment and are not within the
scope of this study. However, a brief review of
the use of the NSC by several presidents is worth-
while and is pertinent to the subject at hand.

A brief comparison of the manner in which the
NSC was used by President Eisenhower and by President Kennedy will be made because the differences
are significant and had a direct bearing on the
manner in which the military and the political
points of view were integrated in the national
policy-making process.

Shortly after taking office, President Eisenhower appointed General Robert Cutler to conduct a
thorough, wide-range reappraisal of the NSC. Several significant innovations resulted from this
study, including the creation of the Office of
Special Assistant to the President for National
Security Affairs, the National Security Council
Planning Board, and the Operations Coordinating
Board.

The special assistant to the president for
national security affairs was made responsible for
determination, subject to the president's desires,
of the Council agenda, for briefing the president
in advance of Council meetings, and for presenting
matters for discussion at the Council meetings.
The Planning Board was designed to prepare policy

papers for the NSC, and the Operations Coordinating
Board was designed to provide the follow-up coordination once a decision had been reached to pursue
a particular course of action.

The NSC became highly institutionalized with
rather firmly fixed procedures for the planning and
coordination of national security policy. One of
the most common criticisms of President Eisenhower's
use of the NSC was that the formalization resulted
only in a requirement for a presidential "yes" or
"no" with no other alternative being immediately
available. It was argued that in the event the
president elected to reject the Council's recommendation, he was left with the unhappy choice of making no decision at all or of improvising, for alternatives were readily available.

President Eisenhower had directed that all decisions on national security policy, except those
evolving out of special emergencies or situations,
would be made within the framework of the NSC.
The Council was very active during the Eisenhower
administration, meeting, for example, 115 times
during the first 115 weeks.

Closely associated with the NSC in the area of
national decision making is the White House Staff
Organization. The role of the assistant for national security affairs is particularly critical.
It was mentioned earlier and will be commented on
subsequently. A few general comments, however,
which relate to the formal organization that contributed to the integration and coordination of
the nation's national security policy, are in order
here. Under President Eisenhower the White House
Staff Organization provided for an unofficial chief
of staff, who held the title of assistant to the
president. Most policy proposals for the president's consideration and decision were routed
through Sherman Adams and later through Wilton B.
Persons, both of whom held the position of assistant to the president. In some respects this was
simply an institutionalization of the role played

by John Steelman in the Truman administration and
of Harry Hopkins in the Roosevelt years. The anal-
ogies are a bit less than perfect but they serve to
illustrate the point. Because of the role of the
assistant to the president in the Eisenhower administration, it has been argued that only those policy conflicts that could not be resolved at the
staff level survived to be argued before the president. Briefly, then, this was the formal and the
informal organization that served President Eisenhower during his eight years in office.

When President Kennedy took office in 1961 he
accepted some of the more significant recommendations of the Subcommittee on National Policy Machinery of the Senate Committee on Government Operations. The Subcommittee studies indicated, among
other things, that "the main work of the National
Security Council has centered largely around the
consideration of foreign policy questions, rather
than on national security problems in their full
contemporary sense."[10] In other words, the Council
was not adequately performing its role of integrating and coordination of the military and the political aspects of the national security policy equation, but was placing too much emphasis on foreign
policy considerations.

President Kennedy, in February 1961, "deinsti-
tutionalized" and "humanized" the NSC, eliminating
the Planning Board and the Operations Coordinating
Board.

> The Planning Board which had been the
> Senior Staff under Truman, gave way
> before the Kennedy Administration's
> notion that plans and operations should
> be integrated and, further, that plan-
> ning is most effective when specifical-
> ly pointed rather than general in char-
> acter. Elimination of the Operations
> Coordinating Board was a protest
> against committee inefficiency in the
> implementation of Council decisions

> in favor of concentrated (in a single
> department or agency) responsibility
> for swift policy execution.[11]

In addition, President Kennedy did not fill
the highly controversial position of assistant to
the president, but named McGeorge Bundy as his
special assistant for national security affairs.
The organizational changes are important but in
many ways the more subtle differences between the
two philosophies are equally or perhaps even more
important.

In an analysis of how policy was determined in
the Kennedy administration, U.S. News and World Report commented as follows, only a few months after
the new Administration had taken over:

> In this administration one thing is
> clear-cut. President Kennedy is the
> boss. He makes the decisions of im-
> portance not Secretaries or subordi-
> nates. . . . The President does not
> believe that the Government can be
> run successfully by organizing it
> into a lot of compartments, hermeti-
> cally sealed. Ideas and proposals
> crop up from all sides in a process
> which the White House group calls
> cross-fertilization. The fact that
> Dean Rusk is Secretary of State does
> not stop key officers such as McGeorge
> Bundy, Walt Rostow, Paul Nitze, Adlai
> Stevenson, and others from turning
> out ideas and suggestions as well.
> Yet the final decision is the Presi-
> dent's.[12]

President Kennedy borrowed a page from military planning and operational concepts and established numerous "task forces" to take over the
planning and execution of specific problems that
he felt would become bogged down in the more institutionalized planning agencies such as the NSC.

The task force method

> has the advantage of direct action,
> one man responsibility, and the follow-
> through momentum of a small group.
> But it removes the planning and the
> operations somewhat out of channels
> (although an effort is made to keep
> everyone informed) and limits the ac-
> tion to a few strong minds, without
> the admittedly slower checks and bal-
> ance system of old fashioned staff
> work in which conflicting views are
> resolved in a seasoning process of
> concurrences and non-concurrences.[13]

The Kennedy administration's shift from formality to informality, from the NSC to the task
force is now a matter of history. In 1962 Lloyd
Norman wrote that

> the National Security Council is no
> longer the policy-making body. The
> Council which was almost ignored at
> first, now meets about every two
> weeks--more to hear about the deci-
> sions already made than to hammer out
> new policies. President Kennedy
> calls upon the entire Council for ad-
> vice only infrequently, preferring
> the concentrated attention of a small-
> er group directly concerned with a
> problem than a wide divergence of
> views in the larger gathering.[14]

Following the strikingly poor example of
politico-military coordination at the Bay of Pigs
in April, 1962, there was a shift toward a more
formal staff organization and toward more reliance
on the NSC system. The overall thrust, however,
of the Kennedy administration remained toward a
less-formally structured system and more dependence
on small and informal task forces than was the case
in the Truman and Eisenhower administrations.

The tragic circumstances and the accompanying suddenness with which President Johnson assumed the duties of the presidency negated serious thought of the sort of changes in national security organization that logically accompany a conventional transfer of power. For a number of reasons, President Johnson found it expedient to rely initially on the personnel and machinery installed by President Kennedy.

Gradually, as would be expected, the personal style of the new president became apparent. In comparison with earlier presidents, however, Johnson came closest to the Kennedy techniques for use of the NSC machinery. While, for practical purposes, President Johnson operated with essentially the same structure as his predecessor, a rather significant change was made in his relationship with key Cabinet officers as he placed increased emphasis and reliance on the secretary of state and the secretary of defense. Early in his administration President Johnson reaffirmed the primacy of the State Department in foreign policy matters. Shortly after McGeorge Bundy's departure from the White House staff in early 1966, the president reiterated this by specifically assigning the secretary of state the responsibility for and the authority to carry out "overall direction, coordination and supervision of interdepartmental activities of the United States Government overseas."[15]

The enhanced positions of the key Cabinet officers in the politico-military field is explained by one writer as perhaps being owing to

> President Johnson's relatively narrower experience in foreign and military affairs than his predecessor and, consequently, his inclination to participate less intimately in the details of policy and operations in these areas than did Kennedy. In any event, these factors combined with the departure of Bundy from the White

House have greatly enlarged the influence of the two key Presidential
advisors on the National Security
Council.[16]

This author would tend to emphasize the "inclination" part of the foregoing explanation at the expense of the "narrower experience."

Until McGeorge Bundy's departure, the duties
and responsibilities of the special assistant for
national security affairs remained essentially unchanged. When Walt W. Rostow was brought over from
the Department of State to replace Bundy, the duties
were somewhat realigned and Rostow was not given
the title of special assistant for national security affairs but was simply referred to by the president as a special assistant. At a news conference
on March 31, 1966, the president described Rostow's
duties as "principally, but not necessarily exclusively, in the field of foreign policy. I will
look especially to him for the development of long-
range plans in that field, . . ."[17] For practical
purposes, however, it was generally accepted that
"Rostow will assume largely the functions formally
performed by McGeorge Bundy. . . ."[18]

From the politico-military point of view the
impact of the White House staff was reduced in the
Johnson years and the role of the two principal
Cabinet officers for politico-military affairs was
strengthened. In theory, at least, this should
have provided for a better balance to the politico-
military equation. In practice it is not at all
clear that this was so. Critics of the Johnson
administration argue that, especially after the
Gulf of Tonkin incident, the equation became unbalanced by unnecessary emphasis on military considerations. An interesting phenomenon was the sometimes
reversed roles played by the secretaries of state
and defense with the secretary of state frequently
being the proponent of more emphasis on the military side of the equation and the secretary of defense arguing at times for political emphasis.

Of significance is the fact that while the machinery for integrating political and military considerations into national security policy remained essentially unchanged, the pressures of external events and the style and personality of the individual players weighed heavily on how the equation was to be balanced.

President Nixon came to the White House in January, 1969, and inherited what is without a doubt one of the most perplexing politico-military problems faced by any president. The problem was an outgrowth of the cold war but the immediate symptom was the war in Vietnam. In this environment the new administration set out to put the nation's politico-military machinery in order as it saw the requirements.

The National Security Council was "revitalized" and Henry Kissinger was named to succeed Rostow. This time the title of special assistant for national security affairs was assigned. For practical purposes it is reasonable to say that Kissinger's duties closely resembled those performed by Rostow but that they probably more closely equated those performed by Bundy for both Presidents Kennedy and Johnson.

One of the favorite exercises of the news media when a new administration takes the reins in Washington, is to comment on what the "new team" will look like and what it will likely do. The advent of the Nixon administration was no exception and the national security functional area was not overlooked.

In January, 1969, one weekly news magazine, generally representative of them all, identified the "foreign policy group." This group consisted of the secretary of state, the under secretary of state, the chief negotiator in Paris, and the Special Assistant for national security affairs. In commenting on Kissinger, the article noted that his duties were to "reorganize White House 'security

planning' machinery; revitalize procedures of National Security Council; do advance planning on
world crises."[19] The article also identified the
"defense team" as consisting of the secretary of
defense and the deputy secretary of defense. In-
terestingly, the article established no connection
between the "foreign policy group" and the "defense
team."

     About the same time a national newspaper quoted
Kissinger as saying: "Our aim is to take the best
features of the past three administrations. We
would like to get back to the formality of Eisenhower, yet keep alive the dynamics of personal
choice created during the Kennedy period."[20] The
new administration did, in fact, roughly restore
the functions performed by the Eisenhower Planning
Board and Operations Coordinating Board but with
different names and in a somewhat more flexible
structural arrangement.

     The same month the new administration took of-
fice a professional military journal published an
article entitled, "The New National Security Team:
Geopoliticians for a Changing World?" The author
of the article did not define geopolitics and one
might question his use of the term in the article,
but a logical assumption is that he intended to suggest the dynamic integration of the elements of national power as opposed to the more static academic
discipline of political geography. In the context
of this study his use of the expression geopolitics
might be construed as the balancing of the politico-
military equation.

     The article identified the requirement for the
secretary of defense to be a "geopolitician" and it
added, "Geopolitics is, of course, also the business of the Department of State and--preeminently--
of the White House."[21] It is interesting, and also
encouraging, to note that an article in a military
journal clearly included the president and his special assistant for national security affairs, the
secretary of state, and the secretary of defense on
the national security team.

Slightly more than a year after the Nixon administration had taken office another professional military journal looked at the existing staff system. It concluded that

> The new NSC system is the culmination of 23 years of experience adopted to the needs of a new President. Viewed in isolation the Nixon NSC system makes a lot of sense. In conjunction with the executive agencies of government the flow of information, deliberations, decisions, and implementation seems to work smoothly.
> The first year's record looks good. Only time and the trials of crises managed--or avoided--will tell in the long run however.[22]

The administration, for the first time since the NSC came into being, clearly and publicly stated its conception of the system in the President's Report to the Congress of February 18, 1970. In the concluding remarks in Part I of the Report, "The National Security Council System," the President said:

> There is no textbook prescription for organizing the machinery of policymaking, and no procedural formula for making wise decisions. The policies of this Administration will be judged on their results, not on how methodically they were made.
> The NSC system is meant to help us address the fundamental issues, clarify our basic purposes, examine all alternatives, and plan intelligent actions. It is meant to promote the thoroughness and deliberation which are essential for an effective American foreign policy. It gives us the means to bear the best foresight and insight of which the nation is capable.[23]

The President reemphasized his reliance on the NSC system in his 1971 Report to the Congress.[24]

The ultimate effectiveness of the national security policy-making machinery in the Executive Office in the current administration remains to be seen. Future trends in the shape of this machinery will depend in great part on the effectiveness of the current system, the international environment at any given time and primarily on the personal style of the White House incumbent. If the machinery, whatever its form may be, produces a meaningfully balanced politico-military equation it can be considered a success. If it fails to achieve and maintain this balance it has not accomplished its purpose and the nation has been poorly served.

Of particular significance is the fact that the NSC is an established part of the U.S. national policy-making machinery, and will in all probability continue to be for some time to come. The NSC came into being primarily as the result of a deficiency that was recognized in World War II, but its true trial by fire was the cold war.

Since World War II a number of factors combined to shift emphasis in the politico-military equation toward the political side of that equation. There are those who believe that the emphasis has been too strong and that the equation is now very much out of balance to the detriment of the military point of view. There are those who feel that it has not gone far enough, and there are those who feel it is about correct. The fact is that the NSC deliberations are a reflection of the politico-military philosophy in vogue at a given time. It is not necessarily the NSC that determines the overall politico-military balance, but it is the accepted politico-military philosophy that determines how the Council will be used by the president at a given time.

A rather vague but nonetheless identifiable thread can then be constructed from the Joint Board

through the NSC. The Joint Board existed at a time
when the necessity for coordinating the several
types of military policy was recognized but the necessity for closely coordinating the nation's military with its foreign policy was not fully appre-
ciated. From this purely military coordinating
agency came the wartime Joint Chiefs of Staff,
which, although a military agency, assumed the role
of coordinator of military and foreign policy when
it was necessary. The predominantly political
problems associated with surrender and occupation
brought into being the State-War-Navy Coordinating
Committee, which was the initial step toward
achieving a national coordinating agency for the
integration of political and military factors. The
NSC then logically followed within the context of
the cold war.

    In the ten-year period from 1937 to 1947 one
can trace the progression from a military-dominated
national planning agency to, in the opinion of
some, the other extreme, but in the opinion of most
observers, to an agency that permits, but does not
insure, the proper integration of the military and
the political points of view. In World War II
military considerations predominated and the coordinating machinery reflected it. In the cold war
political considerations weighed more heavily and
the coordinating machinery also reflected that.

    Up to this point the discussion of organiza-
tion as an exemplification of politico-military
conceptual thinking has been limited to the Executive Office of the President. There have been some
rather significant organizational innovations in
the Departments of State and Defense that also express this concept. Each will be commented on
briefly in the pages to follow.

                THE DEPARTMENT OF DEFENSE

    The Department of Defense came into being as a
result of the National Security Act of 1947. The

primary purpose of the Department was to coordinate
the vast national defense effort that was previously carried out by the War Department and the Navy
Department and was now to be shared with the new
Department of the Air Force. Since its founding,
the Department of Defense has undergone a number of
organizational changes that have generally tended
toward centralization at the departmental level.

Of particular importance here are several organizational innovations that are directly related
to the expanding concept of politico-military affairs. At the Defense Department level there
exists the Office of the Assistant Secretary of Defense for International Security Affairs. This office has been assigned to the overall mission of
seeing to it that the military policy of the United
States is in accord with its foreign policy. In
fact, the internal organization of the office, with
its geographic subdivisions, is not at all unlike
a miniature Department of State. The simple fact
that the secretaries of defense saw fit to organize
and maintain such an office is in itself testimony
of the importance to the Defense Department of the
politico-military function.

In the Department of Defense Directive, which
established the office, the responsibilities of the
assistant secretary of defense (international security affairs) are enunciated. The assistant secretary is identified as "the principal staff assistant to the Secretary of Defense in the functional field of international security. . . ."
More specifically, some of the functions of the office, as they apply to this study, are as follows:

1. Monitor Department of Defense
participation in National Security
Council affairs, . . .

2. Assist the Secretary of Defense, the several components of the
Department of Defense, and other
agencies of the government in establishing defense policies by:

a. Determining . . . the current and emerging international
problems of major significance
to the security of the United
States, and analyzing the range
of possible political-military
actions for dealing with the long-
term aspects of such problems.

b. Identifying the national
security objectives of the United
States and developing the international political-military and
foreign economic implications. . . .

3. Initiate appropriate actions
and measures within the Department of
Defense for implementing approved
National Security Council policies.

4. Develop and coordinate Defense positions, policies, plans and
procedures in the field of international political-military and foreign
economic affairs, including arms control and disarmament, of interest to
the Department of Defense and with respect to the negotiating and monitor-
ing of agreements with foreign governments and international organizations
on military facilities, operating
rights, status of forces and other international political-military matters.

5. Provide policy guidance, as
appropriate, to components of the Department of Defense, DOD representatives on United States Missions and
to international organizations. . . .

In a separate section entitled "Relationships"
the assistant secretary of defense (international
security affairs) is instructed to

2. Maintain active liaison for
the exchange of information and advice with the military departments,
the Joint Chiefs of Staff and other
Department of Defense agencies.

3. Coordinate relations between
the Department of Defense and the Department of State in the field of his
assigned responsibility.[25]

It is emphasized that the above extracts of
the functions and relationships of the assistant
secretary of defense (international security affairs) do not enumerate all of the duties of that
officer. They do, however, demonstrate a recognition at the Department of Defense level of politico-
military requirements and clearly illustrate the requirement for coordination with other agencies of
the Department of Defense and with other governmental agencies, specifically with the National
Security Council and the Department of State. The
last mentioned point of coordination is of particular importance. It will be referred to in a subsequent discussion of the politico-military functions
of the Department of State.

Within the Office of the Joint Chiefs of Staff
(OJCS) and on each of the service staffs there is a
politico-military staff activity. On the Joint
Staff the politico-military function is the responsibility of the director of plans and policy (J-5) who
is "charged with providing assistance to the Joint
Chiefs of Staff . . . by recommendations on political/
military matters. . . ." The deputy director for
plans and policy is designated as "the OJCS representative to the Interdepartmental Political-Military
Group." The chiefs of the several Regional Divisions
"are responsible to the Director, J-5, for . . .
policy matters of a political/military nature pertaining to their geographic areas."[26]

The politico-military function is carried out
on the army staff by the Politico-Military Division

of the Office, Director of International and Civil
Affairs, which in turn is responsible to the Office
of the Deputy Chief of Staff for Operations (ODCSOPS).
The functions of the Politico-Military Division are
spelled out as follows:

> 1. Develops Army Staff views on
> politico-military aspects of national
> security policy and national strategy
> to include National Security Act and
> related statutes, National Security
> Council affairs, Senior Interdepart-
> mental Group affairs, and Interdepart-
> mental Regional Group affairs; matters
> related to international treaty organi-
> zations and international agreements
> to include international and regional
> organizations, international boards
> and commissions, status of forces
> agreements and negotiations, and base
> rights negotiations; policy, plans,
> objectives and requirements related
> to Arms Control and Disarmament and
> outer space; proposed national policy
> papers on individual countries. Sup-
> ports ODCSOPS [Office of the Deputy
> Chief of Staff for Operations] member-
> ship in various international agencies.
> Monitors and, as necessary, acts upon
> politico-military implications in re-
> ports submitted by U.S. agencies over-
> seas. Monitors situational develop-
> ments of a politico-military nature
> in regions and countries as they im-
> pact on relations with the U.S. and
> recommends proposed DA [Department of
> the Army] positions with respect
> thereto. Provides Army Staff contact
> on politico-military matters with ele-
> ments of OSD [Office of the Secretary
> of Defense], JCS [Joint Chiefs of
> Staff], other Services, State Depart-
> ment, and other governmental agencies.
> Discharges ODCSOPS responsibilities

relating to MAAG's [Military Assistance Advisory Groups], missions, and
military group matters and international assistance programs applicable
to individual countries. Advises on
politico-military matters related to
Foreign Internal Defense Policy and
internal defense plans and programs
applicable to individual countries.

2. . . . Provides Army contact
point for foreign assistance policy
matters with OSD, JCS, other Services,
State Department, and other governmental agencies. Monitors, develops, and
coordinates Army views on foreign assistance legislation. . . .[27]

The same function is performed for the navy by
the Politico-Military Policy Division of the Office
of the Deputy Chief of Naval Operations (Plans and
Policy). The mission assigned to the Division is:
"To provide assistance, counsel, representation,
planning and policies on politico-military affairs
of interest to the Department of the Navy."

Some of the functions of the navy's politico-
military agency are as follows:

1. Maintains liaison with the Office of the Assistant Secretary of Defense (International Security Affairs)
[OASD(ISA)] in all international
politico-military matters of interest
to the Navy Department; on such matters which are uniservice in nature
and where appropriate, maintains direct liaison with the Department of
State, keeping OSD(ISA) informed; and
effects similar liaison between the
Navy Department and other U.S. governmental departments and agencies.

2.   Is the Navy Department point
of contact on all matters concerning
the Senior Interdepartmental Group
and the Interdepartmental Regional
Groups.

3.   Effects coordination within
the Navy Department on international
politico-military matters. . . .

5.   Informs responsible officers
of the Navy Department of any politico-
military matter of international interest with which those officers may
be concerned, to insure that appropriate action on all such matters is
taken.

6.   Assists the Secretary of the
Navy, in his position as an adviser
to the Secretary of Defense in the
latter's capacity as a member of the
National Security Council, and CNO
[Chief of Naval Operations], in his
considerations of NSC documents as a
member of the Joint Chiefs of Staff;
and maintains Navy Department records
and files of National Security Council documents and State Department
guidelines for U.S. policy and operations.

7.   Advises and makes recommendations to the Secretary of the Navy to
CNO on matters of an international
politico-military nature.

8.   Provides advisory assistance
on matters of an international
politico-military nature which are
before the Joint Chiefs of Staff for
consideration.

9. Provides liaison with the
State Department with respect to
United Nations matters of interest
to the Navy Department.

10. Provides Navy Department representation on the Washington Liaison
Group in the development of plans for
emergency evacuation of U.S. nationals
from areas abroad. . . .

14. Is the Navy Department point
of contact on the international aspects of nuclear propulsion. . . .[28]

Also within the Department of the Navy a simi-
lar function is carried out on the Marine Corps
Staff in the Office of the Deputy Chief of Staff
(Plans and Programs).

On the air staff the function is performed in
the Office of the Director of Plans and more specifically in the Office of the Deputy Director for
Plans and Policy. At one time there was an International Affairs Division in the Office of the
Deputy Director to serve as the politico-military
focal point on the air staff. That Division has
been abolished and its functions assigned elsewhere,
namely to two regional divisions in the Office of
the Deputy Director. The Department of the Air
Force Organization and Functions Manual assigns the
following as one of several responsibilities of the
deputy director for plans and policy:

Politico-Military Affairs. Concerning national and international
politico-military matters including
regional treaty organizations, foreign aid, foreign base rights, and
clearances; . . . arms control and
nuclear policy.

Each of the two Regional Divisions
(Eastern and Western),

1.   Maintains daily liaison with
the Joint Staff, OASD/ISA and State
Department on regional matters.

2.   Reviews and develops Air
Force positions on politico-military
considerations of a regional nature
resulting from proposals and decisions by joint, combined, interdepartmental agencies, . . .[29]

The names of the several agencies within the
Department of Defense and the military departments
are in themselves of little importance as is the ex-
act wording of the statement of missions and functions of the agencies. It is important, however,
that in each of the military departments and in the
Department of Defense, a specific organization
charged with the responsibility for politico-
military affairs does exist. It is also significant that each of these staff agencies is placed at
a high level in the plans and operations functional
area.

The excerpts from the statements of missions
and functions of the several politico-military agencies are intended to illustrate the similarity of
function of the agencies, although the format and
the wording varies considerably. It is also intended to clearly point up the fact that there are
in existence formal staff organizations, manned
primarily by professional military officers, that
have a function that only a few years ago was considered to be well outside the scope of the interest and even the competence of the military professional.

THE DEPARTMENT OF STATE

Politico-military problems and relationships
are not new to the Department of State. It has,
however, been relatively recent that the Department
has strengthened its capability in this field. The

Policy Planning Council has a history of politico-
military relations. This has been especially apparent in its close dealings with the National Security
Council. Also, most of the geographic bureaus have
for some time had officers or staffs charged with
this general responsibility. Moreover, the deputy
under secretary of state for political affairs has
been the senior departmental officer responsible
for maintaining coordination with the military.
This officer has "had working relations with the
senior officers of the Department of Defense and
the Joint Chiefs of Staff, though on a more or less
'as required' basis."[30]

It became apparent, however, that something
more needed to be done:

> . . . the Department needed a unit
> that could look at politico-military
> problems on a world-wide basis, as-
> sure that regional variations and in-
> terrelations had been taken into ac-
> count, and provide a central point of
> focus and coordination, as required,
> for the politico-military activities
> being carried on by the geographical
> bureaus of the Department. Such a
> unit would not replace regional
> politico-military staffs but rather
> strengthen and tie together their re-
> lated activities.[31]

Such a unit came into being in the spring of
1961 in the form of the Office of the Deputy Assistant Secretary of State for Politico-Military Affairs. This office was abolished in the fall of
1969 and the personnel and functions were transferred to the newly created Bureau of Politico-
Military Affairs.[32] The purpose of the establishment of the Bureau and the importance the Department placed on close coordination with the Department of Defense was clearly stated in a memorandum
by the under secretary of state shortly after the
new bureau came into being. The under secretary
said in part:

A major purpose of the establishment
of the Bureau of Politico-Military Affairs [PM] is to ensure that there is
a central point in the State Department that keeps cognizant of all issues with politico-military implications and abreast of all matters under
joint consideration by the State Department and the Defense Department.
In establishing this Bureau there has
been no intention to alter the current
action responsibilities of the individual geographic bureaus in matters
which fall within their areas. To
the contrary, I look to the Bureau of
Politico-Military Affairs as a major
point for supporting the work of
other offices in the Department in
this functional area by contributing
its expertise and perspective gained
from its across-the-board responsibilities. However, for an effective interaction to take place between PM and
the rest of the Department, it is important that the Bureau of Politico-
Military Affairs be kept fully and
currently informed about all business
with the Department of Defense and is
given an opportunity to coordinate
particularly on those problems between
State and Defense which have new or
major policy implications.[33]

The importance the State Department placed on the
politico-military function is evident in the fact
that the new bureau was to be headed by a director
with the equivalent rank of an assistant secretary.
The next several pages are devoted to a broad examination of the politico-military functions within
the Department of State.

The Policy Planning Council, which came into
existence during the secretaryship of General Marshall, under the title of the Policy Planning Staff,
has had a continuing interest in politico-military

matters. Prior to the creation of the Office of
the Deputy Assistant Secretary of State for Politico-
Military Affairs, the Policy Planning Council (Staff)
was central in the Department of State's participation in the National Security Council. Currently
that function is the responsibility of the Bureau of
Politico-Military Affairs but the Council continues
to be actively engaged in politico-military matters,
especially in relation to its long-range planning in
the field of foreign policy. The Council closely
coordinates its efforts with the Bureau of Politico-
Military Affairs.

Each of the assistant secretaries heading a
geographic bureau has a politico-military function
to perform and has officers or staffs charged with
that specific responsibility. As an example of the
extent to which formal organization for politico-
military affairs has gone, the Bureau of European
Affairs will be examined briefly. It must be recognized that Europe, with its unique interrelations
of political and military strategies, presents more
of a challenge in the area of politico-military coordination than do some of the other regions. This
bureau is used as an example because of its emphasis on this problem. It is by no means intended as
being representative of the politico-military structure of a typical bureau.

In March, 1962, the Office of Regional Affairs,
where the politico-military function is performed
in most bureaus, was divided into two subordinate
units. The reorganization resulted in the creation
of an Office of Atlantic Political-Economic Affairs
and an Office of Atlantic Political-Military Affairs. The latter office provided organizational
support in the Department of State for U.S. participation in the North Atlantic Treaty Organization.

As was pointed out above, the Office of the
Deputy Assistant Secretary of State for Politico-
Military Affairs came into being in the spring of
1961. In addition to performing the function of
coordinating the politico-military efforts of other

agencies in the Department, "it was also felt that
it would be convenient to have one obvious point of
contact within the Department well known to all elements of the Department of Defense."[34] In the most
basic terms, the Office came into existence to assist the deputy under secretary of state for political affairs in carrying out his ever-increasing
politico-military functions. The eventual abolish-
ment of that Office and the establishment of the
Bureau of Politico-Military Affairs clearly emphasized the importance of that function.

Of primary significance in this review of the
Department of State organization for politico-
military affairs is the fact that the requirement
exists at various echelons and that a number of
staff groups have come into being to meet those requirements. The Bureau of Politico-Military Affairs coordinates the politico-military efforts of
the geographical and functional bureaus. It also
works closely with the Arms Control and Disarmament
Agency for International Development. The Bureau
staff periodically meets formally with representatives of the politico-military staffs of the Department's geographic bureaus.

A significant portion of the day-to-day
politico-military work of the State Department is
still done in the several geographic bureaus. The
true significance of the Bureau of Politico-Military
Affairs is that it provides a central, high-level,
point of contact for politico-military matters
within the Department and also provides a point of
contact for agencies outside the Department of
State, especially the Department of Defense. The
extent to which the formal organization of the Department of State has been modified in the last
decade to accommodate politico-military affairs is
testimony of the importance that is attached to the
function.

It is impractical to attempt to draw strict organizational comparisons between the Departments of
State and Defense. The departments exist for

entirely different reasons and have essentially different internal organizations. It is, however, possible to compare favorably the extent to which both
departments have made significant internal organizational changes over the years to take into account
the growing politico-military function.

FIELD ORGANIZATION

It has been pointed out above that the requirement for proper politico-military coordination has
brought about some significant organizational
changes in the U.S. government over the years. The
National Security Council came into being and has
undergone several modifications in search of the
most efficient way of achieving the necessary coordination. The Departments of Defense and State
have both undergone a series of internal organizational changes to insure that the nation's foreign
and military policies are operating in concert. Organizational changes to accommodate politico-military
requirements are not limited to the executive departments. There have been some rather important developments at a lower level that are worthy of brief
comment.

Recognizing the risk of oversimplification at
this point, it can perhaps be said that the "field"
for the Department of Defense is the Unified and
Specified Command, while to the Department of State
it is the diplomatic mission. Politico-military coordination is not limited to the Washington command
post, but exists in the field as well.

On the staff of the Unified and Specified Commander there is a foreign service officer with the
title of political advisor (POLAD). A POLAD is defined as

> A Foreign Service Officer who has
> been assigned to the staff of a U.S.
> unified or specified military com-
> mander on the basis of a formal

agreement between the Departments of
State and Defense and who is responsible solely to the commander. . . .

The POLAD is not an institutional
representative of the Department of
State nor is he a Department of State
liaison officer serving with the command.

The function of the POLAD is to
advise and consult with the commander
on political, political-military and
economic matters affecting the commander's theatre of operations. In
performing this function, he provides
a specialized expertise and source of
information to the commander in the
same way as any other staff officer.[35]

As much as five years ago the Department of
State announced that it had "nine advisors assigned
to unified commands in the U.S. and abroad to advice commanders on political and economic matters."
The Department emphasized the fact that these
POLADS "are neither commissars nor liaison officers, . . . but are on the commander's staff."[36]
The existence of a political advisor on the staff
of the military commander is not necessarily new.
What is new and of special interest is the extent
to which the practice has been accepted by the departments involved, and the degree to which it has
become institutionalized.

While the POLAD is assigned to the military
staff to provide political advice to the commander,
there is also a requirement to provide military advice to the chief of the diplomatic mission. While
the required military advice is normally available,
it is frequently not completely clear who is expected to give it. There is no real military counterpart of the POLAD on the staff of the chief of
mission.

In the environment of the cold war the need
for close coordination between all activities of

the U.S. government in a given country is most essential. From this requirement has evolved the
formalization of the basic concept that the chief
of the diplomatic mission in a given nation is the
responsible American officer on the scene. Especially since the close of World War II this concept
has been strengthened and has been formalized into
what is sometimes called the "country team" concept.
Actually there is little new about the basic concept of the country team. What is new is the extent to which the concept has been formalized and
institutionalized.

One study of the problem comments that

> large-scale problems of coordination
> in United States representation
> abroad did not arise until World War
> II, but this was more because of the
> restricted nature of American activi-
> ties (even, relatively speaking, dur-
> ing World War II) than because of ad-
> ministrative arrangements designed to
> solve problems of coordination. In-
> deed a need for such administrative
> arrangements had begun to be felt in
> the years preceding World War II and
> a start had been made devising them,
> but the improvements made in the co-
> ordination processes were rapidly
> overshadowed by new problems of co-
> ordination arising directly from the
> war.[37]

From this requirement came a series of executive orders and other directives in the post-World
War II administrations. These represent a somewhat
evolutionary process of more specifically spelling
out the responsibilities of U.S. representatives
abroad. A letter sent by President Kennedy to all
chiefs of mission in May, 1961, was perhaps the
most precise guidance provided. It spelled out the
line of responsibility between the political and
the military representation in a foreign nation
rather clearly:

Now a word about your relations to the military. As you know, the United States Diplomatic Mission includes Service Attaches, Military Assistance Advisory Groups and other Military components attached to the Mission. It does not, however, include United States military forces operating in the field where such forces are under the command of a United States area military commander. The line of authority to these forces runs from me, to the Secretary of Defense, to the Joint Chiefs of Staff in Washington and to the area commander in the field.

Although this means that the chief of the American Diplomatic Mission is not in the line of military command, nevertheless, as Chief of Mission, you should work closely with the appropriate area military commander to assure the full exchange of information. If it is your opinion that activities by the United States military forces may adversely affect our over-all relations with the people or government of . . ., you should promptly discuss the matter with the military commander and, if necessary, request a decision by higher authority.[38]

These paragraphs were omitted from the letters sent to ambassadors in nations in which there were no U.S. military forces under an area military commander. In those cases, the chief of the diplomatic mission was responsible for all U.S. government activities in the country concerned.

The Kennedy letter was an obvious effort to achieve clear unity of effort through the technique of unity of command where there was no major military command involved and through coordination where a major military commander had area responsibility.

Unfortunately, this objective was not fully realized.
The achievement of politico-military coordination on
the part of the chief of the diplomatic mission presents a somewhat different problem from that of the
area military commander.

A detailed study of the interworkings of the
typical U.S. diplomatic mission is not considered
desirable. However, this review will point up at
least a few of the more perplexing problems as they
are applicable to politico-military affairs. The
heart of the problem appears to be that while the
chief of the diplomatic mission is without question
the responsible American official in a given foreign
country, the military commanders with whom he deals
are often concerned with a broader geographical area.
Therefore there is no easy, neat match between the
overseas responsibilities of the diplomat and the
professional military officer.

As an example, the chief of mission may deal
with service attaches, military assistance advisory
groups, and military area commanders on politico-
military affairs within the country in question.
No one military officer is designated as "the" military advisor to the chief of mission. Here is a
case where the organizational structure of the military and the diplomatic forces overseas is not compatible and sometimes presents a knotty problem.

This is clearly an area in the formal organization for politico-military affairs where lines of
responsibility and chains of command are less than
clear. Some actions that are now being taken along
these lines are worthy of comment. In overseas diplomatic missions, where there are important military
problems confronting the ambassador, foreign service
officers with the necessary politico-military education and experience are now being assigned to political sections or as special assistants and advisors
to the ambassadors in the field. In the same vein,
an experiment has been conducted with the assignment of Department of Defense civilian officials to
some of the major embassies.

The use of the foreign service officer and the Department of Defense civilian official as politico-military advisors to the chief of the diplomatic mission is pointed out because it illustrates a point and at the same time it raises a question. The point is that the deficiency in the formal organization for politico-military affairs is recognized and action is being taken to correct it. The question it raises has to do with the use of other than professional military officers to perform the military part of the politico-military function. Specifically, why is a military professional not assigned this task?

Still in the area of formal coordination, although not necessarily an organizational matter, is the State-Defense exchange program, initiated in January, 1961, by Secretaries Christian Herter and Thomas Gates. Military officers are assigned by the Department of Defense to duty with the Department of State and similarly foreign service officers are assigned by the Department of State to the Department of Defense. The purpose of the program is to foster mutual understanding and respect and to enhance both the necessary formal and informal coordination which takes place between the two departments. The secretaries of state and defense both commented most favorably on the exchange program. The secretary of state commented on the program as follows:

> There is no doubt that the Department of State's handling of politico-military problems has benefitted significantly from the contributions of the Defense exchange officers. In many cases, their efforts have been quite outstanding.[39]

The secretary of defense commented:

> I doubt that there has ever been closer coordination, cooperation and mutual understanding between the two

Departments than we are now experiencing. Certainly, this is not attributable entirely to the State-
Defense Officer Exchange Program, but
that program has done its share in
achieving this result.[40]

The number of foreign service and military officers
who have served in politico-military positions is
increasing constantly and "cooperation and mutual
understanding" is significantly enhanced by that
experience.

Although this portion of the study is concerned
with formal organization, the existence of considerable informal coordination between the officers of
the Departments of State and Defense should not be
completely ignored. A 1964 questionnaire addressed
to military officers in the Washington area who were
involved in politico-military assignments asked
about the working relationships between the military
officers and the officers of the Department of State.
Of the ninety-six officers replying to the questionnaire, all but three indicated that there was an excellent official and unofficial working relationship. Of the three who replied in the negative, two
explained that their particular assignment simply
did not call for direct contact with the Department
of State and therefore they answered in the negative.[41]

NOTES

1. David C. Rapoport, "A Contemporary Theory
of Military and Political Types," in Changing Patterns of Military Politics, ed. Samuel P. Huntington
(New York: The Free Press of Glencoe, 1962), p. 97.

2. Harold D. Lasswell and Abraham Kaplin,
Power and Society (New Haven, Conn.: Yale University Press, 1950), p. 252.

3.   J. W. Fulbright, "Public Policy and Military Responsibility." An address given at the opening session of The National War College and the Industrial College of the Armed Forces, August 21, 1961. Congressional Record, Vol. 107, No. 144 (August 21, 1961), pp. 15356-59.

4.   Stanley L. Falk, The National Security Structure (Washington: Industrial College of the Armed Forces, 1967), p. 1; the Neustadt quote is from U.S., Congress, Senate, Committee on Government Operations, Conduct of National Security Policy, Hearings before the Subcommittee on National Security and International Operations, Part 3, 89th Cong., 1st sess. (Washington: U.S. Government Printing Office, 1965), p. 130.

5.   Herman Finer, The Presidency, Crisis and Regeneration--Essay in Possibilities (Chicago: University of Chicago Press, 1960), p. 35.

6.   Rocco M. Paone, "Foreign Policy and Military Power," Military Review, November, 1964, p. 9.

7.   William R. Emerson, "F.D.R. (1941-1945)," in The Ultimate Decision, ed. Ernest R. May (New York: George Braziller, 1960), pp. 136-37.

8.   Samuel P. Huntington, The Soldier and the State (Cambridge, Mass.:   The Belknap Press, 1959), p. 318.

9.   Ibid., p. 320n.

10.   U.S., Congress, Senate, Committee on Government Operations, The National Security Council, Study by the Subcommittee on National Policy Machinery, 86th Cong., 2d sess. (Washington: U.S. Government Printing Office, 1960).

11.   J. C. Heinlein, Presidential Staff and National Security Policy (Cincinnati, Ohio: University of Cincinnati, 1963), p. 53.

12.   "The Way U.S. Foreign Policy Is Made Under Kennedy," U.S. News and World Report, April 10, 1961, p. 196.

13.   Lloyd Norman, "The Commander-in-Chief and National Security Policy," Army, February, 1962, p. 2.

14.   Ibid.

15.   U.S., Department of State, "Direction, Coordination and Supervision of International Activity Overseas," Foreign Affairs Manual, Circular No. 385 (Washington: U.S. Government Printing Office, March 4, 1966).

16.   Falk, op. cit., p. 54.

17.   Presidential News Conference, March 31, 1966. Text in The New York Times, April 1, 1966, p. 1.

18.   John D. Pomfret, "Kintner and Rostow Get Posts as Johnson Aides," The New York Times, April 1, 1966, p. 1.

19.   "Washington Now: Who's In, Who's Out of Power," U.S. News and World Report, January 27, 1969, pp. 26-29.

20.   George Sherman, "Kissinger Maps Firm Path," The Washington Star, January 1, 1969, p. 23; see also John Osborne, "Nixon's Command Staff," The New Republic, February 15, 1969, pp. 13-15.

21.   John B. Spore, "The National Security Team: Geopoliticians for a Changing World?" Army, January, 1969, p. 15.

22.   Brooke Nihart, "New Staff System After One Year," Armed Forces Journal, April 4, 1970, p. 29. See also U.S., Congress, Senate, Committee on Government Operations, The National Security Council: New Role and Structure, February 16, 1969. Submitted by the Subcommittee on National Security

and International Operations, 91st Cong., 1st sess. (Washington: U.S. Government Printing Office, 1969).

    23.   Richard Nixon, <u>U.S. Foreign Policy for the 1970's: A New Strategy for Peace</u>. A Report to the Congress by the President of the United States, February 18, 1970 (Washington: U.S. Government Printing Office, 1970), p. 23.

    24.   Richard Nixon, <u>U.S. Foreign Policy for the 1970's: Building for Peace</u>. A Report to the Congress by the President of the United States, February 25, 1971 (Washington: U.S. Government Printing Office, 1971), p. 226.

    25.   U.S., Department of Defense, <u>Department of Defense Directive: Number 5132.2</u>.   "Assistant Secretary of Defense (International Security Affairs)," May 20, 1961, p. 1.

    26.   U.S., Department of Defense, <u>JCS Pub 4, Organization and Functions of the Joint Chiefs of Staff</u> (Washington: U.S. Government Printing Office, January 1, 1969), pp. III-5-3, 5, 6.

    27.   U.S., Department of the Army, <u>Chief of Staff Regulations: Number 10-34</u>. Office of the Chief of Staff, September 9, 1968, p. 13.

    28.   U.S., Department of the Navy, <u>OPNAV 90B63-P1</u>, Office of the Deputy Chief of Naval Operations (Plans and Policy), pp. 06-16.

    29.   U.S., Department of the Air Force, <u>Organization and Functions Manual (HP 21-2)</u>, December 31, 1969, pp. 129-30.

    30.   Burton M. Sapin, "The Political-Military Affairs Staff: Its Organization and its Duties," <u>Department of State Newsletter</u>, No. 30, October, 1963; see also U.S., Congress, Senate, Committee on Government Operations, "Memorandum on the Department of State's Politico-Military Organization and Staffing." Part 6, December 11, 1963, 88th Cong., 1st sess. (Washington: U.S. Government Printing Office, 1963).

31. Sapin, loc. cit.

32. U.S., Department of State, Foreign Affairs Manual Circular; No. 536, "Establishment of
Politico-Military Affairs (PM)," September 18, 1969.

33. Memorandum by Elliot L. Richardson, Under
Secretary of State, "State-Defense Relations,"
November 3, 1969.

34. Sapin, loc. cit.

35. "POLAD's Role with the Military," Department of State Newsletter, No. 31 (November, 1963),
pp. 7, 30.

36. "'Political Commissars' at U.S. Military
Bases," U.S. News and World Report, January 11,
1965, p. 13.

37. U.S., Congress, Senate, Committee on Government Operations, The Ambassador and the Problem
of Coordination. Study by the Subcommittee on National Security Staffing and Operations, 88th Cong.,
1st sess., Document No. 36 (Washington: U.S. Government Printing Office, 1963), pp. 3, 18. This
reference gives the general background of the concept and the initiation of the term.

38. Ibid., p. 156.

39. U.S., Congress, Senate, Committee on Government Operations, Hearings Before the Subcommittee
on National Security Staffing and Operations, part
9, June 25, 1964, 88th Cong., 2d sess. (Washington:
U.S. Government Office, 1964), pp. 597-98.

40. Ibid., p. 599. The value of the program
was reasserted by Secretaries William Rogers and
Melvin Laird. U.S., Congress, Senate, Committee on
Government Operations. The State-Defense Officer
Exchange Program. Analysis and Assessment submitted
by the Subcommittee on National Security and International Operations, 91st Cong., 1st sess. (Washington: U.S. Government Printing Office, 1969).

41.   Survey in the form of a written questionnaire submitted by the author to professional military officers assigned to politico-military duties
in the Washington area, September, 1964.

5

POLITICO-MILITARY
EDUCATION
OF THE
AMERICAN
MILITARY PROFESSIONAL

One of the central themes of the study up to this point has been the gradual increase of participation by the professional military officer in the formulation processes as well as in the implementation of the nation's foreign policy and of the ever-constant balancing of the politico-military equation. This trend has, of course, been more pronounced in the years following World War II. A typical statement of the effect of this phenomenon on the national security policy maker was made by Senator J. W. Fulbright in the address to the combined student bodies and faculties of The National War College and the Industrial College of the Armed Forces cited in the preceding chapter. The senator said:

> The politician must acquire knowledge
> and sensitivity to every aspect of
> national security, including the mili-
> tary, while military officers are un-
> der a heavy obligation to bring to
> the performance of their tasks much
> of the wisdom of history and state-
> craft.[1]

More recently a military professional published an exceptionally thoughtful article entitled, "On Understanding War." In it he commented on an observation by Liddell Hart as follows:

> B. H. Liddell Hart once observed that the old Roman maxim, "if you wish for peace, prepare for war" has not insured peace, either for the Romans or for anyone else since. Thus, he reasoned, the argument must either be fallacious, or else it is put too simply--without sufficient depth of thought. Liddell Hart then submitted that his studies of war suggest that a truer maxim would be, "if you wish for peace, understand war."[2]

He then further commented:

> Pacifists completely condemn war and make no attempt to understand it, believing it to be intrinsically sinful. Soldiers, on the other hand, study war, but their studies are almost exclusively devoted to the tactics and techniques of military operations-- military strategy in the narrowest sense--as opposed to an examination of the nature of war and its relationship to society. Neither group really understands war. [Emphasis added.]

The senator and the soldier seem to arrive at the same general conclusion but have travelled considerably different routes to arrive there. In keeping with the scope of this study, the emphasis in this chapter is on the educational measures the military profession has taken and continues to take to insure that professional military officers are prepared to meet this "heavy obligation" and to truly "understand" war. The acquisition of "knowledge and sensitivity to every aspect of national security" by the "politician" and his "understanding" of war is perhaps not fully within the scope of this chapter but some aspects of this particular problem are addressed along with the commentary on military education. The immediate question that comes to mind is: Where and how does the military professional gain this "wisdom of history and statecraft" and this "understanding" of war that he is obliged to bring with him to the performance of his tasks? Formal education and practical experience are the two broad avenues of approach. While it is fully recognized that practical experience is in itself an invaluable educational experience, this chapter concerns itself primarily with formal in-service education.

When, during World War II, the military profession came to realize that it was expected to participate in the formulation as well as the pure implementation of national security policy in its broadest sense and to participate in politico-military deliberations, it found that, with few exceptions, it did not possess the politico-military sophistication to assume the added responsibilities. General Omar Bradley stated the problem clearly when he commented on his experiences in World War II: "At times, during the war, we forgot that wars were fought for the resolution of political conflict, . . . we sometimes overlooked political considerations of vast importance."[3] While it is recognized that the Joint Staff in Washington was engaged in making foreign policy, this comment by General Bradley rather typifies the view of the majority of the professional military officers. For the most part, the United States operated on the assumption that the truly knotty political problems, the ones that have subsequently caused so much consternation, would be settled by the victor after the war. In the years since World War II the military profession in the United States has come a long way toward understanding this new dimension more fully and accepting it more willingly, but this understanding and willingness is still less than complete.

The virtues and pitfalls of military participation in the foreign policy process are not argued

in this chapter. The participation is accepted as
an established feature of the nation's contemporary
national security policy-making process. It is
further accepted that this involvement will likely
continue for some time to come. This chapter is
based on the premise that the professional military
officer now has a requirement to be well versed in
the various aspects of foreign affairs and international relations so that he can better perform his
military duties.

As has already been suggested, there are two
broad avenues through which a professional military
officer might be exposed to some of the more important foreign affairs facts of life. While there is
much to be said for practical experience as an educational device in any endeavor, there are certain
realistic limitations that make it impractical for
most officers to gain this experience in the course
of a normal career. Furthermore, practical experience is frequently quite narrow and related only to
a given set of conditions, at a given time, in a
given situation. A little experience, therefore,
may well be a negative influence if the officer
does not have the educational background to fully
appreciate the limitations of his experience. The
politico-military implications of the U.S. commitment in Europe are, for example, quite different
from those in the Far East, and experience in one
area does not in itself necessarily qualify one as
an expert in the other. It is, on the other hand,
reasonably certain that the officer will be subjected to and influenced by the military educational
system at several stages in his career.

This chapter will briefly evaluate the effectiveness of the military educational system in
preparation of the professional officer for the
politico-military role that he may be expected to
play during his service. It will also comment much
more briefly on the formal education to which the
foreign service officer may expect to be exposed by
his service in preparation for his contribution to
the politico-military equation. The evaluation will

be attempted, not through a detailed analysis of
comparative curricula, programs of instruction, and
other academic accouterments, but rather through an
examination of the overall educational trends of the
military services and the Department of State. It
is emphasized that this chapter deals with the formal, in-service military and foreign service educational systems as they affect professional officers
in their politico-military functions. The vast
specialist and purely military training programs
are not addressed.

HISTORY

The complex formal military educational system
in existence today is the result of more than a century of growth and experience. Each of the three
services operates a comprehensive school system
that is designed to meet that service's unique
needs. Just as the role and structure of the military establishment has changed through the years
and the role of the professional military officer
has likewise changed, the military educational system has undergone a series of significant alterations to meet contemporary demands.

Prior to the Civil War, truly professional military education was mostly limited to the two service
academies. The Military Academy at West Point had
been established in 1802 and the Naval Academy at
Annapolis in 1845. It is important to note that
these two institutions served as the source, not
exclusively however, for regular army and navy officers. There existed nothing like the vast educational system of today that is designed not only to
provide the precommission education for potential
officers but also to keep the commissioned officer
professionally competent throughout his career.
Prior to the Civil War the service academies were
the military educational system. Now they are but
a very small part of it.

Following the Civil War, interest in military
education, at any level, dropped sharply. By the

1880's, however, the armed forces awakened slowly
when the nation began to turn from internal affairs
as it felt the stirrings of a sense of national
power. New technological developments in the art
of warfare placed the requirement on the services
to educate their officers more thoroughly. This
resulted in the creation of new military schools of
various descriptions. These new institutions, however, concerned themselves primarily with the technical aspects of the application of military power.
The services had become aware of the need for greater technical competence on the part of their officers but there was still little concern for an appreciation of politico-military factors.

Fortunately for the services, and for the nation they served, a few thoughtful officers did
fully comprehend the requirement for a corps of professionally well-rounded officers. They saw the
need for theoretical and scholarly study of the
role of military power and for the development of
career officers prepared not only in the technical
aspects of military affairs but also in the broader
areas of national policy as well.

The greatest contribution to military education during the period between the Civil War and
World War I was the introduction of what might be
called the postgraduate, or postcommission, level.
Of special importance was the establishment of the
two service war colleges. The navy was the first
of the services to establish a war college, doing
so in 1884. In the words of Captain (later Rear Admiral) Stephen B. Luce, the college was founded

> so that there might be a place where
> our officers would not only be en-
> couraged, but required to study their
> profession--war--in a far more thor-
> ough manner than had heretofore been
> attempted, and to bring to the investi-
> gation of the various problems of the
> modern naval warfare the scientific
> methods adopted in other professions.[4]

The naval officer corps as a whole, however, did not accept the concept of a war college initially and it was only through the dogmatic efforts of a few officers that the college was not relegated to the scrap yard early in its career. As one naval officer put it, "The College was tolerated, but it was not looked upon as being one of the most essential features of the navy."[5]

The army, although late in accepting the idea of a war college, brought its institution into being in 1903 as part of a sweeping reform of the entire service under the secretaryship of Elihu Root.[6] Generally speaking, the army's educational system had the support of the majority of the professional officer corps.

The experiences of the two services in the Spanish-American War, just before the turn of the century (which was commented on in an earlier chapter), had a profound effect on their respective views on professional education. A reevaluation of the army educational system was one of the significant corrective actions taken after that war. Recognition by professional army officers that their service did not perform well had a profound effect on the support they gave to the new educational reforms. The navy, on the other hand, having performed relatively well in the war, was perhaps less inclined to support an educational system designed to improve something that, in the view of many professional naval officers, needed no improvement.

The military services of the United States approached World War I with the navy in its historic relatively high state of readiness and the army now possessed of a corps of professional officers who had at least been exposed in the classroom to the problems of contemporary war.

Following World War I the military educational system was modified again to meet the new requirements that were made apparent by that experience. The courses at the two service academies were

broadened to include greater emphasis on nontechni-
cal military matters. In 1920 a separate air service school was established at the intermediate
level in response to the introduction of the new
dimension in warfare. The Army Industrial College
was created in 1924 to educate officers

> in the useful knowledge pertaining to
> the supervision of procurement of all
> military supplies in time of war and
> to the assurance of adequate provi-
> sion for the mobilization of material
> and industrial organization essential
> to wartime needs.[7]

This college was later to become the Industrial College of the Armed Forces.

Both services continued to revise and modify
their respective educational systems during the in-
terlude between World Wars I and II. By the time
the United States became involved in World War II
it had the potential of fielding a military force
led by a professional officer corps equal to any.

This very general review of the development of
the military educational system up to the beginning
of World War II points out the dynamic nature of
the system. However, many of the changes did not
come about easily. The inherent conservatism that
is native to the military profession produced many
highly competent and influential officers who were
skeptical of the whole concept of education at best
and often actually hostile to the development of an
educational system. When a major modification in
the system came about it was normally the result of
a specific requirement that advanced military technology had imposed on the service. Necessity was
the mother of invention in the armed forces educational system. After it had become necessary for
the professional military officer to increase his
expertise in various areas, the school system was
modified, after the fact, to meet those requirements. Prior to World War II, while it was fully

accepted that military and political factors were inseparable at the highest level, it was not generally accepted that the average professional military officer needed any special politico-military expertise, so the school systems made no particular provisions for it.

As was suggested previously, the military professional was for the most part unprepared by experience, and by training, for the new responsibilities that were presented to him. The military educational system rose to the challenge and, over the years since World War II, has placed increased emphasis on the subject of international relations in general and politico-military affairs in particular.[8]

The emphasis thus far has been on the "military" educational system and the preparation of professional military officers to deal with politico-military problems before World War II. The educational system designed to serve the nonmilitary participants in the politico-military equation also must be mentioned to complete the picture. Within the context of this brief historical sketch it is quite simple to comment on the in-service formal education for foreign service officers and other civilian officials involved in politico-military affairs by saying that, for all practical purposes, it was nonexistent during this period. This point was made quite clearly by Ambassador Robert Murphy when he commented on his own formal educational preparation for the politico-military duties he was assigned in World War II in comparison with a professional military colleague who was later appointed under secretary of state.

> Those thirty days and twenty minutes
> included all the educational assign-
> ments of my career. By contrast,
> General Bedell Smith, Eisenhower's
> Chief of Staff who later was appointed
> Under Secretary of State, enjoyed
> eleven years as student and instructor
> in a number of Army-financed courses.[9]

Ambassador Murphy and others in the Department
of State recognized this shortcoming and, as will
be pointed out in subsequent pages, the Department
undertook remedial action.

CONTEMPORARY POLITICO-MILITARY EDUCATION

During World War II the military educational
system was modified to meet the immediate requirements of the war. Courses of instruction were
shortened or eliminated, all but the most essential
material was eliminated from the surviving curricula,
and the student population was greatly increased.
It was in brief, a mass-production training mill.
In a sense, the military educational system reflected the overall national philosophy that was
expressed in the concept of "unconditional surrender." Maximum effort was devoted to training the
largest possible number of officers in those techniques that were necessary to win the war while
little or no effort was devoted to international
political matters or to serious consideration of
professional military requirements in the postwar
period. The experiences of World War II heavily
influenced the shape the postwar educational structure would take. The two quotes that follow, one
by an academician and one by a high-ranking military professional, are illustrative of the thinking
of the time.

> During the war the services had
> learned the techniques of combined
> military operations. Military and
> diplomatic personnel had also worked
> together, with officers of the armed
> forces frequently making decisions of
> political consequence and civilian
> officials handling problems of con-
> cern to the military.[10]
>
> We need men who understand the causes
> of war and conflict, who understand
> the fundamentals of our aims and

ideals, who understand the interrela-
tion of international politics, internal politics, trade and finance
and the true significance of military
power. . . .[11]

Following the war the military educational system was reconstructed in essentially the same pattern as in the prewar period. One major exception
to this was that three "joint" institutions were
brought into being as a direct result of wartime
experience in joint and combined operations and as
a consequence of the National Security Act of 1947.
With the exception of the creation of the new National War College, the politico-military experiences of the war were reflected more in the subject
matter incorporated into the educational system and
the composition of the student bodies than in the
organizational structure itself.

For purposes of discussion, it can be said
that the existing system was, and continues to be,
divided into two broad categories: precommission
and postcommission education. The postcommission
category further divides into three smaller areas:
basic, intermediate, and advanced. These are by no
means universally accepted categorizations. The
semantics are unimportant so long as any chosen
grouping depicts the progressive educational levels
that generally correspond to a normal career pattern.

In one very descriptive work, the military educational system is likened to a pyramid, with precommission education providing the broad base of
the model. Moving upward toward the apex of the
pyramid, the basic level of postcommission education is next encountered. Here the pyramid narrows
very slightly from the precommission base. Narrow-
ing now more precipitously, the intermediate level,
involving considerably fewer officers, is reached.
At the very narrow apex of the pyramid, one finds
the advanced (senior service college) educational
level that involves still fewer professional officers than the preceding level.

As a general statement it can be said that all military professionals receive some sort of precommission formal education and virtually all receive the basic level of in-service postcommission schooling. Those officers remaining in the service, and otherwise eligible for intermediate-level education, are subjected to a screening process that significantly reduces the number of those selected to participate. Another, and significantly more rigorous, selection process identifies those officers who are later offered advanced-level education.[12]

A model designed to demonstrate the breadth of the curriculum at the various levels would be essentially the converse of the above, with the basic postcommission courses being very narrow and concentrating on the technical aspects of military operations. The intermediate level would be broader and the advanced level the broadest. Again, as a general rule, it can be said from the point of view of politico-military exposure, that the exposure increases as the apex of the pyramid is approached.

The pyramid, as a device for illustrating the military educational system, is not at all unreasonable. The same pyramid roughly depicts the distribution of professional officers in the services. The most junior officers, who are the recipients of basic-level education, represent the largest group of officers. The intermediate group is smaller in number and the senior officers who receive advanced-level education represent the smallest group. Quite obviously, the patterns of length of service, experience, and level of responsibility also roughly equate to the pyramid. At the apex of the perfect model one would find the most senior officers, who have the broadest experience, who will receive the most responsible assignments, and who are most likely to be involved in decision making requiring knowledge of politico-military affairs. In the educational system they are exposed to the broadest curriculum with the most emphasis on politico-military matters.

It must be recognized, however, that the pyramid illustrating the educational system narrows more precipitously than does one showing the numerical distribution of officers. While essentially all junior officers receive basic-level education, something less than half of those who eventually become colonels or navy captains receive advanced-level education. Also, it is generally true today that completion of advanced-level education is a prerequisite for selection to general or flag rank.

In more conventional terms, precommission education may be described as the undergraduate level of the military educational system. For the most part this level is attained at one of the service academies or through one of the several ROTC programs associated with the many civilian colleges throughout the country. With some exceptions, the attainment of a degree at a civilian institution implies a certain amount of exposure to a liberal education. In the service academies this has not always been the case. It is significant, however, that the academies have experienced a steady inclination toward broadening their curricula in order to offer a more liberal education, even though the extent to which the trend has been implemented varies somewhat among the academies. Ideally the newly commissioned officer enters the service with a broad educational base and at least a basic appreciation of the role and position of the military forces in the overall national structure. Recognizing considerable variances between the services, it can be generally stated that the newly commissioned officer is an "educated" man and not a "trained" military technician.

Moving now into the postcommission category, the basic level is encountered first. For the most part the courses at this level are designed to train young officers in specific military techniques. The emphasis is on "training" rather than "education." Training, as the word is used in this chapter, implies those activities that result in the acquisition of some specific military skill or skills.

Education includes those activities that result in the acquisition of the ability to <u>understand</u> the military profession and the role of military force in the resolution of national security problems.[13] Schooling at this level comes early in the new officer's career. Depending upon the particular service, this general level may involve actual attendance at a formal school or it may consist primarily of practical experience. In overall perspective, however, it may be said that at this educational level the young officer receives little instruction in other than purely military matters. Military technology is emphasized.

When the professional military enters the educational phase identified above as intermediate, he has moved onto a level at which the academic horizons commence to broaden considerably. At this level the student is exposed to the roles and missions of the sister services and the fundamentals of joint and combined operations. He is also exposed, often for the first time, to a rather healthy bloc of politico-military instruction. The emphasis at this level shifts from training to education.

In the opinion of the author, this is the most critical phase in the military educational system because it represents the highest level at which the majority of the professional officers participate in formal education. This is often referred to as the "command and staff" level. It includes the Army Command and General Staff College, the Air Force Command and Staff College, the Naval School of Command and Staff, the Marine Command and Staff College, and the Armed Forces Staff College.

The advanced educational level, normally referred to as the "war college" or "senior service college" level, is the most comprehensive from the politico-military point of view. Subsequent to World War II The National War College and the Industrial College of the Armed Forces came into being and after some internal adjustment within the military establishment the war college educational

level came to include the Army, Navy and Air Force
War Colleges, the Industrial College of the Armed
Forces, and The National War College.

Attendance at each of the war colleges is by
military officers from each of the services and
civilian governmental officials, namely foreign service officers. The student bodies of the war colleges of the three military departments consist primarily of officers of the parent service with a
relatively small representation from the other services, the foreign service, and other civilian
agencies of the government. The student composition of the Industrial College of the Armed Forces
and The National War College, the two senior institutions of the Joint Chiefs of Staff, is essentially one quarter military officers from each of the
three military departments and one quarter civilian
officials.*

The faculty composition of each of the war colleges is on essentially the same ratio as the student body. Each of the colleges has a career foreign service officer of ambassadorial rank, who
serves--under differing titles--as the foreign affairs advisor to the military commandant. At The
National War College, the ambassador is the deputy
commandant for international affairs.

Ambassador Raymond L. Thurston, who served as
the foreign affairs advisor at the Air War College,
commented on this level of education:

---

*Reference is intentionally made to the educa-
tional structure of the military departments as opposed to the armed services. The Marine Corps,
which is part of one of the three military departments, but is considered as a separate armed service, has its own educational system at the basic
and intermediate levels but has no separate war college. The Marine Corps also leans heavily on the
Army's educational system at all levels.

The overall mission of the war colleges is to prepare senior military
officers for the important responsibilities many will assume shortly in
the various service, joint, and international commands and in other policy-
making roles in the defense establishment. In a ten-month course the Air
Force and Army colonels or lieutenant
colonels and the Navy captains and
commanders achieve through lectures
by national leaders and prominent
specialists, reading assignments,
group discussion, and problem-solving
a better understanding of the contemporary international scene with emphasis, of course, on United States objectives and programs and on military
and politico-military factors. At
the Industrial College, however, primary attention is given to the economic component of the defense spectrum. The curriculum of the National
War College has a heavy non-military
content. . . .
          . . . The principal aim of all
these institutions is to broaden the
outlook of senior military officers
with respect to the nature and direction of the dynamic forces in our contemporary world and, more concretely,
to the importance of, and imperative
need for, cooperative working relations among all branches of the armed
forces and all other agencies and instruments of our national security.[14]

     The similarities of the curricula of the sev-
eral war colleges are more apparent than are the
differences, yet each has its area of special emphasis. The Army, Navy, and Air War Colleges emphasize the role of land, sea, and air forces respectively in the resolution of national security
problems. The Industrial College of the Armed

Forces emphasizes the economics of national security and The National War College emphasizes the
politico-military aspects of the national security
problem. Because of the peculiar emphasis of The
National War College it will be commented on in
greater detail in subsequent paragraphs. The mission statements* of the several war colleges follow:

> Army War College. To prepare selected
> senior officers for command and high-
> level staff duties with emphasis on
> Army doctrine and operations and to
> advance interdepartmental and inter-
> service understanding.
>
> Air War College. To provide instruc-
> tion which will prepare senior offi-
> cers for high command and staff duty.
> To develop sound understanding of the
> elements of national power to insure
> the most effective development and em-
> ployment of aerospace power.
>
> Naval War College. To provide Naval
> officers advanced education in the
> science of naval warfare and related
> subjects in order to improve their
> professional competence for higher re-
> sponsibilities.
>
> The National War College. To conduct
> a course of study of those agencies
> of government and those military, eco-
> nomic, scientific, political, psycho-
> logical, and social factors of power
> potential, which are essential parts

---

*The mission statements are taken from a 1966
document in which they were all included. In subsequent years some of the wording has changed but
the substance remains the same and the different
emphasis at each of the war colleges has not
changed.

of national security in order to enhance the preparation of selected personnel of the Armed Forces and State
Department for the exercise of joint
and combined high-level policy, command and staff functions, and for the
planning of national strategy.

Industrial College of the Armed Forces.
To conduct courses of study in the
economic and industrial aspects of
national security and in the management of resources under all conditions, giving due consideration to
the inter-related military, political, and social factors affecting
national security, and in the context
of both national and world affairs,
in order to enhance the preparation
of selected military officers and key
civilian personnel for important command, staff, and policy-making positions in the national and international security structure.[15] [Empha-
sis added.]

In the introductory comments to this chapter,
Senator Fulbright was quoted as saying that "the
politician must acquire knowledge and sensitivity
to every aspect of national security, including the
military. . . ."[16] The foreign service officer
gains this "knowledge and sensitivity" in the same
manner as the military professional gains the "wisdom of history and statecraft," through practical
experience and formal education. The basic limitations of practical experience that are identified
above for the military professional are also applicable to the foreign service officer. He, like his
military counterpart, must depend to a great extent
on in-service formal education either to substitute
for or at least complement his practical experience.

A formal educational structure of the Department of State did not exist prior to World War II.

As a result of the experiences of that war and on the urging of senior professional foreign service officers, a structure patterned roughly after the military system was instituted in 1947. The Department of State's Foreign Service Institute was established in March, 1947, by Section 701 of the Foreign Service Act of 1946. The act instructed the secretary of state to establish an institution

> to furnish training and instruction
> to officers and employees of the For-
> eign Service and of the Department
> and to other officers and employees
> of the government for whom training
> and instruction in the field of for-
> eign affairs is necessary. . . .[17]

The Institute was, at the outset, divided into two schools, the School of Foreign Affairs and the School of Language and Area Studies. It is within the purview of the School of Foreign Affairs where the most significant activity in the field of politico-military affairs is centered so the comments that follow will be limited to that portion of the Foreign Service Institute.

The general career training courses of the School of Foreign Affairs can be likened to the pyramid used earlier to describe the military educational concept. The basic foreign service course is mandatory for all newly appointed foreign service officers. This course forms the base of the pyramid. The foreign affairs program management seminar, which in 1965 replaced the mid-career course in foreign affairs, constitutes the intermediate educational level and is attended by those officers who are expected to move into middle-grade executive positions in foreign affairs. The apex of the pyramid is represented by the senior seminar in foreign policy. This level of education is experienced by only a relatively few officers each year and is designed to prepare them for high positions of responsibility in policy recommendation and execution and in executive management roles at home and abroad.

The basic foreign service officer course is heavily oriented toward the teaching of techniques that a junior officer must know in the performance of his duties. Politico-military exposure at this level is extremely limited. As early as 1965, the year the foreign affairs program management seminar came into being, one seven-day period was devoted to "United States Military Policy and Program Co-ordination." The scope of that bloc of instruction was described as follows:

> The coordination in political-military matters between State and Defense will be examined, together with the Defense role in operations and programs abroad. This will include United States mili-tary concepts and operations, the Mili-tary Assistance program operating through ISA [International Security Affairs] in Defense and MAAG [Military Assistance Advisory Groups] in the field, the role of military intelli-gence, military programs in develop-ing states concerned with internal de-fense, Defense interests in space and missilry, the problems involved in the operation of the United States alliance systems, and the question of disarmament.[18]

The same general philosophy toward exposure to mili-tary thinking exists today in the construction of the curriculum of this intermediate-level seminar.

As would be expected by the trend suggested above, the senior seminar in foreign policy devotes even more of its time to problems that have a politico-military connotation. The senior seminar is a ten-month course that generally equates to the war-college level in the military educational sys-tem. It is unlikely that a foreign service officer would attend one of the war colleges in the mili-tary system and also attend his own service's senior seminar. The Department of State identifies the "ob-jective and scope" of the senior seminar as follows:

> The Senior Seminar in Foreign Policy
> is the most advanced educational pro-
> gram in the field of international re-
> lations and foreign policy offered in
> the United States Government. Its
> purpose is to assist in the prepara-
> tion of officers for positions of high
> responsibility. The Seminar provides
> an opportunity for a free and vogorous
> inquiry into some of the complexities
> of foreign policy and US domestic
> problems. It aims to broaden and
> deepen the thinking of its Members
> with regard to domestic and foreign
> affairs. It seeks to stimulate their
> creative powers and to enhance their
> capacity to make thoughtful judgments.[19]

Ambassador Thurston sees fit to more closely equate
the senior seminar to The National War College:

> The similarity in broad outline of
> this [Senior Seminar] curriculum to
> that of The National War College will
> be noted. However, the emphasis on
> diplomatic history, the American do-
> mestic scene, international trade and
> finance, and development diplomacy is
> a distinguishing characteristic of
> the Senior Seminar course.[20]

While it is true that conceptually the senior
seminar is the war-college level of the Department
of State's educational system it is also true that
both the Departments of State and Defense see the
seminar as a bit above the war colleges. This is
apparent from the assignment of foreign service
officers in grades 1 and 2 to the seminar and grades
2 and 3 to the war colleges. Although it is not a
specific requirement, the army, which sends one officer to the seminar each year, selects an officer
who is a graduate of one of the war colleges. As
the army sees the senior seminar, it is post-war
college formal education.

The preceding pages encompass by far the largest part of the in-service educational system that
contributes to politico-military understanding on
the part of professional military officers and associated civilian officials of the government. There
are, however, several closely related formal educational programs that deserve mention in the context
of politico-military education.

The first is a program of post-war college
formal education that was mentioned in the preceding paragraphs in conjunction with army representation at the senior seminar of the Foreign Service
Institute. Each year the Departments of Defense
and State are invited to nominate officers to spend
an academic year on a fellowship at distinguished
academic centers in the foreign policy area, such
as the Center for International Affairs at Harvard
University and the Council on Foreign Relations in
New York. The military officers appointed to these
fellowships are war college graduates and normally
have graduate degrees in related areas from civilian
institutions.

In relation to the pyramid model discussed
earlier, these programs rest outside and a step
above the apex of the pyramid. The number of officers involved each year is extremely limited. Of
significance to this program is the fact that the
military professionals who attend are senior colonels or navy captains who can anticipate high-level
politico-military assignments.

Another program to be mentioned is the "civil
schooling" employed by the several services. Each
year a number of officers of varying grades are
sent to civilian educational institutions to pursue
advanced degrees in a wide variety of subjects
ranging from the sciences to the humanities. Each
year a varying number of graduate degrees in some
phase of international studies are earned by military professionals.

Selection for graduate work in international
studies was at one time closely associated with

successful completion of the intermediate level of
in-service education. In recent years this has not
been so and the officer students and generally
younger and more junior. This trend, in the author's
view, is healthy. Exposure to politico-military education at an early stage in a career should make the
officer's subsequent practical experience and in-
service education more meaningful to him and his
associates. This program rests off to the side of
the previously mentioned pyramid and complements it,
though it is not an integral part of it.

Each of the war colleges also has an advanced-
degree program in association with a civilian college or university. Participation in the program
is voluntary for the student. Most officers who do
not have a graduate degree do elect to participate
in the program and some use the opportunity to earn
a second graduate degree. With the exception of
the associated graduate work offered at the Industrial College of the Armed Forces, the degrees offered are primarily in the social sciences and are
at least indirectly related to politico-military
understanding on the part of the participant.

The value of the graduate-degree programs is
argued annually as each of the war colleges takes
stock of its year's work and contemplates the coming year. The governing, but by no means unanimous,
view is that the graduate degree programs do in
fact complement the war college courses and are an
overall positive contribution to the individual officer and to the professional educational system.[21]

So far it was demonstrated that the in-service
military educational system has undergone changes
in basic philosophy, particularly at the higher
levels, in reaction to the requirement for a broader politico-military expertise by the professional
officer. The essential question is whether the educational system, with all its changes, is in fact
succeeding in educating the officer for his expanded
role in national policy making, and at the same time
keeping him adequately trained in the highly complex
field of military technology.

The search for an answer to this question is
directed through an examination of the professional
requirements of military officers at various levels
in their careers. The effectiveness of the educational system in meeting these requirements is then
evaluated.

EDUCATIONAL REQUIREMENTS

As a general statement it can be said that the
military officer needs to be more of a generalist
and less a specialist as he advances in rank. Several "levels" of professionalism with varying professional demands in each can be identified. The
lower level is that in which technical military expertise is the most demanding factor. It is applicable primarily, but not limited exclusively, to
the more junior and consequently less experienced
officers. It is at this level that an officer is
less likely to be called upon to deal with politico-
military matters. The higher level has to do with
the weaving of military skills into the politico-
military equation. It emphasizes "what" is to be
done with military power in the resolution of some
national problem as opposed to the "how." This
level is most applicable, but by no means limited,
to the more senior, more experienced officers who
are more likely to be called upon to wrestle with
knotty politico-military problems than with the
more narrow, but not necessarily less important,
technical military problems.[22]

Still dealing in very general terms, it would
appear that the educational system is constructed
to support this basic concept. At the lower levels
military technology is emphasized while at the
higher levels a broad approach is taken. Directing
the evaluation specifically to the politico-military
requirements of the officer, a similar conclusion
may be drawn. For the most part, the officer who
is involved in the making of national policy, and
is in need of politico-military sense, is not the
newly commissioned ensign or lieutenant but rather

a relatively senior officer in the higher level suggested above. Again it is apparent that the emphasis on politico-military affairs at the higher educational levels is consistent with the basic requirements.

   In that great center area, between the basic
and the advanced educational levels, there is a
mixture of military and political education that
should serve to keep the officer professionally
solvent from a technical point of view and at the
same time expose him to some of the more important
facts of international life. In the author's opinion, it is in this intermediate area where the
politico-military educational balance is most critical.

   A brief examination of this middle area, however, raises an interesting question. Are the duties that the officers in this group will be called
upon to perform primarily military or primarily
political? The obvious answer is that for many of
the officers the duties will be primarily military,
while for others they may well be primarily political. The bulk of the assignments will, however,
require some reasonable appreciation of politico-
military affairs. This "appreciation" must be more
complete than that of the average junior officer,
but it need not be as comprehensive as that of the
senior officer.

   The officers who fit into this middle area are
of the age and rank that are normally associated
with attendance at the intermediate (command and
staff) level of education. Assuming that one of
these officers is faced with the not unlikely possibility of having to make a decision or offer a
staff recommendation that has politico-military implications, it would be comforting to know that he
has at least been exposed to politico-military concepts, and it must be hoped that within whatever
freedom of action he may have, he would propose a
wise solution from the political as well as from
the military point of view. It should not be

difficult to muster support for the thesis that the
chances of his making a sound politico-military
recommendation would be much better if he had received some meaningful intermediate-level politico-
military instruction somewhere in the educational
process.*

The evaluation up to this point illustrates a
possible weakness in the educational system at the
basic level. The logical remedial action would
simply appear to be the inclusion of additional
politico-military instruction at the basic level.
Such an action must, however, be viewed with a certain amount of caution.

In view of the trend to broaden undergraduate
education and place less emphasis on military technology, and in the light of recent trends at the
senior educational levels to emphasize politico-
military matters at the expense of military technology, it happens that the only place military
technology is still heavily emphasized is at the
basic level. Any action that would tend to dilute
this level must be taken with great care. In the
article cited above (see Note 22) the following observation was made about professionalism and
politico-military expertise at varying stages of an
officer's career:

---

*While serving as the chief of the Interna-
tional Affairs Division, J5, Hq MACV, from September, 1968, to June, 1969, the author experienced
the problem of identifying military officers with
the necessary educational background to effectively
participate in activities in close coordination
with the U.S. Embassy in Saigon and with the negotiating team in Paris. Subsequently, while serving
with a tactical unit in the field, he became pain-
fully aware of the necessity for politico-military
education of some sort at the basic educational
level so that the junior officers could cope intelligently with the many politico-military demands
placed on them in a war such as the one the nation
is experiencing in Vietnam.

The newly commissioned lieutenant of
infantry with a deep academic understanding of the theory of international politics and the role of military force in the affairs of state
but without the technical expertise
to perform the basic military skills
necessary to command the rifle platoon
to which he is assigned is not a military professional in any sense of the
word. He is, in fact, a "technician"
who may be capable of serving as a
technicial somewhere on a politico-
military staff.

By the same token, a senior officer who possesses a wealth of technical military knowledge and skills resulting from many years of experience,
but who fails to understand the
politico-military implications of
military force in the contemporary
world is equally non-professional.
He too is a military "technician"
with a narrow area of competence.[23]

The article then proceeds to evaluate the effect of this misguided professionalism as follows:

The former "technician" may be incapable of serving his country well at a
given moment but the shortcoming is
correctable and he can likely be made
into an effective professional. The
command influences in our hierarchical organization will likely serve to
at least modify the impact of errors
made while he is learning. The latter "technician," however, is in a position to do his country and his profession a great disservice. Because
of his very rank and experience there
is much less modifying influence on
him and he is likely to be in a position where his decisions will have

great impact and his views will be
heard and carry significant weight.[24]

Ideally, all professional military officers of
all ranks should be thoroughly versed in the technical details of their profession and at the same
time be all-wise in the ways of international politics. The ideal is impractical to attain but the
military educational system has proven itself to be
dynamic and flexible. It has adjusted to meet the
requirements of a changing national and international
environment to serve the military profession as a
whole, and the several services in particular, by
reasonable emphasis and balance.

The trend toward a broader liberal education
at the precommissioned level is sound and should
continue, primarily because a broad undergraduate
background will provide a more meaningful intellectual base upon which the newly commissioned officer
can build. The trend toward a politico-military emphasis at the senior educational level also is
sound and should continue. Some politico-military
instruction must be taught at the basic level, but
the emphasis must remain emphatically on military
technology. The amount of politico-military education at the intermediate level must strike a delicate and rather elusive balance. It is especially
important here because this is the highest level of
formal military education to which many professional
officers are exposed.

The primary danger to the military educational
system is that the politico-military trend will continue to the point where military education is diluted to a dangerous degree. The military educational system exists for the purpose of providing
the nation with professionally competent military
officers. The Department of State's system exists
for the purpose of providing the nation with professionally competent foreign service officers. While
these two systems are complementary, neither one
should attempt to assume the role of the other.

The professional military officer who understands only the military technology of the "ordered
application of force" or the "management of violence" is of very limited value to his profession.
On the other hand, the officer who has lost his expertise in these areas is likewise of very questionable value. Responsibility for maintaining the
proper balance between military technology and
politico-military expertise rests, in great part,
with the military educational system.[25] In the
final analysis the responsibility is with each individual professional officer. The in-service educational systems can at best serve as a guide for
him to follow.

A survey of the alumni of The National War College in 1969 revealed a surprising acceptance of
politico-military emphasis on the part of the graduates.

> The study of our national strategy,
> to include the integration of mili-
> tary and foreign policies ". . . is
> clearly seen as the most important
> base of study for the course, regard-
> less of year of graduation, service,
> branch of government or rank of the
> respondent. . . ." The alumni poll
> gives the suggestion that less empha-
> sis need be given, at The National
> War College level to military capa-
> bilities and plans and the employ-
> ment of joint and combined military
> forces.[26]

The survey conducted by the author, of The
National War College classes of 1968 and 1970, suggests an interesting possibility concerning the
politico-military sophistication of the student before he attends the college. The last query on the
questionnaire completed by the students was: "If
you had answered this questionnaire last September
do you believe you would have answered it any differently?" The students were given the questionnaire

approximately one month before graduation in both
cases. The obvious intent of the question was to
determine if attendance at The National War College
had in any way affected the individual's view of
politico-military factors.

In the class of 1968 approximately two thirds
of the respondents indicated that they would have
answered differently, and those who explained their
answer pointed out how the course had significantly
broadened their horizons. Only slightly over one
third of the respondents of the class of 1970 answered the same way. The respondents' comments suggested that because of exposure to politico-military
problems on previous assignments, military and foreign service officers as a group may be becoming
more politico-militarily sophisticated earlier in
their service.[27]

ASSOCIATED PROBLEMS

The major portion of the discussion in this
chapter has thus far been limited to the formal in-
service military educational system as it affects
and is affected by the current concept of politico-
military relationships. There are, however, several associated problems that are on the periphery
of the formal educational system. They are commented on briefly in the following pages as they
are applicable to politico-military affairs and
military professionalism.

Civilian educational institutions, for the
most part, serve two functions. First they are
teaching institutions at which knowledge is transmitted from the instructor to the student. Secondly they are sources of original thought. It is interesting, although not too flattering, to the military profession that the bulk of the original writing in the area of national security policy comes
out of the civilian educational institutions and
not the military. This is, of course, a generalization to which there are some, but unfortunately

too few, exceptions. Why is this so? Why does the
professional military officer not contribute more
to the overall understanding of the problems of national security by writing and lecturing? Is it
because the military mind is not intellectually
capable of original thought? Is it because the
military educational system does not encourage original thought? Or is it because the contemporary
concepts of politico-military affairs in general
and civil-military relations in particular discour-
age it?

The possibility that the military mind is intellectually deficient will be dealt with by reference to a statement by a former deputy assistant
secretary of defense (education):

> The military mind, of course, really
> isn't unlike other professional minds.
> It deals with intellectual problems
> in basically the same way that an aca-
> demic mind or a medical mind or an
> engineering mind or a legal mind at-
> tack their respective problems. It
> deals with very real, intellectual
> problems concerning the profession of
> arms. . . .
> There is no profession which is
> more intellectual than this one, and
> that is why I suggest that the mili-
> tary mind really doesn't have very
> much time on its brain cells, so to
> speak, to be worrying about taking
> over the government or starting world
> wars. It is really much more con-
> cerned with meeting the ever-increasing
> demands and responsibilities thrust
> upon this nation.[28]

Assuming the validity of the above view, what
then is the problem? While there is general agreement as to the overall effectiveness of the military educational system especially at the war college level as instructional institutions, there is

some concern that they fail as centers of formula-
tive politico-military thinking and writing.[29]

While the military educational system may serve
to bring the military professional more in touch
with the realities of international politics, is
this really enough? Bernard Brodie commented that
"any real expansion of strategic thought . . . will
. . . have to be developed largely within the military guild itself."[30] Where else but in the academic environment of the senior military colleges
could this be better done? The students at these
institutions are not beset with day-to-day operational problems and are in an excellent position to
do some serious thinking and writing. In fact, one
of the strong justifications for the war college
level of professional military education is that it
gives the officer an opportunity to reflect and exchange views.

There are many professional military officers
who take full advantage of the opportunity offered
and do some really serious thinking and writing. A
major problem is, however, that the effect of this
thought and writing is shared with relatively few
fellow students and faculty members. The discussions in a seminar at a senior service college may
be as penetrating as those at any educational institution; however, the views exchanged are seldom
heard by anyone outside the seminar room or the lec-
ture hall. There is some sound original thought in
the many student theses that find their way into
the archives of the several military colleges. The
thoughts, unfortunately, most often stay in the archives to which they are relegated.

In the early 1960's the author was assigned to
a university in the Washington area and had occasion to conduct some research in politico-military
affairs. He was most surprised to find that he, as
a professional military officer with the necessary
security clearance, did not have reasonable access
to the unclassified student theses on file in the
library of The National War College. They were

closely controlled, and only the students and the
faculty of the College had the requisite clearance
to study them freely. If a professional military
officer must gain special permission to browse
through the unclasified writings of his fellow professionals in search of new ideas, is it any wonder
that the product of the military mind does not get
wide distribution within the military establishment
and seldom appears on the shelves of the public or
university libraries. This is not to say that all
student theses prepared at the war colleges end up
in a vault where they are infrequently seen. There
are, for example, copies of unclassified student
theses from the Army War College on the open shelves
of the army library in the Pentagon and selected
papers do appear from time to time in professional
journals. One example is The National War College
Forum in which selected student papers are published.
The Forum, however, is printed in a limited number
of copies and receives a limited distribution. It
is not for sale and not normally available to the
public.

    While those in the military profession believe
in the intellectual capacity of their fellow professionals, and feel that they have something to
offer in the way of original thought, they make it
rather difficult for their members to disseminate
their views. They might well do some hard thinking
about whether they really mean it when they say they
welcome and encourage original thought.

    In this regard, two military professionals sev-
eral years ago expressed concern that "there has
been too little solid contribution from military
pens to national security policy thinking for this
new age. . . ."[31] They recognized that the ever-
present problem of security clearance may be a major
contributor to this shortcoming. There is a constant conflict between the desirability for a free
exchange of ideas and information, the requirements
of security, and policy. When there is any doubt
as to which is to take precedence in a given situation, security is normally the overriding factor.

They also believe, however, that there is a lack of
intellectual stimulation in the services of the
type required to cause contribution to national
security thinking. If this is true, the military
educational system must accept its share of the
blame.

Closely allied to the military educational system and overall intellectual stimulation, is the
question of professional military journals. Some
of the more common publications are official organs
of the service involved and are most often prepared
at one of the military educational institutions.
Others are unofficial but nonetheless are very representative of current military thought. An examination of several periodicals over the years since
the close of World War II to the present indicates
a definite trend. The trend has been away from articles on purely military technology to articles
with a much broader content; away from purely military articles written by military professionals to
articles with a much broader politico-military coverage written by military professionals and civilians alike. This shift in emphasis is not really
surprising as it is in keeping with the overall
trend toward a recognition of the importance of
politico-military affairs.*

While the shift in emphasis in military periodicals is encouraging it must, in all fairness, be
pointed out that these are "professional journals"
that are subscribed to and read primarily by military professionals. They serve a most useful purpose in disseminating information within the military profession but they are unfortunately of

---

*The United States Naval Institute Proceedings,
an unofficial publication of the navy, moved from
about 3 percent of its articles in Volume 71 (1945)
to approximately 40 percent in Volume 95 (1969).
The Military Review, an official army publication,
shifted from less than 1 percent in Volume 25 (1945)
to about 45 percent in Volume 49 (1969).

limited value in acquainting governmental officials, scholars, and the general public of military thinking.

It is worthy of note that the libraries of the universities in the Washington area carry a very small number of the military periodicals. Strangely enough, the same is true of the Department of State library. The author was informed, however, at the Department of State library that the requests for military publications has been increasing rapidly and that they are obtained for the user through interlibrary loan.

An examination of several of the more prominent journals devoted to international affairs reveals essentially the same pattern as indicated for the service journals. The number of articles that deal directly or indirectly with military matters has greatly increased. However, it is worthy of special note that while the number of articles concerning military affairs has increased significantly, most of these articles are written by civilian authors. It is rare indeed to find an article in one of these publications authored by a military professional. While there is every reason to be thankful that the idea of politico-military coordination is being disseminated in these publications, there is also reason for concern as to why the military pen is not contributing more.

PROFESSIONAL EFFECT

The shift in basic educational philosophy as exemplified in the formal educational system, the trend toward politico-military writing in service journals, and the emphasis on civil education in international relations for professional military officers clearly illustrate the importance that the military profession places on politico-military affairs.

The military educational system has made, and will continue to make, a solid contribution to the

effort of broadening the professional military base.
Some idea of the impact of the nation's war colleges
on the governmental services as a whole is suggested
by the distribution of The National War College
graduates as of 1970. There have been 3,064 graduates of the College through the class of 1970. Of
that number, 1,574 remain in active government service. Add to this the graduates of the other war
colleges and the impact is apparent.[32] As indicated above, however, there is the ever-present danger of increasing the politico-military expertise
of the professional officer at the expense of his
purely military expertise.

While it is absolutely essential that a military staff officer or commander fully understands
the international political ramifications of a given
situation, the nation will be poorly served if he
has learned his international politics at the expense of his ability to translate national policy
decisions into military action when necessary. In
addressing the graduation class at the United States
Military Academy in June, 1956, Secretary of the
Army William Brucker cautioned the new officers:
"You must guard with jealous care your most price-
less possion--your soldier's soul. You are a fighting man."[33] So long as the military educational
system recognizes that the professional military
officer must achieve a certain expertise in international politics as a means to an end--the creation
of a better "fighting man"--the profession is on
solid ground. If, however, it strives for expertise
in international politics as an end in itself it
will have lost its effectiveness. The military educational system carries much of the responsibility
for keeping this concept in perspective.

In his January, 1965, message to the Congress
on national defense, President Johnson commented on
military education as follows:

> It is imperative that our men in uni-
> form have the necessary background
> and training to keep up with the

complexities of the everchanging military, political, and technical problems they face each day. To insure
this, the Secretary of Defense is undertaking a study of military education to make certain that the education available to our men and women
at their Academies, at their War Colleges and at the Command and Staff
Colleges, is excellent in its quality.[34]

A valuable commentary on the status of in-
service military education is found in the following critique by a military professional:

The low regard in many places for the
military intellect is in part our own
fault. We have earned the image because too many of us have neglected
for too long the study of those facets
of national security once considered
none of the officer's concern. At
least since the close of World War II,
change has been the watchword in national security affairs. Unfortunately, the impact of what has been hap-
pening has been slow to reach the educational arena of the military. Education programs have tended to lag
behind the military leader's present
environment, let alone anticipate the
challenges he will face in the future.
Only now is change moving in full
swing in all our institutions responsible for professional military education.[35]

NOTES

1.   J. W. Fulbright, "Public Policy and Military Responsibility," an address given at the opening session of The National War College and the Industrial College of the Armed Forces, August 21, 1961, Congressional Record, Vol. 107, No. 144 (August 21, 1961), pp. 15356-59.

2.   R. L. Gidding, Jr., "On Understanding War," United States Naval Institute Proceedings, July 7, 1968, p. 27; for a commentary on the need for an intellectual orientation toward the profession of arms see Roger Hilsman, "Research in Military Affairs," World Politics, April, 1955, pp. 490-503.

3.   Omar N. Bradley, A Soldier's Story (New York: Henry Holt and Company, 1951), pp. 528-36.

4.   Quoted in John W. Masland and Laurence I. Radway, Soldiers and Scholars (Princeton, N.J.: Princeton University Press, 1957), p. 82.

5.   Admiral W. V. Pratt, quoted in Masland, ibid., p. 83.

6.   Russell F. Weigley, History of the United States Army (New York: The Macmillan Company, 1967), p. 320.

7.   Masland, op. cit., p. 90.

8.   See ibid., pp. 76-99.

9.   Robert Murphy, Diplomat Among Warriors (Garden City, N.Y.:   Doubleday and Company, 1964), p. 453.

10.   John W. Masland, "The National War College and the Administration of Public Affairs," Public Administration Review, December, 1952, p. 267.

11.   Walter Millis, ed., The Forrestal Diaries (New York: Viking Press, 1951), p. 62.   The quote

is from a letter written by Admiral Halsey to Congressman Woodrum, chairman of the Committee on Postwar Military Policy.

12. Harold F. Clark and Harold S. Sloan, Classrooms in the Military (New York: Teacher's College, Columbia University, 1964), p. 8.

13. See R. L. Gidding, "The Neglected Task of Officer Education," Air University Review, July-August, 1965, pp. 54-59. For still another professional view, see John P. Lisack, "Air Force Education," Air University Review, November-December, 1964, pp. 84-91.

14. Raymond L. Thurston, "Education at the Top of Government," Political Science Quarterly, June, 1966, pp. 255-56. See also Lincoln P. Bloomfield and Barton Whaley, "The Politico-Military Exercise: A Progress Report," Orbis, Winter, 1965, pp. 854-70.

15. U.S., Department of the Army, "Report of the Department of the Army Board to Review Army Officer Schools" (Haines Board), February, 1966, p. 486.

16. Fulbright, op. cit.

17. U.S., Department of State, Foreign Service Institute, Programs of Instruction; 1963-64.

18. U.S., Department of State, Foreign Service Institute, Foreign Affairs Program Management Seminar, O/FSI-October 6, 1964.

19. U.S., Department of State, Foreign Service Institute, Senior Seminar in Foreign Policy; 1969-70 Session, description and outline.

20. Thurston, op. cit., p. 259.

21. U.S., Department of Defense, The National War College, The Commandant's Annual Report; 1969-1970, p. 12.

22. Donald F. Bletz, "Military Professionalism: A Conceptual Approach," <u>Military Review</u>, May, 1971, pp. 9-17.

23. <u>Ibid</u>., p. 13.

24. <u>Ibid</u>., p. 14.

25. Edward L. Katzenback, Jr., "The Demotion of Professionalism at the War Colleges," <u>United States Naval Institute Proceedings</u>, March, 1965.

26. U.S., Department of Defense, The National War College, <u>Survey of National War College Alumni</u>. A General Report of a Survey of Views and of Attitudes of National War College Alumni Concerning the College, December 1969, p. 9.

27. See Appendix.

28. U.S., Congress, Senate, Committee on Government Operations, Hearings Before the Subcommittee on National Security Staffing and Operations, Part 9, June 25, 1964. 88th Cong., 2d Sess. (Washington: U.S. Government Printing Office, 1964), p. 555.

29. For an expansion of this view see C. M. Fergusson, Jr., "Strategic Thinking and Studies," <u>Military Review</u>, April, 1964, pp. 9-24; see also by the same author, "The Study of Military Strategy," <u>Military Review</u>, April, 1965, pp. 35-44.

30. Bernard Brodie, <u>Strategy in the Missile Age</u> (Princeton, N.J.: Princeton University Press, 1959), p. 9; and Joseph Kraft, <u>Profile in Power: A Washington Insight</u> (New York: The New American Library, 1966), p. 62.

31. George A. Lincoln and Richard G. Stilwell, "Scholars Debouch into Strategy," <u>Military Review</u>, July, 1960.

32. Figures from the Department of Defense,
The National War College, The Commandant's Annual
Report, 1969-1970, Appendix H.

33. William Brucker, quoted in U.S., Congress,
Senate, op. cit., p. 545.

34. Lyndon B. Johnson, "Text of President's
Message to Congress on Defense," The Washington
Post, January 19, 1965, p. A10.

35. John Tucker Hayward, "The Second-Class
Military Advisor: His Cause and Cure," Armed
Forces Management, November, 1969, p. 67.

6

MILITARY
THINKING
IN THE
UNITED
STATES

     In August, 1970, the news department of a
major television network carried a short segment
of the proceedings of the President's Commission on
Campus Unrest as part of its normal news coverage.
In the segment, a distinguished member of the Commission deplored the excessive violence on the part
of the Ohio National Guard at Kent State University
earlier that year and made reference to the "execution" of unarmed dissidents by the armed military
forces. He then asked the witness appearing before
the Commission (the adjutant general of the State
of Ohio) if such "executions" were consistent with
the thinking of the military in the United States.

     Although not directly related to the question
of politico-military affairs as it is being addressed in this study, the incident is cited here
for several reasons. First, assuming the sincerity
of the distinguished member who asked the question,
the fact that he, or anyone, would feel it necessary to ask such a question is by itself significant. Secondly, the wording of the question in-
ferred some sort of monolithic military structure
in which all members think as one on all issues to
include the "execution" of students. Finally, it

is significant, or at least an interesting coincidence, that the network news editors chose that particular segment of the proceedings to air to the public.

The first point could perhaps be explained as an overemotional reaction on the part of the distinguished citizen. The second, possibly, is consistent with an apparently widely held belief that the military profession is in fact a monolith in its thinking. The final point was certainly consistent with popular contemporary views of the nation's military profession and was, therefore, a logical and dramatic segment to include.

Analysis of the "why" of the above is not the central issue and will not be pursued further here. The significant point is that what and how the nation's military professionals think and the nation's perception of what and how its military professionals think is extremely important. Equally important is how the nation itself thinks about military matters and the military professional's perception of what and how the nation thinks. Both have a highly significant bearing on the structuring and balancing of the nation's politico-military equation.

The preceding chapters have shown the historical development of the military profession in the United States and have pointed out how the integration of the political and military aspects of a given national problem have made these elements evermore inseparable. As Professor Thomas Schelling has pointed out:

> Military strategy can no longer be
> thought of, as it could for some countries in some eras, as the science of
> military victory. It is now equally,
> if not more, the art of coercion, of
> intimidation and deterrence. The instruments of war are more punitive
> that acquisitive. Military strategy,
> whether we like it or not, has become
> the diplomacy of violence.[1] [Emphasis
> added.]

In the contemporary international environment the politico-military equation must be delicately balanced within the context of the "diplomacy of violence." As has been suggested in Chapter 1, it is virtually axiomatic that it is essential for the professional military officer to have a deep appreciation for the "diplomacy" (or political) as well as the "violence" (or military) sides of the equation.

In order to develop the concepts of how the nation thinks about things military, how the military professional thinks about things national, and how they both relate to the politico-military equation, two emotionally charged, yet operationally definable, terms will be used. American <u>militarism</u> will be examined from the point of view of how it affects the nation's thinking about things military with emphasis on its relationship to the military profession and to politico-military affairs. The <u>military mind</u> will be looked at from the point of view of how it affects the thinking of the professional military officer with emphasis on its relationship to the nation as a whole and to politico-military affairs.

At the outset of this study the military professional was defined as "the career officer who devoted himself to the expertise, responsibility, and corporateness of the profession of arms."[2] This definition was suggested as a synthesis of several thoughts on military professionalism and on the military professional. Using the initial definition as a reference point and considering some of the factors brought to light in the intervening chapters, it would appear that a further refinement of the definition is in order here. Possibly what is being suggested, rather than a definition of a military professional, is a description of what a military professional ideally should be. The two thoughts are not necessarily synonymous nor are they mutually exclusive. A refined definition is: <u>a commissioned officer on active duty who possesses the requisite level of training, education, experience, and intellect to perform the duties that he might logically be assigned.</u>[3]

The first definition emphasizes the professional officer's <u>commitment</u> to his profession. The latter one stresses his <u>competence</u> to honor that commitment with emphasis on his perception--his "thinking"--of his professional commitment.

To reiterate the thoughts in Chapter 5, the newly commissioned lieutenant of infantry, highly educated in the theory of international relations and the role of military force in the affairs of state but without the technical expertise to command his rifle platoon, is not a military professional.

By the same token, a senior officer who possesses a wealth of technical military knowledge and skill resulting from many years of practical experience, but who fails to understand the politico-military implications of military force in the contemporary world, is equally, and it can be argued even more, nonprofessional. Both are, at best, military technicians with narrow areas of competence. The latter of the two technicians is by far the more dangerous as he is in a position to do the nation and the military profession a great disservice. Because of his seniority and experience, and the respect and attention commanded by both, there is much less modifying influence on him and he is more likely to be given assignments where his decisions will have great impact and his views will carry more weight. In the contemporary international environment, this senior technician must be made into a professional, or closely supervised by a competent professional. Neither alternative can be implemented with ease.

A reasonable conclusion seems to be that there are multiple levels of professionalism with varying professional demands at each level. The word <u>level</u> is used intentionally to connote a vertical as opposed to a horizontal separation. For the purpose of this study, two levels will be developed briefly.[4] The first level, that in which technical military expertise is the most demanding factor, is the one applicable primarily, but not exclusively, to

the more junior officer. It is at this level of
military professionalism that an officer is least
likely to be called upon to deal with comprehensive
politico-military problems on his own. This is the
level of professionalism associated primarily with
the "how" of the "management of violence." It emphasizes the application of military skills.

The second level of professionalism has to do
with the weaving of military skills into the
politico-military equation. It centers more on
"what" is to be done with military force in the
resolution of some national problem as opposed to
"how." This level is most applicable, but by no
means limited, to the more senior, more experienced
officer who is most likely to be called upon to
wrestle with knotty politico-military problems than
with the more narrow, but not necessarily less important, technical military problems. The question
of whether a given tactical operation, no matter
how "professionally" it may have been conducted,
was a valid "ordered application" of available military force in the resolution of a given national
problem belongs to this second level of military
professionalism.

The purpose of the suggestion of levels of professionalism is to emphasize the point that professional officers do not think in the same terms simply because they both belong to the same profession.
The nation has every right to expect a different
level of professionalism and a different sort of
thinking from the general or flag officer than it
would expect from the newly commissioned ensign or
lieutenant. In this sense the military profession
is analogous to the professions of law or medicine
where society's expectations from the seasoned lawyer or doctor are different from those it has from
the medical intern or neophyte lawyer.

AMERICAN MILITARISM

Concern with militarism in the United States
is by no means unique to contemporary times.
Throughout the history of the United States things

military, and especially anything with the term
"militarism" attached to it, has been looked on
with varying degrees of disfavor depending on the
international and domestic political milieu at any
given time.

In Chapter 2, which presented a brief historical sketch of the growth of the military profession
in the United States, Admiral Mahan's observation
that "the trouble with the United States as a country was that we are perhaps the least military, but
not behind the foremost as a military one," is identified.[5] In the context of this chapter one might
take a bit of editorial license to update and para-
phrase Mahan as expressing the view that "while the
United States is not intentionally a 'militaristic'
nation it is not behind the foremost as a proponent
of the 'military way.'" For the time being, the
somewhat ambiguous meaning of the terms is intentionally left unattended and vague.

In Alexis de Tocqueville's classic, Democracy
in America, he commented on why "democratic nations
naturally desire peace and democratic armies, war."[6]
De Tocqueville, after giving some sound psychological and sociological reasons for his observation,
enunciated his thinking as follows:

> All the ambitious spirits of a demo-
> cratic army are consequently ardently
> desirous of war, because war makes
> vacancies and warrants the violation
> of that law of seniority which is the
> sole privilege natural to democracy.[7]

He then arrived at what he called "this singular
consequence"

> that, of all armies, the most ardent-
> ly desirous of war are democratic
> armies and, of all nations, those
> most fond of peace are democratic
> nations; and what makes these facts
> still more extraordinary is that

> these contrary effects are produced
> at the same time by the principle of
> equality.

His line of thinking is perhaps best summarized by
the following passage:

> All the members of the community, be-
> ing alike, constantly harbor the wish
> and discover the possibility of chang-
> ing their condition and improving
> their welfare; this makes them fond
> of peace, which is favorable to indus-
> try and allows every man to pursue
> his own little undertakings to their
> completion. On the other hand, this
> same equality makes soldiers dream of
> fields of battle, by increasing the
> value of military honors in the eyes
> of those who follow the profession of
> arms and by rendering those honors ac-
> cessible to all. In either case, the
> inquietude of the heart is the same,
> the taste for enjoyment as insatiable,
> the ambition of success as great; the
> means of gratifying it alone are dif-
> ferent.[8]

This formulation was developed in the context
of early nineteenth-century America and in contrast
to the European aristocratic societies of that era.
The thesis was that in the aristocratic society
military rank was held in relation to a man's social standing in the aristocratic hierarchy and
there was virtually nothing he could do to improve
his standing. In the democratic society, however,
a man's station in life could be improved if he
had an opportunity to prove himself. In the military profession this meant in some form of warfare.

What de Tocqueville identified was the source
of one kind of militarism that arose from within
the military profession itself. It is paradoxical
that it was to be the very same liberalism and

equalitarianism, essential to the successful democracy, that was the wellspring of that particular
form of militarism.   It goes without saying that the
America of today is quite different from that of
which de Tocqueville wrote so favorably and that all
his thoughts are not fully applicable today.   The
concept, however, of the propensity of the military
profession in a democracy to welcome war in order
to exercise its equalitarianism, is worthy of some
sober thought by the nation's political and military
leaders.   It will be commented on later.

American militarism took many forms over the
years and had a diverse body of supporters and critics.   When war with Spain was threatening in the
spring of 1854, spurred on by the excesses of Senator Pierre Soulé, and fanned by the Black Warrior
embroilment, Major General Ethan Allen Hitchcock expressed his objections to the militarism of Soulé
and his supporters.   He spoke of "a war with Spain
. . . forced on us by the headstrong ambition of
false policy of the Cabinet in Washington. . . ."
He was "in principle opposed to the war, not only
as unjustifiable towards Spain but as impolitic and
injurious as respects ourselves."[9]

Morris Janowitz has pointed out that

> Military criticism of civilian politi-
> cal leaders for their "reckless mili-
> tary adventurism" and "blind faith in
> the manifest destiny of the Republic"
> continued to recur until the Japanese
> attack on Pearl Harbor.[10]

Militarism, in its many forms, has by no means
been an exclusive characteristic of the military
profession.   One author, writing shortly after World
War I, commented:

> Militarism is the characteristic, not
> of an army; but of a society.   Its
> essence is not any particular quality
> or scale of military preparation, but

a state of mind, which, in its concen-
tration on one particular element in
social life, ends finally by exalting
it until it becomes the arbiter of
all the rest. The purpose for which
military forces exist is forgotten.
They are thought to stand by their
own right and to need no justification. Instead they are being regarded
as an instrument which is necessary
in an imperfect world, they are ele-
vated into an object of superstitious
veneration, as though the world would
be a poor insipid place without them,
so that political institutions and social arrangements and intellect and
morality and religion are crushed
into a mold made to fit one activity,
. . . which in a militarist state is
a kind of mystical epitome of society
itself.[11]

From these few examples, which cover a very
large span of the history of the United States, an
identification of several forms of militarism is
seen. First is militarism that is inherent in the
armies of democracies. Second is the sort of militarism that is the outgrowth of national imperial-
istic tendencies and proposed by the civilian leadership while opposed by the very military profession
that would supposedly gain personal benefit from a
foreign adventure. Finally there is an example of
a point of view that sees militarism as a characteristic of society as a whole. The society tends
to place military considerations to the fore and in
so doing creates a military establishment that becomes an end in itself rather than a means to an
end. As will be seen when contemporary American
militarism is examined, each of these patterns can
be identified in today's environment in varying
degrees.

Any attempt to define the emotionally charged
concept of "militarism" has intentionally been

avoided to this point so as to not unnecessarily re-
strict the preceding more general observations.
However, before examining contemporary militarism
in the United States, a more specific identification of terms is in order.

Militarism means many things to many people
and the meaning one chooses to attach to it is normally a direct function of the use to which the individual intends to put it; a good or a bad influe-
ence, a positive or a negative connotation, and the
like. The standard dictionary definition of militarism is

> predominance of the military class or
> prevalence of their ideals; the spirit
> which exalts military virtues and
> ideals; the policy of excessive mili-
> tary preparedness.

Alfred Vagts distinguishes between the military
way and militarism. Of the military way he said:

> The military way is marked by a pri-
> mary concentration of men and materi-
> als on winning specific objectives of
> power with the utmost efficiency, that
> is, with the least expenditure of
> blood and treasure. It is limited in
> scope, confined to one function, and
> scientific in its essential qualities.[12]

"Militarism, on the other hand," he continued

> presents a vast array of customs, in-
> terests, prestige, actions, and
> thought associated with armies and
> wars and yet transcending true mili-
> tary purposes. Indeed, militarism is
> so constituted that it may hamper and
> defeat the purposes of the military
> way. Its influence is unlimited in
> scope. It may permeate all society
> and become dominant over all industry

and arts. Rejecting the scientific
character of the military way, militarism displays the qualities of
caste and cult, authority and belief.[13]

In relating militarism to pacifism Vagts observed:

Militarism is thus not the opposite
of pacifism; its true counterpart is
civilianism. Love of war, bellicos-
ity, is the counterpart of the love
of peace, pacifism; but militarism is
more, and sometimes less, than the
love of war. It covers every system
of thinking and valuing and every complex of feelings which rank military
institutions and ways above the ways
of civilian life, carrying military
mentality and modes of acting and decision into the civilian sphere.[14]

A social science encyclopedia says of militarism that it is

a doctrine or system that values war
and accords primacy in state and society to the armed forces. It exalts
a function--the application of vio-
lence--and an institutional struc-
ture--the military establishment. It
implies both a policy orientation and
a power relationship.[15]

"Militarists," the article continued, "cannot be
identified with military or uniformed personnel."[16]

The differences in the definitions or descriptions of militarism are apparent. The word does
not mean the same thing to everyone. The similarities, however, are at least equally apparent and
considerably more significant. In each case, the
connotation of "excessive" emphasis on things military is present--either stated or implied. Radway
identified the similarities when he stated:

In ordinary usage "militarism" has a
derogatory meaning. Like legalism or
clericism it suggests excess: a lack
of proportion in policy or, when ex-
hibited by warriors, a disregard for
appropriate professional bounds.[17]

In something of the same vein, Hans Morgenthau
observed that

militarism is the conception that the
power of a nation consists primarily,
if not exclusively, of its military
strength, conceived especially in
quantitative terms. The largest army,
the biggest navy, the biggest and
fastest air force in the world becomes the predominant, if not the exclusive symbols of national power.[18]

A working definition of militarism, for the purpose of this study, is proposed then as a politico-
military doctrine that places excessive reliance on
the military aspects of the politico-military equation in resolving both national and international
differences. A militarist, it follows, is an individual, be he military or civilian, public official
or private citizen, who espouses militarism.

The suggested definition has one very obvious
weakness that is inherent in the adjective "excessive." The essential value judgment of what is excessive and what is not still remains very much a
matter of individual choice within some very broad
parameters. The author accepts this weakness and
points out that when he chooses to identify a policy
as militaristic, or an individual as a militarist,
in his judgment the requisite excessiveness exists.

The great American author, Ernest Hemingway,
in commenting on his personal experiences in the
Spanish Civil War, is quoted by one scholar as saying: "It gave you a part in something that you
could believe in wholly and completely and in which

you felt an absolute brotherhood with the others
who were engaged in it." The same scholar then observed that

> in the hands of Hemingway and other
> exponents of the strenuous life of
> the late nineteenth and twentieth cen-
> turies, war offered a new opportunity
> for heroic action, brotherhood, com-
> munity, dedication, selflessness, or-
> der, command, ritual, and aristocracy
> in an era when all these were being
> eroded by bourgois liberal society.
> For in the hands of such writers, war
> represents the antithesis of the lib-
> eral society. . . .[19]

One sees in these words the "spirit that exalts
military virtues and ideals." This feeling is not
uncommon to many men when they directly participate
in war, regardless of the ideological factors involved, or the part of the political spectrum with
which they identify. There can be no doubt that
Hemingway's words just as precisely describe the
feelings of many young men fighting on the side of
Hemingway's enemies. Who were the militarists?

According to his own secretary of state, the
great liberal American president, Franklin Roosevelt, literally gloried in his role as commander in
chief of the U.S. armed forces during the militarily
exciting period of World War II. The secretary revealed that

> the President continued not to invite
> me to his military meetings. He
> loved the military side of events,
> and liked to hold them in his own
> hands. Following Pearl Harbor, he
> preferred to be called Commander-
> in-Chief rather than President.
>   At a Cabinet dinner, probably in
> 1942, where I was to propose the
> toast, the President asked me, before

I rose to speak: "Please try to address me as Commander-in-Chief, not
as President."[20]

Put in a somewhat different context and related to
an American "Colonel Blimp" sort of character, this
would serve as a perfect example of popularly accepted comic militarism at its very best.

In his Presidential Power, which has been sometimes equated to Machiavelli's The Prince, in the
coldly prescriptive practical advice it gives to
American presidents, Richard Neustadt addressed the
question of personal power.[21] He saw Franklin
Roosevelt as a strong and effective president because he desired and actively sought personal power
and manipulated his Cabinet officers and other advisors accordingly. President Eisenhower was
viewed as something of a high-minded idealist who
disdained power and was above it all. He was considered an ineffectual president, moved by the decisions of other men and circumstance.

President Kennedy, who called Neustadt to
Washington at the outset of his administration to
assist in the transition from the Eisenhower administration to his own, apparently read and understood the lessons of Presidential Power. It was
Kennedy, another great liberal president, who, by
threat of the use of the most destructive military
force in the history of mankind, brought the world
closer to the brink of mutual annihilation than
ever before or since. This was the "diplomacy of
violence" of the greatest magnitude. Never had the
threat of the use of such destructive military
force been used by anyone.

The exaltation of war and the desire to gain
and retain great personal power are characteristics
frequently attributed to the militarist. The same
charge is made of the person who sees military
power, or the threat of it, as the solution to a
problem in international relations. Were Ernest
Hemingway, Franklin Roosevelt, and John Kennedy

militarists because they demonstrated some of the characteristics of militarism? The author would argue that the answer must be an emphatic "no" because in his judgment the word <u>excessive</u> does not apply in light of the circumstances in each individual case, and also because, within the context of the definition suggested earlier, militarism becomes a meaningful concept only when it affects the "unbalancing" of the politico-military equation. The exaltation of war, the love of rank and prestige, the desire for personal power, and the threat of the use of military force are each militaristic characteristics, but in themselves do not make a militarist.

Whether or not there is such a phenomenon as American militarism is really not the critical issue. The meaningful consideration is that there are pressures inherent in the contemporary American industrialized democracy that do emphasize the military side of the politico-military equation and these pressures must be clearly identified, understood, and constantly studied. Within the past few years the charges of an existing American militarism have mounted. In many respects this is a resurgence of the sort of highly critical commentary that followed World War II and other wars in American history. Now, however, because of the relative "unpopularity" of the war in Vietnam, charges and warnings of a new American militarism have not awaited the end of that conflict. Militarism as a contemporary socio-psychological-political phenomenon, has been addressed by sociologists and political scientists in the academic community and by distinguished members of the government, the news media, and the military profession.

A rather profound observation on the root cause of modern-day militarism by Raymond Aron is that in an industrial society "the army industrializes itself, industry militarizes itself; the army absorbs the nation; the nation models itself on the army."[22] Aron's comment is not directed to the United States specifically but the Western industrialized democracies in general. The source of American militarism can, however, be found, for the most part, in the same roots.

More directly addressing the American experience, President Eisenhower identified the influence of the rather complete integration of the American military establishment into society as a whole. In his farewell address of January 18, 1961, he said:

> A vital element in keeping the peace is our military establishment. Our arms must be mighty, ready for instant action, so that no potential aggressor may be tempted to risk his own destruction. . . .
> Until the latest of our world conflicts, the United States had no armaments industry. American makers of plowshares could, with time as required, make swords as well. . . . we have been compelled to create a permanent armaments industry of vast proportions. . . .
> This conjunction of an immense military establishment and a large arms industry is new in the American experience. The total influence-- economic, political, even spiritual-- is felt in every city, every state house, every office of the federal government. We recognize the imperative need for this development. Yet we must not fail to comprehend its grave implications. Our toil, resources and livelihood are all involved; so is the very structure of our society. . . .
> We must never let the weight of this combination endanger our liberties or democratic processes. . . . Only an alert and knowledgeable citizenry can compel the proper meshing of the huge industrial and military

> machinery of defense with our peace-
> ful methods and goals, so that secur-
> ity and liberty may prosper together.[23]

Walter Millis commented on the Eisenhower address:

> Eisenhower not only pointed to the po-
> tential danger to democracy inherent
> in the new giant "military-industrial
> complex," but saw as well the ulti-
> mate necessity for disarmament and
> the infeasibility of the war system
> itself as the governing element in in-
> ternational relations. He regretted
> his failure to accomplish more toward
> the resolution of these great issues;
> but few earlier American soldiers
> would have even recognized their ex-
> istence.[24]

In a sense this was the same thought developed
by Janowitz when he identified and compared various
models of politico-military elites. While the democratic model, in which the military and political
functions of society remain completely separate, is
identified as the ideal, it is also recognized as
not an historical reality but only an objective of
political policy.

> Elements of the democratic model have
> been achieved only in certain Western
> industrial countries, since it re-
> quires extremely viable parliamentary
> institutions and broad social consen-
> sus about the ends of government.[25]

Of the models suggested by Janowitz, the garrison state model, which he borrowed from Harold Lasswell, more closely fits contemporary America.[26]
The term garrison state is not used by Janowitz as
an emotionally explosive expression with a purely
negative connotation, but as a practical and descriptive articulation. In the garrison state the

thesis is that the military establishment, because
of the highly complex technological and political
aspects of contemporary military organization and
strategy, has become so integrated with all aspects
of American society that it does, as a consequence,
exert an unprecedented degree of influence on society as a whole. This influence may be direct or
rather circumspect, it may be intentional or unintentional and it may be excessive or within acceptable bounds. In other words it may be militaristic
or it may not, but it does exist. It is what President Eisenhower identified and warned the nation of
in 1961.

Professor Janowitz further commented on the
concepts of "designed militarism" and "unantici-
pated militarism." He suggested that "unantici-
pated militarism" is perhaps more critical in the
American situation because it

> develops from a lack of effective tra-
> ditions and practices for controlling
> the military establishment, as well
> as from a failure of civilian politi-
> cal leaders to act relevantly and
> consistently. Under the circumstances
> a vacuum is created which not only en-
> courages an extension of the tasks and
> power of military leaderships but ac-
> tually forces such trends.[27]

The nature of the dilemma is further identified
by an observation made by Janowitz in an article
written several years after the one cited above.
His concern was with the political and social aspects of military operations and the requirement
for military professional to be politically and
sociologically astute. He said:

> [I]t is still a question as to how
> realistic such a concern will be.
> One can say for better, since it
> could contribute to a rational for-
> eign policy; for worse, because

> politically sensitive military lead-
> ership could be more difficult to
> subject to civilian control.[28] [Empha-
> sis added.]

The concern is a valid one and is but one more factor to be considered in evaluating militarism in the
United States. It must be understood by the nation's civilian and military leadership alike.

In April, 1969, General David M. Shoup, in col-
laboration with Colonel J. A. Donovan, spoke out
against American militarism.[29] General Shoup is a
retired Marine Corps general and, at the time of
his retirement, was serving as the commandant of
the Marine Corps. In that capacity he was not only
the nation's senior marine but was in a position to
participate in most of the deliberations of the
Joint Chiefs of Staff as well. Colonel Donovan is
also a retired Marine Corps officer and the author
of a book on the same subject.[30] While the words
in the article are apparently primarily those of
Colonel Donovan, General Shoup has certainly given
his unqualified blessing to the thoughts expressed.

In one paragraph, the Shoup-Donovan article
summarizes the history of American militarism since
World War II:

> Our militaristic culture was born of
> the necessities of World War II, nur-
> tured by the Korean War, and became
> an accepted aspect of American life
> during the years of the cold war emer-
> gencies and real or imagined threats
> from the Communist bloc. Both the
> philosophy and institutions of mili-
> tarism grew during these years be-
> cause of the momentum of their own
> dynamism, the vigor of their ideas,
> their large size and scope, and be-
> cause of the dedicated concentration
> of the current military leaders upon
> their doctrinal objectives.[31]

The description is completely consistent with the
findings of scholars in the field and carries additional credence because of General Shoup's personal
experience in the military establishment at the
highest levels.

In a two-part article in a national magazine,
which appeared a few months after the Shoup-Donovan
piece was published, many of the same points were
raised and General Shoup was liberally quoted. A
portion of Part I of the series was entitled, "American Militarism: What is it Doing to Us?" In it the
author pointed out the extent to which military matters have come to dominate much of what the U.S.
government does or fails to do. He added:

> No conspiratorial cabal planned it
> that way. There is no monolithic
> "power elite" in this country.
> There is no set of "historical im-
> peratives," inherent in modern Ameri-
> can capitalism, irrevocably driving
> us to militaristic imperialism abroad
> or an "authoritarian rule of piety
> and iron" at home. . . .[32]

Both of the articles cited say essentially
that this influence does exist to an unprecedented
degree in the United States and that it is the result of a number of complex political, economic,
sociological, philosophical, and military factors
that have been recognized and identified by astute
observers for a number of years. The author is of
the opinion that these articles do, in fact, represent the thinking of a significant segment of that
portion of the American body politic that concerns
itself with national security and related international and domestic political matters.

The danger of militarism, as perceived by
many, has been identified. The reaction of significant segments of the population in the form of
"antimilitaristic" expressions of all sorts ranging
from rational argumentation to radical acts of

violence against persons and property is an observ-
able fact. If militarism is <u>excessive</u> emphasis on
the military side of the politico-military equation,
antimilitarism would logically consist of efforts
to bring the equation back into balance. In practice, however, antimilitarism may well be <u>excessive</u>
rejection of the essential military factors in the
equation. There is a practical danger in both.

     The military professional's view of militarism
is quite likely to be significantly different from
that held by many. The most basic difference is
that the military professional, and one might also
include his civilian colleagues in the defense establishment, often has a different perception of
what is "excessive" and what is not. The professional whose duty it is to see to the national defense would be expected to define "excessive" in
more all-inclusive terms than would the political
scientist who theorizes about national security but
shares none of the responsibility for it, or the
politician who feels political pressure to shift
some of the available national resources from national security into other critical areas, or the
medical researcher who is competing for resources
in his field.

     Additionally, when confronted with the word
<u>militarism</u>, in any of its many variations, the aver-
age military professional goes on the defensive.
He will usually dismiss the possibility that there
is such a thing as American militarism and will argue that the American "military-industrial complex"
is a myth. The author has discussed this fact with
many of his colleagues and has concluded that the
primary reason for the out-of-hand rejection is
that most military officers make the semantic connection between "military" and "militarism" without realizing that there is a truly basic difference. They do not make the distinction between the
"military way" and "militarism" as suggested by Vagts.

     The reaction to the Shoup-Donovan and the
Sevareid articles, by what the author believes to

be an all too typical representative of the military profession, supports the thesis suggested in the preceding paragraph. With few exceptions, the reaction of military professionals to the Shoup-Donovan article was extremely negative. The article was viewed as antimilitary, ill-founded, irrational, emotional, and the like. General Shoup, once the "grand old man" to thousands of proud marines, soon became "a senile old man" who was being "used" by somebody for evil purposes. Most of the critics with whom the author spoke had not read the article but had heard about it. The title was "antimilitary" so it could not have been a valid article. A few officers did read the article in detail and agreed that there was a great deal of truth in some of the arguments. These officers either accepted or rejected the article in part or in full but knew what it was they were agreeing or disagreeing with. It caused them to do some thinking and some professional soul-searching.

Reaction to the Sevareid article in Look was essentially the same. One general officer, commenting on Part I, said, "Did you read what they said about us?" The general took it as a personal attack on himself and his profession and he apparently gave little or no thought to the substantive content. Many military professionals fail to see the threat of "militarism" as an understandable social-economic-political phenomenon of both the military and civilian sectors of contemporary democratic industrial societies. Instead they view references to militarism as a direct attack on themselves and their profession to include derogation of all those virtues that are so much a part of their lives. Rather than attempting to understand the meaning of militarism and its impact on the military profession, American democratic society, and the politico-military equation they simply deny its existence.*

---

*The author's "findings" here are as much the result of subjective evaluation as specific empirical evidence. Informal discussions with colleagues and inferences drawn from student papers at The National War College serve as the primary source.

One final thought from the Shoup-Donovan article must be commented on here. The article asserted that it is the large nucleus of "aggressive, ambitious professional military leaders who are the root of America's evolving militarism." It was further asserted that despite arguments to the contrary, ambition (not to be confused with intentionally evil) military officers do not "dislike" war but welcome it as an opportunity to prove themselves to the nation and gain rank, honor, and prestige. The inference is that they automatically would be prone to give advice at the highest councils of government that would lead to more, rather than less, emphasis on military force in balancing the politico-military equation. Eric Sevareid commented on the same thought, with a somewhat different twist, by saying, "It remains eternally true that professional soldiers say they hate war but hate it no more than does a trained surgeon hate his often tragic trade."[33] The similarities between the thoughts identified in this paragraph and those expressed by Alexis de Tocqueville a century and a half ago are more than coincidental.

The author, at the outset of this project, would have completely disagreed with General Shoup's thesis on the military professional's desire for war, and would have only reluctantly accepted the Sevareid assertion. Now, however, the author has modified his views.

The preceding pages have identified two basic sources of possible "excessive" military emphasis. The first was identified by de Tocqueville and restated by General Shoup and Eric Sevareid--plus many more in the intervening years. That source is the psychological and sociological impact of democratic liberalism and equalitarianism on the military professional as an individual. The second source was identified as the increasingly close relationship of the nation's military establishment with other segments of American society resulting from the growing technological and political complexity of national defense. This is the phenomenon of which President Eisenhower warned the nation--

the garrison state. The essential conditions that
contribute to increased emphasis on the military
side of the politico-military equation do exist in
the United States today. Whether these pressures
are strong enough to cause "excessive" emphasis and
consequently to be labeled "militarism" is a value
judgment that will vary with each individual and
with each situation. What one wishes to call it is
not important so long as the existence of the pressures is recognized and understood.

Militarism, by its very excessiveness, de-
tracts from the national security. National security is the business of the military professional.
Militarism is incompatible with military professionalism. An officer who possesses the "requisite
level of training, education, experience, and intellect" to perform his duties cannot be a militarist.

THE MILITARY MIND

The expression militarism was used as a basis
for considering how the American body politic thinks
about things military and how this may affect the
politico-military equation. The expression military
mind will be used as the basis for examining how
military professionals think and how that thinking
may affect the same politico-military equation.

As is the case with militarism, the military
mind means many things to many people and like militarism it normally carries a negative connotation.
Seldom does one person credit another with posses-
sion of a military mind if his intention is to pay
a compliment. One writer put it quite well when he
said, "Critics malign the term, but they do not define it precisely. Instead they call forth an as-
sortment of adjectives asserting that these describe it."[34]

The late Charles Lerche, in an article published in a military professional journal, commented on the military mind:

> The "military mind" is generally ac-
> cepted by Americans to be technically
> proficient, dedicated, patriotic,
> tenacious, and courageous. These are
> the positive virtues that popular cul-
> ture grants to the officer corps.
> Negative impressions, however, far
> outweigh the positive, and to be
> marked as possessing a "military
> mind" is to be the victim of a pre-
> dominantly critical verdict.[35]

This particular comment very graciously states the
positive virtues of the military mind, while most
authors are content to list the many negative impressions that Lerche said "far outweigh the positive."

Some typical comments and observations on the
military mind follow. They are arranged chronologically and reflect a variety of views. The comments
are by a former secretary of war, a Supreme Court
justice, a journalist, two scholars, and a military
professional. They cover the period of two decades
following World War II.

Former Secretary of War Robert Patterson observed:

> I have been in close touch with the
> military for ten years of my life--
> three in the Army and seven as Sec-
> retary of War. I give it as my ex-
> perience that there is no set type
> of military mind. There are marked
> characteristics. There is a highly
> developed sense of duty, a standard
> of behavior stricter than the aver-
> age. . . . But I have never seen
> the signs of a military mind that
> could be identified as a single type,
> any more than there is a lawyer's
> mind, an engineer's mind or a mer-
> chant's mind. Mental equipment and

outlook on life vary as much in the
Army and Navy as with other occupa-
tions or callings.[36]

Hanson W. Baldwin, former military editor of
The New York Times, commented:

> With some persuasiveness, it has been
> claimed that there is no such thing
> as the military mind, and it is true
> that the term has been generalized
> and misapplied. But there is a scien-
> tific mind; there is a religious mind;
> there is a creative mind; there is
> even a stockbroker's mind. And there
> is a military mind.
>   The military mind is the product
> of its training and thought processes
> and environment and sometimes of its
> heritage. It has assets and it has
> liabilities. It is a rational mind
> but not an intuitive one. It is a
> pragmatic mind. It is a mind disci-
> plined to obedience and to order, to
> system and to logic. . . . It can
> grapple with tangibles but not so
> well with intangibles.
>   . . . In the formulation of for-
> eign policy, the military mind and
> military opinions are essential in-
> gredients, but if the military mind
> dominated, over any long-term period,
> war is likely to result.[37]

The next observation is by Justice of the U.S.
Supreme Court Willam O. Douglas:

> They [military men] are men of high
> character and fine ideals. But the
> military mind is too narrow, and mili-
> tary techniques too limited to deal
> with the vast problems of this age. . . .
>   The military mind, in other words,
> has two distinctive characteristics--

first, it tends to put every problem
in the perspective of war; second, it
tends to regiment people, to have one
orthodox creed and to leave no room
for diversity of opinion, the strength
of democracy. . . .[38]

The next two observations are from the academic
community. In the first, the authors list several
items that would appear to register a severe indict-
ment of the intellectual capability of the professional officer:

To summarize, the most serious criticisms of the military mind appear to
be of alleged tendencies toward
(a) rigidity in thought and proper
analysis--the rejection of new ideas
and reliance on tradition rather than
lessons learned from recent experience; (b) inadequate weighing of nonmilitary factors in military problems,
and inability to understand complex
politico-military relationships; (c)
an authoritarian approach to most social issues and situations, accompanied by disrespect for and regard
of civilian authority; (d) insulation
from nonmilitary knowledge and anything beyond what is narrowly defined
as militarily relevant; and (e) judgment of policy goals and techniques
primarily in terms of military force
and military strategy.[39]

Another expression from the academic community:

Nevertheless, there is a military mind
and all military men, to one degree or
another, possess it. It is a mind
that is used to order and predictabil-
ity, that insists on decisions being
made, that cannot abide procrastina-
tion, that is comfortable in the

>   manageable world of a military post
>   and often unconsciously makes over
>   any other setting--the home, the
>   office, even the Presidency of the
>   United States--with the same charac-
>   teristics of punctuality, rank and
>   simplicity.[40]

The final comment is by a distinguished former member of the military profession in the United States. It was made in a speech to the Fellows of the American Bar Association in February, 1964.

>   Personally, I've never been overly
>   exercised by the charge of possess-
>   ing a military mind. How would you
>   lawyers feel if you were said not to
>   possess a legal mind? By the same
>   token we soldiers, sailors and air-
>   men regard a military mind as some-
>   thing to be sought and developed--an
>   indispensable professional asset
>   which can only be acquired after years
>   of training in reflecting and acting
>   on military and related problems. We
>   hope that such a mind, when properly
>   matured, will prove itself analytical,
>   accurate and decisive in time of
>   crisis because history has shown that
>   neither the battlefield nor the na-
>   tional council table is the place for
>   conjecture, vagueness or obscurity of
>   thought.[41]

Perhaps the best source of perceptions of what the military mind is all about is the contemporary professional military officer himself and his civilian colleague in the government who associates with him. For an examination of the military mind from the point of view of those who are accused of possessing it, the survey made by the author of the 1968 and 1970 classes and faculties of The National War College will be examined. (See Appendix for full survey.)

The respondents were asked the following question:

"In your view is there such a thing
as a 'military mind'?"   Yes _____
No _____

"If you answered 'yes' above, what
connotation do you attach to the term
military mind?"

Generally detrimental to the
national interest _____?
Generally contributory to the
national interest _____?

The respondent was then invited to define the concept "military mind."

Of those who responded, 53 percent said there was a military mind while 46 percent said there was not--1 percent answered in some other way. Of those who answered "yes," 43 percent saw the military mind as a negative factor and therefore detrimental to the national interest. The positive, or contributory, view was taken by 48 percent while 9 percent of those who answered "yes" to the basic question did not attempt to express themselves on the latter part.

Generally speaking, those who said there was no military mind but still elected to define it, did so as they thought others saw it and this was almost exclusively in negative terms. Of those who defined the military mind in negative terms, there was a strong tendency to be defensive by saying, "but the situation is improving" or words to that effect. Not surprisingly, those who saw the military mind as a negative factor used many of the same uncomplimentary expressions suggested above to describe it and those who saw it as a positive element used the generally complimentary adjectives in their definitions.

There were exceptions, however. One respondent, for example, "associated the 'military mind' with a hawkish viewpoint," and another saw it as a mind "conditioned to the winning of the military victory at all costs." Both of these respondents said the military mind, as they defined it, was contributory to the national interest. Much more often, however, those same characteristics were used in the derogatory sense, rather than in the positive. In the responses there was no significant difference between the several military services. The civilian respondents were slightly more prone to see the negative, rather than the positive, aspects of the military mind. Of those, civilian and military, who defended the military mind, many equated it to the legal mind, the religious mind, the academic mind, and the medical mind to name but a few. There was nothing significantly different in the responses of the 1968 and 1970 groups. A slightly more positive view of the military mind was noted in the 1970 responses.

Some typical responses follow:

1. There is a military mind. It is contributory. An attitude that places duty, honor, country above any personal bias or ambition. (air force officer)

2. There is not a military mind. Alleges as a mind that believes that political problems can be resolved by solely military means. (air force officer)

3. There is a military mind. It is contributory. A mind that thinks in military terms. I respect it. (foreign service officer)

4. There is not a military mind. If there is such a thing--take any mind of a SAC [Strategic Air Command] general. (foreign service officer)

5.   There is a military mind. It
is contributory. A mind trained to
evaluate problems in a logical, sys-
tematic manner. (army officer)

6.   There is a military mind. It
is detrimental. Only a few people in
each service have it and they normally are kept out of Washington. (army
officer)

7.   There is a military mind. It
is contributory. Possessed by an individual who puts loyalty and the
security of the country above all
else. (naval officer)

8.   There is not a military mind.
Term generally associated with an un-
yielding, unimaginative, rigid individual whose opinions are formed in
an earlier period and doesn't want to
be confused with facts now. (naval
officer)*

It is not the intent here to contribute to the
perpetual and totally useless polemic about the existence or nonexistence of the military mind or
about its competence or incompetence. Clearly,
there are patterns of thinking associated with the
military professional, but the preceding paragraphs
suggest that that association includes the complete
spectrum of negative and positive characteristics.
While, as suggested earlier, the term is usually
used in a noncomplimentary sense, instances of its
use in a complimentary manner have also been noted.

---

*For a more complete indication of how the
minds of a representative group of war college-
level officers work, the responses to the remaining questions asked of The National War College
classes and faculties of 1968 and 1970 should be
examined. See the annotated questionnaire in the
Appendix.

The previous section of this chapter dealt with some of the semantics of militarism and quoted Alfred Vagts in citing the difference between the "military way" and "militarism." The far-ranging connotations assigned to the military mind suggest a possible compatibility between the concept of the military way, militarism, and the military mind. In what is intended to be something more than academic sleight-of-hand, in the form of a useless semantic exercise, it will be argued that the military mind, in its positive connotation, does very reasonably equate with the military way. The military mind, in its more negative sense, deserves nothing better than to be called the "militaristic mind" and to be equated squarely with militarism. For the purpose of this study, the military mind is considered in its positive sense and is defined as: <u>that mind which is conditioned by training, education, experience, and intellect to recognize and place in perspective the military implications inherent in a given national security problem.</u>

The similarity between this definition and the refined definition of the military professional suggested earlier in the chapter is not unintentional. As the terms have been defined, a military mind is a requisite for a military professional.

From the survey previously mentioned, a number of general thought patterns, representative of the military profession as a whole, can be identified. The reader is reminded of the levels of professionalism suggested earlier in this chapter. The comments that follow are related rather specifically to the second level. Fourteen broad generalizations that can be drawn from the empirical data derived from the survey are suggestive of the thinking of the professional military officer at the war college level.

1. The national security interests of the United States will be best served by an increasing emphasis on the thorough integration of political and military considerations. Further, there will

be an ever-increasing requirement for military officers to become intimately familiar with the processes of the formulation as well as the implementation of the nation's foreign policy.

2. Adequate governmental machinery does exist
for the integration of the nation's foreign and
military policies.

3. The average civilian official, who is involved in politico-military affairs, does not have
an adequate appreciation of the military side of
the politico-military equation.

4. The average military officer, who is involved in politico-military affairs, does not have
adequate appreciation of the political side of the
politico-military equation.

5. There has been a discernible trend in the
past five years toward more mutual understanding
between the military officer and the civilian governmental official in the area of politico-military
affairs.

6. The military point of view is being heard
at the highest decision-making levels in the country.

7. The military point of view is not only being heard but is being given adequate weight at the
highest decision-making levels in the country.

8. Continued emphasis on politico-military
factors will strengthen the professionalism of individual military officers.

9. There is not a place for a politico-
military specialist in the military profession in
somewhat the same sense that there are logistical
specialists, etc.

10. There is a place for a politico-military
specialist in the foreign service in somewhat the
same sense that there are area specialists, etc.

11. In the Korean War and the Vietnam War, the
U.S. national objective was (and is) primarily a
political as opposed to a military one.

12. The "unconditional surrender" concept of
World War II is not valid in the contemporary international environment.

13. Following the Vietnam War there will be a
strong isolationist reaction in the United States
and this will not be in the national interest.

14. The following thought is not valid in the
contemporary international environment: "In the
old days, war was war and peace was peace. Our nation did not ask leaders for a definition. Is this
a 'limited war' or a 'general war' or a 'total war'?
When the nation was at war, Americans were at war,
and the nation did what was necessary to win."[42]

The reader is reminded that the responses that
served as the empirical base for these fourteen generalizations are from a somewhat select group of
about 200 military professionals. By their very
selection to attend The National War College, they
are not fully representative of the officer corps
as a whole, even at the second level of professionalism. It is significant, however, that by their
selection, these officers are destined for positions
of greater command and staff responsibility. A number of them have already been selected for flag and
general officer rank. The reader is also reminded
that not all of the officers responding are in accord with the generalizations. It is noted, however, that only in the case of points 9 and 10 was
there anything approaching parity of opinion. Even
then, the viewpoints were separated by 18 and 10
percentage points respectively.

As one reviews the positions, he finds it difficult to relate what these military professionals
have said that suggests "rigidity of thought," "rejection of new ideas," "reliance on tradition,"
"inadequate weighting of nonmilitary factors,"

"inability to understand complicated politico-
military relationships," and "authoritarian approach
to most social issues," to name but a few. Assuming
the generalizations do, in fact, represent those
military minds that are destined to be among the
most influential, have we not identified a mind
that is "conditioned by training, education, experience, and intellect" to function in today's complex
politico-military environment? Using the definition
of a military mind developed earlier, it can be argued, on the basis of some empirical evidence, that
the military mind is very much in evidence in the
military profession and that it is indeed a positive
factor.

Some speculation as to why the all-too-
frequently held opinions of the military mind do
not equate with the evidence found in the author's
survey may in itself be revealing. If the military
mind is truly that which is "conditioned by training, education, and experience," as the author believes it to be, it must then be suggested that the
military mind, possessed by the professional military officer today, is just as different as the
military profession itself is different, from that
of twenty, forty, or sixty years ago. The professional military officer attaining flag or general
officer rank today (the category covered in the
survey) has not had the same training, education,
and experience as an officer reaching that rank
twenty, forty, or sixty years ago. Therefore, it
seems to follow that the contemporary military officer would not be possessed with the same mind as
was his predecessor.

Most of the criticisms of the military mind
seem to imply that while the rest of the world has
moved forward, both chronologically and intellectually, the mind of the military professional is
still the vintage of about the turn of the century.
If this is in fact true, then all the criticism
that can be leveled is justified. However, the preceding chapters have shown that the basic factors
that condition the military mind by training,

education, and experience are no longer of turn-of-
the-century vintage.

The formal politico-military organizational
structure, in which the military mind can be expressed, now exists. The military educational system, which is designed to broaden the military mind,
likewise exists. It remains only for the military
professional to speak his mind and for the civilian
leadership to hear it. This is admittedly more
easily said than done. In this connection Robert
A. Lovett commented as follows:

> Military advice is only one--although
> on occasion, the most necessary--type
> of guidance needed today and the
> decision-making process involves a
> system of checks and balances in the
> Executive Branch deliberately de-
> signed to keep any one economic or
> social group or any one governmental
> department from becoming dominant.
> Therefore, every judgement made at
> the decisive level requires a weigh-
> ing of several often-conflicting and
> competing factors.
>   For these reasons, the ability of
> the military expert to give wise ad-
> vice--and to get it listened to by
> policy-making officials--depends in
> great measure on his possessing
> knowledge in key non-military fields
> and in seeing issues in broad perspec-
> tive.[43]   [Emphasis added.]

The current organizational structure provides
the framework within which the military advice can
be "given." The educational system provides the
sources of knowledge so that the advice will be
worthy of being "listened to."

Recognition of the requirement for broadening
professional military thinking was officially expressed by the Department of Defense in 1959:

> The Secretary of Defense, in December
> 1959, issued a directive that, ". . .
> all officers . . . will serve a nor-
> mal tour of duty with a Joint, Com-
> bined, Allied or OSD (Office of the
> Secretary of Defense) Staff before be-
> ing considered qualified for promotion
> to general or flag officer rank." The
> directive made some exceptions based
> upon scientific and technical exper-
> tise.[44]

This directive is significant in two ways.
First, it required that officers who were to attain
high rank have some experience in working with the
other services. This is part of a broadening process to break down some of the rather stiff and unproductive interservice antagonism. Alternatively,
it required that the officer serve on a combined
staff or in the office of the secretary of defense.
This would expose him to some of the facts of international life or at least to some of the facts of
life in the United States so far as civil-military
relations are concerned. We see then, in this
directive an effort to broaden the base of military
thinking by exposing the candidate for high rank to
the views of the other services, to the views of
other nations, and to the views of our own civil
authorities. There can be no question that the
military mind possessed by officers with such experience will be different from that of the more
traditional military "hero."

Several years later, in giving guidance to the
Navy Flag Board, the secretary of the navy said in
part:

> After giving special consideration to
> qualification for sea command and re-
> quired specializations, I believe the
> selection board should place great
> stress on seeking evidence, in the
> past performance of prospective
> flag officers, of the qualities of

<u>flexibility of mind, analytical</u>
<u>thought processes, creativity and</u>
<u>imagination</u> which will best qualify
them to compete with the increasingly professional and intellectual
civilian leadership within an increased integrated Defense Department. I think that the evidence of
such qualifications can be found in
many categories of billets. However, I can think of none where the
naval officer is put to the greater
test of ability to rise above his
background and possible prejudices
than by demonstrated outstanding performance in Joint and International
Staffs and Agencies. It is here that
the common dogma of any one service
must give way to the give and take
analysis from differing perspectives.
It is here that he must rely less on
the lessons of past experience and
more on his basic qualities of intellect and thoughtfulness.[45] [Emphasis
added.]

It is interesting to note that the adjectives
that are used to describe what characteristics the
candidate for advancement to flag rank should possess are essentially the same ones used by critics
in commenting on what is missing in the military
mind. The position of the Department of Defense
cited above, and the statement by the secretary of
the navy, which is representative of all the services, makes it quite clear that the nation came
to expect something more from the military officer
of 1964 than it did in the past. This is even more
true in 1971.

Also inherent in the above comments, although
not explicitly stated, is the concept that the professional military officer has the responsibility
to inject into his deliberations the effect a given
military action may have on the revered civil institutions of the nation. Of this David C. Rapoport
commented:

It is essential to stress that both
military and political institutions
are manifestations of something deeper and more vital than themselves--a
conception of community. A military
innovator must be prepared to accept
the possibility that civil life may
have to be reconstructed to vouchsafe
his military reforms.[46]

All too often in the past the military professional concerned himself with the relatively narrow
considerations of military expediency. If and when
these considerations trod on cherished civil institutions, normally the same ones the military professional was supposed to be defending, the pacification of wounded civilian feelings was the responsibility of civil authorities. Now, it is indeed
difficult to conceive of a significant military
policy decision that does not cross over into the
realm of the civilian. The new military professional, possessed of the new military mind, must
recognize this and take it into account in his deliberations.

An excellent example of the new type of military leader that is emerging in the nation is to be
found by an examination of the evolving composition
of the Joint Chiefs of Staff. With the retirement
of General Curtis LeMay as chief of staff of the
air force on the last day of January, 1965, an era
came to an end. All of the members of the Joint
Chiefs of Staff were then of a new breed. While
they all differed greatly in personality and background they all had one major quality in common:
They were experienced staff officers who had gained
prominence in that capacity rather than in the
field with the fighting units. All may be expected
to state their views strongly and candidly, and
then to support publicly whatever decisions may be
made by the secretary of defense or the president.
The experience and temperament of each of the members of the Joint Chiefs gives them the qualifications that are a requirement for the military professional today. Time magazine said, "All can cooperate in the overlapping area between military

and political policy without breaking a lot of
crockery."[47] In the same article the secretary of
defense is quoted as saying, "The application of
power in a nuclear age takes a great deal of sophistication. It requires men with knowledge of and
sensitivity to politico-military considerations,
not just military." That composition of the Joint
Chiefs of Staff was an indication of what the contemporary military professional was expected to be,
and it hinted strongly at the broad view that was
then expected of the military professional. In the
view of the author, the differences between the "old"
and "new" Chiefs is overstated in these articles.
Certainly, there was a trend that may have taken a
pronounced turn in 1965. Today in General William
Westmoreland, chief of staff of the army, we see
something of a reappearance of the "warrior" image.
In Admiral Elmo Zumwalt, chief of naval operations,
we see the military intellectual image. The trend,
however, is clear.

A visualization of what an ideal military mind
should be has been suggested and it was further indicated that progress toward that goal has been significant. The author would be remiss, however, to
even infer that there are still not more than a few
members of the military profession who fit the older,
and more negative, military mind concept. There are
army and marine officers who suffer from a vicious
"body count" mentality, there are naval officers who
still think in terms of the "great white fleet" of
the late nineteenth century, and there are air force
officers who feel that the only solution to international differences is to "bomb the opposition back
to the stone age." Fortunately, this mentality is
being eroded away and replaced by that identified
by the survey at The National War College. Unfortunately, however, and infinitely more dangerous to
the nation, is the fact that there are a number of
prominent civilians in the nation, in and out of
government, who support and encourage the "militaristic" minds within the military profession.

There is a military mind. Without it military
professionalism, as defined in this study, would be

a myth. The military professional must constantly
strive to improve his military mind and be constantly alert to the dangers of the militarist mind. The
civilian community must fully comprehend the difference between the military and the militarist mind
just as it must comprehend the difference between
the proponents of rationalism and irrationalism in
any other profession or social grouping. The
politico-military equation will be well served by
the military mind. It will be destroyed by the
militaristic one.

INTERACTIONS

Military thinking in the United States is as
diverse as are the political, social, and personal
philosophies that manifest themselves in the nation.
The appearance of the politico-military equation at
any given time is a mirror reflecting the nation's
military thinking and acts directly on the nation's
foreign policy. Military force, by use or threat of
use, is a given factor in this era of the "diplomacy
of violence." It cannot be wished away. The factors that contribute to the excesses leading to
"militarism" do exist in the United States--not because it has become an "evil" nation but because it
is a powerful, highly industrilaized democracy trying to remain powerful, industrialized, and democratic.

There are militarists and proponents of the
military way in the United States spread throughout
the military and civilian sectors. There are militaristic minds and military minds within the military profession and they are spread throughout all
parts of the vast military establishment. The line
that divides the militarist and the proponent of
the military way and the militarist mind from the
military mind is imprecise and discussion of it is
frequently highly emotional. In the minds of many,
a military professional is a militarist simply because he is a military professional. In the minds
of others, an intellectual--as an example--is antimilitary simply because he warns of the excessiveness

of military considerations in the councils of government. Both generalizations are, of course, unfounded and emotionally based.

The professional military officer cannot possess a militaristic mind--because he then joins the ranks of the militarists--and still perform professionally. The military mind of the professional military officer is one of the most meaningful safeguards the nation has for keeping the politico-military equation in balance and preventing militarism.

NOTES

1.   Thomas C. Schelling, Arms and Influence (New Haven, Conn.: Yale University Press, 1966), p. 34.

2.   See page 6 of this book.

3.   See Donald F. Bletz, "Military Professionalism: A Conceptual Approach," Military Review, May, 1971, p. 11.

4.   The thought is developed in greater detail in ibid., p. 14.

5.   See page 16 of this book.

6.   Alexis de Tocqueville, Democracy in America, Vol. II (New York: Vintage Books), especially Chapter XXII, pp. 279-85.

7.   Ibid., p. 281.

8.   Ibid.

9.   Quoted in Morris Janowitz, The Professional Soldier (New York: The Free Press of Glencoe, 1960), p. 259.

10.   Ibid.

11.   R. H. Tawney, The Acquisitive Society (New York: Harcourt, Brace and Company, 1920), p. 44.

12.   Alfred Vagts, A History of Militarism: Civilian and Military, rev. ed. (Greenwich, Conn.: Meridian Books, Inc., 1959), p. 13.

13.   Ibid.

14.   Ibid., p. 29.

15.   Laurence J. Radway, "Militarism," in International Encyclopedia of the Social Sciences, Vol. 10, ed. David L. Sills (New York: The Macmillan Company and The Free Press of Glencoe, 1968), p. 300.

16.   Ibid. Also see Samuel P. Huntington, The Soldier and the State (Cambridge, Mass.: The Belknap Press, 1959), pp. 69-71.

17.   Radway, loc. cit.

18.   Hans J. Morgenthau, Politics Among Nations, 4th ed. (New York: Alfred A. Knopf, 1966), p. 157.

19.   Quoted in Leon Bramson and George W. Goethals, eds., War: Studies from Psychology, Sociology, Anthropology, rev. ed. (New York: Basic Books, 1968), p. 297.

20.   Cordell Hull, Memoirs, Vol. II (New York: The Macmillan Company, 1948), pp. 1110-11.

21.   Richard E. Neustadt, Presidential Power: The Politics of Leadership (New York: John Wiley and Sons, 1960). The relationship with Machiavelli is made by William T. Bluhm, Theories of the Political System (Englewood Cliffs, N.J.: Prentice-Hall, 1965), pp. 224-59.

22.   Raymond Aron, The Century of Total War (Garden City, N.Y.: Doubleday and Company, 1954), p. 88.

23. *Public Papers of the Presidents of the United States, Dwight D. Eisenhower, 1960-1961* (Washington: U.S. Government Printing Office, 1961), pp. 1036-40.

24. Walter Millis, ed., *American Military Thought* (New York: The Bobbs-Merrill Company, 1966), p. 508.

25. Morris Janowitz, "Military Elites and the Study of War," *Journal of Conflict Resolution*, March 1, 1957, pp. 9-18; reprinted in Bramson and Goethals, *op. cit.*, p. 347.

26. Harold D. Lasswell, "The Garrison State," *The American Journal of Sociology*, XLVI (1941), 455-68.

27. Janowitz, *op. cit.*, p. 349.

28. Morris Janowitz, *Sociology and the Military Establishment* (New York: Russell Sage Foundation, 1959), p. 97.

29. David M. Shoup and J. A. Donovan, "The New American Militarism," *The Atlantic Monthly*, April, 1969.

30. J. A. Donovan, *Militarism U.S.A.* (New York: Charles Scribner's Sons, 1970).

31. Shoup and Donovan, *op. cit.*

32. Eric Sevareid, "American Militarism: What is it Doing to Us?" *Look*, August 12, 1969, p. 15.

33. *Ibid.*

34. Gordon K. Fleischman, "The Myth of the Military Mind," *Military Review*, November, 1964, p. 4.

35. Charles O. Lerche, Jr., "The Professional Officer and Foreign Policy," United States Naval Institute Proceedings, July, 1964, p. 71.

36. Robert P. Patterson, "The Military Mind," Infantry Journal, July, 1947, p. 13.

37. Hanson W. Baldwin, "When the Big Guns Speak," in Public Opinion and Foreign Policy, ed. Lester Marke (New York: Harper and Brothers, 1949), pp. 118-20.

38. William O. Douglas, "We Have Become Victims of the Military Mind," Look, March 11, 1952, p. 34.

39. Burton M. Sapin and Richard C. Snyder, The Role of the Military in American Foreign Policy (Garden City, N.Y.: Doubleday and Company, Inc., 1954), p. 20.

40. Gene M. Lyons, "The Military Mind," Bulletin of the Atomic Scientists, November, 1963, p. 19.

41. Maxwell D. Taylor, "Military Advice--Its Use in Government," Vital Speeches, March 15, 1964.

42. The quotation is from Nathan F. Twining, Neither Liberty nor Safety (New York: Holt, Rinehart and Winston, 1966), p. 104. The questionnaire did not identify the source of the quotation.

43. U.S., Congress, Senate, Committee on Government Operations, Hearings Before the Subcommittee on National Staffing and Operations, Part 9, June 25, 1964, 88th Cong., 2d sess. (Washington: U.S. Government Printing Office, 1969), p. 552.

44. U.S. Department of Defense Directive 1320.5, reprinted in The Army, Navy, Air Force Journal, December, 1959.

45. Secretary of the Navy Paul Nitze, quoted in U.S., Congress, Senate, Committee on Government Operations, op. cit., p. 553.

46. David C. Rapoport, "A Comparative Theory of Military and Political Types," in Changing Patterns of Military Politics, ed. Samuel P. Huntington (New York: The Free Press of Glencoe, 1962), p. 97.

47. "Defense: The Management Team," Time, February 5, 1965, p. 22. A somewhat similar view was expressed by Drew Pearson, "Last of the Heroes," The Washington Post, February 7, 1965.

7

**THE
ELUSIVE
CONCEPT
OF
VICTORY**

Certainly one of the most elusive concepts associated with the politico-military equation today is the concept of "victory"--the meaning of "win" in the contemporary international environment.* Even a casual examination of the news media makes it quite apparent that there is something considerably less than universal understanding of the meaning of victory for U.S. policy throughout the world. Recent administrations are on the one hand accused of having a no-win policy and on the other of over-emphasizing military victory. While the current involvement in Southeast Asia serves as the primary source of much of the contemporary consternation, it is only a symptom of a more basic problem that lies very deep in the American national heritage and basic philosophy.

The purpose of this chapter is to explore some of the fundamental reasons for the elusiveness of a viable concept of victory and to put them into some

---

*The word <u>win</u> is synonymous with and is used interchangeably with <u>victory</u> in this chapter.

sort of meaningful perspective in the context of
military professionalism and the politico-military
equation. The task is approached essentially within the politico-military framework established in
the preceding chapters and proceeds by way of an
inquiry into the concepts of "total war and total
victory" and "limited war and limited victory."
These concepts are then studied against the background of the conceptual relationships between victory and national objectives.

Quincy Wright, in commenting on the pattern of
behavior of groups carrying on a conflict, has observed that

> the pattern therefore involves a com-
> bination of separation and unity:
> separation in the fact of antagonism
> and hostility between entities; union
> in the fact of recognition by all en-
> tities concerned of a common objective
> (victory) and the procedure by which
> it is to be obtained (armed force).[1]

The ever-continuing confrontation between nations in the international system makes it essential
that Americans come to realize what victory means in
contemporary international relations. The era of
total war with its total victory in the context of
unconditional surrender may well be an anachronism
in today's nuclear dominated milieu, but what is to
take its place? What is the contemporary concept
of victory? In the answer to this question is to
be found the key to a valid politico-military balance.

"In war, indeed, there can be no substitute
for victory."[2] These words were spoken by the general of the armies, Douglas MacArthur, on the occasion of his address to the Congress subsequent to
his relief from command by President Truman in 1951.
On the surface the MacArthur expression would appear to be a basic truism fully in keeping with the
American experience and philosophy of war. Yet

today the United States, as a nation, seems to be much disturbed by the real meaning of victory as it applies particularly to the nation's military commitments throughout the world. The American citizen is daily subjected to conflicting and confusing statements on victory from the government, the press, the academic community, the clergy, the military, the Congress, and many other, sometimes obscure but always prolific, sources. The truly serious citizen who earnestly attempts to inform himself of the issues of the day will find many ambiguous and ambivalent views of the contemporary concept of victory. As was suggested above, most of the current commentary on the subject relates to the nation's present involvement in Southeast Asia but the issue is considerably more fundamental than that.

From a former chairman of the House Armed Services Committee, the American citizen has heard:

> I was taught, from the time I was a
> child, that when I entered a conflict
> of any kind--from a baseball game to
> a fist fight--I should try to win. . . .
> It is about time we adopted the same
> policy in North Vietnam.[3]

General James Gavin, another critic of the nation's Asian policy expressed a somewhat different view in a statement to the Congress in which he said: "Military victory in the terms we usually conceive of it is impossible today."[4] General Nathan Twining, in a book in which he expressed sharp disagreement with the Kennedy-Johnson administration's concept of victory commented:

> In the old days, war was war and
> peace was peace. Our nation did not
> ask its political leaders for a def-
> inition, "Is this a 'limited war,' or
> a 'general war,' or a 'total war'?"
> When the nation was at war, Americans
> were at war, and Americans did what
> was necessary to win.[5]

The same Twining quote served as the basis for one
of the questions in the questionnaire mentioned in
the preceding chapter. It is interesting to note
that General Twining's book was published in 1966
and The National War College classes of 1968 and
1970 (two and four years later respectively) over-
whelmingly disagreed with this part of it. Of possible significance is the fact that the respondents
to the questionnaire were of an age group that
served in World War II either not at all or in a
very junior status.

General Harold Johnson, former chief of staff
of the army, saw victory in a somewhat different
context. In a speech to a civilian audience he
asked the following rhetorical questions to which
he replied in the negative:

> Is our objective there [in Vietnam]
> to destroy the enemy totally, to
> widen the war, to pay a double price
> --one for destruction, one for recon-
> struction? . . . Do we seek uncondi-
> tional surrender as in World War II?
> Do we march to the belief that there
> is no substitute for [military] vic-
> tory and that a military short cut
> must exist to the attainment of our
> objective?[6]

Admiral Arleigh Burke, former chief of naval
operations, reportedly expressed the view that

> the United States can win in Vietnam
> --if it destroys the Viet Cong's sup-
> ply lines, and employs "the old rule
> of hot pursuit and destroys those
> units which attack us and then go to
> a sanctuary" in Cambodia and Laos.[7]

More recently, on the occasion of his retirement
from the army and from his position as commanding
general (United States Army Pacific), General John
Waters said: "The time has been long overdue for

the United States to take the necessary aggressive and offensive action on the ground to win the war in South Vietnam."[8]

A civilian author, in a militarily oriented technical journal, wrote very emotionally a few years ago:

> I have seen [a pilot] go into the combat area willingly, aggressively, and with a fine patriotic attitude, only to be stifled in his desire to finally be able to deliver a sound blow at communism for his country. . . . Your true patriots are there trying to fight a war. There is no other name for it, the men there want to be given half a chance to win.[9]

A view expressed by a U.S. civilian official in Vietnam was reported as follows:

> And in another Vietnamese provincial capital, a U.S. civilian official frets. "We could still lose this war because of curruption. We've proved we can beat the Communists militarily, but if we can't lick corruption all the effort will be wasted."[10]

The late Everett Dirksen, former Senate minority leader, was not exempt from frustrations over "victory" in Vietnam. In a speech in Grand Rapids, Michigan, he said:

> We have been in Vietnam too long and there is something wrong with that picture. There is no substitute for victory. We need a victory or we need to come to the peace table in an honorable way.[11]

Even when in an earlier war the United States had shown an inclination to "come to the peace

table in an honorable way" there was less than full
support for it. Following the election of Dwight
Eisenhower in November, 1952, the following thought
on his promise to end the Korean War appeared in
The New Leader:

> Our greatest delusion is that we still
> think we have a choice between peace
> and war. When candidates for the high-
> est office in the land offer us "solu-
> tions for peace" either they have not
> understood one of the fundamental ques-
> tions of our time or they are fooling
> the electorate. For there is no real
> choice between war and peace--there is
> only victory or submission, the ulti-
> mate Munich.[12]

A final view on the philosophy of victory in
the framework of the war in Vietnam is expressed by
a distinguished academician:

> The American people, like their lead-
> ers, have very little familiarity
> with losing national enterprises.
> Although they have been commonly un-
> easy about the war in Vietnam almost
> from the beginning, they are equally
> uneasy with the idea of national
> failure, and an American "defeat"
> seems to many of them unthinkable and
> absurd.[13]

The above are but a few of the many expressions of national frustration over the concept of
victory as it exists in the United States today.
The views are representative of civilian and military thinking and are expressed by men in and out
of government. Some are obviously emotionally conceived and others represent a more pragmatic orientation. Most, but not all, relate directly to the
war in Vietnam. It seems quite clear that the
American concept of victory today is indeed elusive.

The will to win totally and completely has historically been an inherent and fundamental part of the American character in both the theoretical and absolute sense. Applied to war, this will to win found its fulfillment in the two great total wars of this century with their total victories. It found confusion and frustration in the limited war in Korea with its inconclusive termination only to be further frustrated by the even more limited and less conclusive effort in Vietnam.

TOTAL WAR AND TOTAL VICTORY

In this study the term total war is synonymous with general war as defined by the Joint Chiefs of Staff:

> General War: Armed conflict between the major powers of the communist and free worlds in which the total resources of the belligerents are employed, and the national survival of a major belligerent is in jeopardy.[14] [Emphasis added.]

It has been posited that the American experience in the two great world wars of the century serves as the basis for much of the total war-total victory philosophy that is in turn very likely at the heart of the present-day frustration suggested in the introductory pages. World War II particularly provides excellent examples of this philosophy and will serve as the primary vehicle for discussion in this section. However, a few comments designed to place the philosophy of World War II in perspective appear to be appropriate.

There is little argument that World War I was to Americans total war and the object was total victory. One author suggests that, while the Allies had some specific war aims, the United States, as an associated power, took a more idealistic view and had total victory as its only goal.

> The Americans had no concrete war
> aims, no precise territorial demands.
> This, too, made them, paradoxically,
> less eager for an armistice. They
> wanted only the "unconditional sur-
> render" of Germany, and were ready to
> go on until this was achieved. The
> Allies also wanted the defeat of Ger-
> many; Britain and France wanted the
> liberation of Belgium; the French
> wanted the liberation of north-eastern
> France; the British wanted the elimi-
> nation of the German fleet. All
> these [objectives] could be secured
> by an armistice. How could the two
> governments justify further blood-
> shed to their war-weary peoples?
> Even apart from this, an armistice,
> as sought by the German government,
> would satisfy the more general aims
> of the Allies.[15]

The United States was on a crusade to fight the
"war to end all wars" and total defeat of the enemy
was the only acceptable way to "end" wars.

When on December 7, 1941, the United States
was fully and irrevocably committed in World War II,
the nation again went to war totally and completely
with the clear intent of totally and completely defeating its enemies. Prior to the attack on Pearl
Harbor, the United States had been gradually committed on the side of the Allies, and it was generally conceded by the nation's policy makers that
it would not be in the national interest to permit
Britain to be defeated. It is quite possible that
had it not been for the Japanese attack in 1941,
the United States would have found itself gradually
drawn deeper and deeper into the war on the side of
Great Britain until it would have been equally totally committed through that avenue.

In today's terminology, the United States, before Pearl Harbor, was in a "limited war" with

Germany and in a very warm "cold war" with Japan. The national objectives at the time were limited as were the resources the nation was willing to commit. During this period there was considerable debate in the United States concerning the actions that had been taken by the administration and the degree to which the nation had been committed by executive action. There were those, in the Congress and elsewhere, who felt very strongly that the involvement was well beyond anything that could be supported in defense of the national interest, and there were those who felt just as strongly that immediate and decisive action should have been taken toward Germany and Japan in defense of the national interest. There was at this time a "constitutional crisis" not unlike the one that many observers feel exists today over the Vietnam commitment. One diplomatic historian called it "the constitutional conflict."[16]

The administration, in an effort to live with the "isolationists" and the "interventionists" as well, steered a course between the two extremes on a cautious, but deliberate heading toward deeper involvement. Although there are many differences between the situations in 1941 and the 1960's, a crude analogy can be drawn between the position of the Roosevelt administration and the later commitment in Southeast Asia. In 1941, as in the 1960's, it was most difficult for the administration to gain any sort of true consensus in support of its policies in the context of limited war or cold war. In 1941, the Japanese attack on Pearl Harbor immediately transformed the struggle into "total war" and provided the administration with virtually instant consensus. The events leading to the Tonkin Gulf Resolution of 1965 served somewhat the same function, but had considerably less force at best. Their impact as a solidifying influence evaporated rapidly as time passed.

In many respects, the development and hardening of the total war-total victory concept is found in the historical sketch suggested in Chapter 2 with emphasis on the latter part of the chapter. The

reader's attention is specifically called to the
statement of objectives found in the "Joint Board
Estimate of United States Over-all Production Requirements" of September, 1941, and the discussion
that follows it.[17]

In a book published in the midst of World War
II, a British author, commenting on the war's objectives, observed that

> the men of 1914-1918 fought and died
> for something more than military vic-
> tory. Many of them believed that
> they were fighting a war to end war,
> and that is a political, not a mili-
> tary, objective. . . .
>   Therefore the achievement of a
> military victory cannot of itself
> guarantee victory in the fullest
> sense of the word. Military victory
> is not necessarily Total Victory.[18]

In retrospect, and with full advantage of
hindsight, it is rather generally accepted that undue emphasis was placed on winning a military victory in World War II at the expense of practical
political objectives. Whether the civilian side of
the U.S government was at fault for not providing
adequate political leadership, or at least guidance,
or whether the military leadership was at fault for
not insisting on clear political objectives is not
really relevant here. It would appear that all
U.S. policy makers eventually surrendered to the
concept of total war and total victory. The national wartime objective became identified virtually exclusively with military victory.

The total war-total victory concept was perhaps best exemplified by President Roosevelt when
he enunciated the "unconditional surrender" policy
at Casablanca in 1943. Whether or not the issuance
of the unconditional surrender declaration had any
real bearing on the outcome of the war is problem-
atical and is argued both ways by scholars. It

will not be argued further here. However, if there
was still any flexibility left in American thinking
in January, 1943, the unconditional surrender declaration eliminated it. The "if," however, is a
big one. From the point of view of this study, the
declaration is important, not because of any effect
it may have had on the outcome of the war, but because it revealed a philosophy that was apparently
fully compatible with the thinking of the American
people at the time.

One scholar commented on unconditional surrender:

> The Casablanca formula of Uncondi-
> tional Surrender is symptomatic of an
> attitude toward war which tends to
> divide [military] strategy from po-
> litical goals. In the Second World
> War American long range political ob-
> jectives played a secondary role. In
> the major conferences of the war, at
> least until the last year, strategy
> took precedence over diplomacy. De-
> cisions of the greatest political im-
> portance were made primarily, even
> solely, on the basis of military con-
> siderations. . . . It is true that
> American planners were dedicated to a
> final goal in the war, but they per-
> ceived the goal as simply total vic-
> tory, the total destruction of the
> military power of the Axis enemy.[19]

The same author goes on to identify three roots of
this "win the war first" mentality as "military,
political, and ideological." The military root is
related to the "psychology of 1943 which . . . can
at least make the error intelligible." The political root is related to the fear that the alliance
might crumble, especially that the Soviet Union
might pull out if there were any hint of a settlement involving less than total victory. Finally,
the ideological root is associated with "a doctrine

of total war defeat of the enemy, that is, in the
doctrine of moral war," which "seems to lie in the
nature of a modern democracy."[20]

In commenting on the same psychological root,
Raymond Aron said "Alexis de Tocqueville had already noted this inclination to double extremism,
few soldiers in peacetime, little diplomatic sub-
tlety once the guns speak--and has considered it
the expression of the democratic spirit."[21] In
further support of the political root, still another author commented:

> In the President's mind, unquestion-
> ably, preservation of American unity
> of opinion was an indispensible condi-
> tion both of [military] victory and
> of success in the peace to follow.
> The two major threats to this unity,
> as the President saw it, were: domes-
> tic indifference, arising from a
> failure to grasp the nature of the
> issues in this total war; and inter-
> national resentment and hostility
> arising from a conflict of aims be-
> tween the United States and above all
> other allies, the Soviet Union.[22]

This is an interesting example of the linkage between domestic and international politics in the
World War II milieu. The president, in 1943, determined that a clearly defined "escalation" of the
terms of the conflict was essential to both Allied
and domestic political consensus. Today, an American administration can hope to achieve some meaningful political consensus only through a very deliberate and demonstrable "de-escalation" of the
Indochina struggle.

There seems to be little doubt that the concept of unconditional surrender was completely acceptable to the American people and if any of the
more sophisticated policy makers, military or civilian, felt strongly against it there is little

evidence that they pressed their views at the time.
In an excellent work on American strategic thinking
Urs Schwarz found that

> diplomacy and foreign policy planning
> remained until a very late date--say,
> 1945--separated by a deep gulf from
> military planning. Foreign policy
> planners in the United States were
> slow to overcome the traditional view
> that military power is not an element
> to be dealt with on a day-to-day basis,
> but rather an auxiliary to which one
> may have recourse in an emergency.[23]

Even though, as pointed out above, a group of
military planners showed an exemplary insight into
politico-military concepts in constructing wartime
national objectives it did not necessarily follow
that military professionals, as a whole, saw the
war in anything but military terms. As an example,
one of the most distinguished military professionals of the period had this to say of politico-
military thinking during the war:

> At times, during the war, we forgot
> that wars are fought for the resolu-
> tion of political conflicts, and in
> the ground campaign for Europe, we
> sometimes overlooked political con-
> siderations of vast importance.[24]

General Bradley further commented that

> we were less concerned with postwar
> political alignments than destruction
> of what remained of the German Army.
> . . . As soldiers we looked naively
> on this British inclination to com-
> plicate the war with political fore-
> sight and nonmilitary objectives.[25]

Sixteen years later another military professional
writing on American military strategy commented
in somewhat different terms:

> A primary fault in the last war in
> Europe was that we brilliantly fought
> and implemented what turned out to be
> an obscure, contradictory and finally
> nonexistent end. Peace,* in and of
> itself, is not necessarily a proper
> objective, . . .[26] [Emphasis added.]

The total war-total victory concept of World
War II had something for everybody. The administration found it convenient as a vehicle to explain
the war to the public. The public liked it because
it satisfied both the liberal and conservative
philosophies of war and it was easy to understand.
The foreign-policy planners apparently liked it
because they could turn the running of the war over
to the military professionals and concern themselves
with what to do with whatever kind of peace the
military eventually turned back to them. The military professionals liked the concept because it
permitted them to get on with their business of
"winning" the war in a relatively uncomplicated
manner by not having to plan around troublesome political constraints. Although there is an element
of facetiousness in the above oversimplification it
is nonetheless illustrative of the relatively sim-
plistic American view of war and politics in World
War II.

History will eventually be the judge of the
validity of the total war-total victory concept.
Circumstances were to usher in a new era shortly
after the close of World War II that would give
birth to a limited-war-limited victory concept. It
is important to keep in mind that most of the political and military leaders who occupied positions

_____

*The concept "peace" as used by Admiral Wylie
is itself elusive. What he is making reference to
is the termination of the war as it would be clearly exemplified by unconditional surrender of the
enemy. "Peace" in the sense it is used here is a
military and not a political objective.

of responsibility in the first nuclear-age application of the limited war-limited victory concept had
won their spurs in the total war-total victory,
pre-nuclear, environment.[27] The new concept is addressed in detail in the following section.

LIMITED WAR AND LIMITED VICTORY

Almost before the smoke of World War II had
lifted, it became all too apparent that there were
deep and basic differences of opinion between the
two superpowers that emerged from the war. The
United States and the Soviet Union saw the postwar
world in two entirely different lights. There were,
however, two basic points on which they seemed to
reach some sort of tacit, though tenuous, agreement. One was that it would not be in their mutual
interests to become engaged in a direct, overt military confrontation with one another and the other
was that it would be equally to their mutual disadvantage to permit the other to have his way in
the world unchallenged. The cold war resulted.
Since the end of World War II there have been a
number of U.S.-Soviet confrontations. Significantly, these confrontations have seldom been direct
and overt and each has been characterized by limited objectives and limited commitment of resources.
It is most significant that in none of the confrontations was the survival of either of the two
superpowers immediately at stake.

The concept of limited war grew out of the
cold war environment. The accepted Joint Chiefs of
Staff definition of limited war is: "Armed conflict short of general war, exclusive of incidents,
involving overt engagement of the military forces
of two or more nations."[28] Without becoming involved in a pointless exercise in semantics it is
simply pointed out that limited war is something
less than the total war described in the preceding
paragraphs and something more than mere incidents
mentioned in the above definition. Although not
specifically considered in the above definition,

one might infer that if a total war breeds total
victory a limited war possibly must lead to some
sort of limited victory. One might also reflect on
the logic of expecting total victory from a limited
war.

Before examining the Korean War as an example
of a limited war fought within the overall framework of the cold war, it is perhaps advisable to
narrow down the meaning of limited war as it is
viewed in this study. The views of Bernard Brodie
will be borrowed rather extensively for this purpose. In answer to a rhetorical question as to
what distinguishes limited war from total war he
said:

> The answer is that limited war in-
> volves an important kind and degree
> of restraint--deliberate restraint.
> As a rule we do not apply the term
> "limited war" to conflicts which are
> limited naturally by the fact that
> one or both sides lacks the capabil-
> ity to make them total. . . . We
> generally use it to refer to wars in
> which the United States on the one
> side and the Soviet Union or Commu-
> nist China on the other may be in-
> volved, perhaps directly but usually
> through proxies on one or both sides.
> In such wars the possibility of total
> or unrestricted conflict is always
> present as an obvious and immediately
> available alternative to limited op-
> erations. That is why we must em-
> phasize the factor of deliberate re-
> straint.[29]

With respect to objectives in limited war the same
author echoed a generally accepted view when he
said: "Limited war has sometimes been defined as a
war fought to achieve a limited objective."[30]

Historically there have been many wars fought
for limited objectives. This is nothing new

although at times there seems to be the perception that the idea was conceived in the post-World War II period. A valid example in U.S. history is the Spanish-American War just before the turn of the century. The U.S. objective in that war was not the total defeat of Spain but something much more limited than that. In this example the objective of the United States was relatively fixed. The amount of force to be applied to achieve the objective was the variable element. At no time in the war was the continued existence of Spain or the United States as independent international actors really in question. However, had Spain chosen to contest the United States to the limit of her ability, in other words, to lay her national existence on the line with a total effort, it is quite likely that the United States would have raised the level of effort accordingly and a total war to achieve what was initially a limited objective could conceivably have resulted.

The point is that the basic objectives of the participants were themselves relatively limited and relatively fixed. In oversimplified form, the United States had the objective of wresting control of Cuba from Spain and the Spanish objective was the retention of control of Cuba. Control of Cuba was the object. The variable in this situation was the level of conflict either side was willing to endure to achieve the objective. This, however, is not the sort of limited war with which the international community must deal today. Again borrowing from Brodie: "We shall have to work very hard to keep it [war] limited. We should be willing to limit objectives because we want to keep the war limited, not the other way around."31

With full recognition of the dangers of oversimplification it is suggested that limited wars today are limited primarily because of the nearly certain disastrous consequences of a total war in the nuclear age on all participants. Today the restraint to keep the level of conflict below the total war level is the relatively constant factor while the degree of limitation of objectives that

will support this restraint is the variable factor.
The Korean War provides an excellent example of
this.

On June 25, 1950, the North Korean armed
forces crossed the 38th parallel and invaded the
Republic of South Korea. Almost immediately U.S.
forces and later U.N. forces were committed and
limited objectives were quickly announced by the
U.S. administration and the United Nations. Essentially the objectives were to cause an immediate
cessation of hostilities and force the withdrawal
of North Korean forces north of the 38th parallel.
In other words, the reestablishment of the status
quo ante bellum. Here was an example of limited
objectives the achievement of which would restore
the tenuous line of demarcation in Korea, but more
importantly, ones that were calculated to avoid a
total war.

By October, 1950, U.N. forces had driven north
of the 38th parallel and the North Korean armed
forces had virtually ceased to exist as an effective
military force. For practical purposes the status
quo ante bellum had been achieved, and done without
recourse to total war. In the first blush of this
military success, however, U.S. and U.N. policy
makers abandoned the initial limited objectives and
expanded them to include reunification of a "free"
Korea. The climate in the United Nations at the
time was such that reference to a free Korea meant
a noncommunist Korea. Up to this point the constant
goal of keeping the conflict limited had been
achieved and had not changed. The objective was
the variable and it had in fact changed.

In pursuit of the revised objective, the U.N.
forces drove northward toward the Yalu River.
Watching the movement from across the Yellow Sea
the Chinese Communists apparently saw the northward
drive as a direct threat to their national security
and made the political decision to intervene. It
is not the intent here to argue the Chinese decision to intervene. The fact is that intervene they

did and the U.N. command had a new war on its hands.
The level of conflict had been raised nearer the
danger point and the whole concept of limited war
and limited objectives had to be thoroughly reevaluated. Now the level of conflict had been raised
considerably and the political leadership in the
United States was under heavy pressure from its
military commanders in the field and segments of
the public to further raise the level of conflict
to permit a "win" in the new environment. In other
words, to allow the objective to become the constant and the level of conflict to become the variable. Rightly or wrongly the administration did
not yield to the pressure.

The Korean War brought to light a number of
most perplexing politico-military problems--not the
least of which was the relief of General MacArthur
by President Truman. Although not debated publicly
in this setting, the differences between the president and the general centered on the meaning of
"win" in a limited war. The Korean War was fought
very much in the Clausewitzian tradition as an integral part of the nation's foreign policy. War
did not take over where diplomacy left off, as was
the case in World War II, but complemented diplomacy throughout the conflict.[32]

It was suggested earlier in this study that in
the Korean War there would be a "substitute for
victory" and that what that substitute would be was
not immediately clear but it was evident that the
United States and the United Nations would be willing to settle for something short of traditional
complete military victory. It was further suggested that considering the past experience of the professional military officers who provided the leadership in the Korean War it is not difficult to appreciate the frustrations they endured in the
prosecution of that war. Those who had learned
their trade in total war were now called upon to
practice it in the unfamiliar environment of limited war. The decision was made, however, to keep
the war limited and it was played out to the bitter
end in that context.

Although General Eisenhower campaigned for the
presidency in 1952 for an honorable settlement of
the war in Korea there was some thought among military officers that he would remove the frustrating
restrictions and permit the "winning" of the war.
When president-elect Eisenhower went to Korea in
December, 1952, however, "his determination to obtain a settlement one way or another" was strengthened.[33] What he hoped that "way" would be was
quite clear to General Mark Clark who was the U.N.
commander in Korea at the time of the visit. General Clark had prepared a detailed estimate of the
resources that he felt would be required to carry
out his overall plan for victory in Korea, however,
as General Clark reported later:

> The most significant thing about the
> visit of the President-elect was that
> I never had the opportunity to present
> this estimate for his consideration.
> The question of how much it would
> take to win the war was never raised.
> It soon became apparent, in our many
> conversations, that he would seek an
> honorable truce.[34]

When attempts to arrive at some sort of an
"honorable truce" were continuously frustrated by
the Chinese Communists, the administration had
reached the end of its patience and General Clark
reports that one final offer was to be made. If,
however, the Communists rejected this final offer
and made no constructive proposals of their own,
"I was authorized to terminate . . . the truce
talks rather than recess them," and carry on the
war in new ways never yet tried in Korea.[35]

According to Sherman Adams, this message was
transmitted to the Chinese Communists through India:

> In May, during talks with Nehru in
> India, Dulles said that the United
> States could not be held responsible
> for failing to use atomic weapons if

> a truce could not be arranged. This
> message was planted deliberately in
> India so that it would get to the
> Chinese Communists, as it did. Long
> afterwards, talking one day with
> Eisenhower about the events that led
> up finally to the truce in Korea, I
> asked hom what it was that brought
> the Communists into line. "Danger of
> an atomic war," he said without hesi-
> tation. We told them we could not
> hold it to a limited war any longer if
> the Communists welched on a treaty of
> truce. They didn't want a full-scale
> war or an atomic attack.[36]

On July 26, 1953, after having been informed
that the truce had been signed, President Eisenhower went on the air and spoke to the American
people:

> For this nation the cost of repel-
> ling aggression has been high. In
> thousands of homes it has been in-
> calculable. It has been paid in
> terms of tragedy. . . . We have
> won an armistice on a single battle-
> field--not peace in the world. We
> may not now relax our guard nor
> cease our quest.[37]

Moscow noted the end of the war also. In a message
to the Chinese Communist and North Korean leaders
Malenkov congratulated them on winning "a great
victory in the cause of defending peace in the Far
East and throughout the world." The author dryly
added, "There was no celebration on Broadway."[38]

The debate as to who "won" the Korean War
still goes on. The Chinese Communists can take
considerable comfort from the war in that one of
its results was the emergence of Communist China as
one of the great powers. David Rees adds:

> But given that on balance the [Chinese
> Communist] regime gained by crossing
> tye Yalu and winning a politico-
> military victory almost as great as
> crushing the KMT [Kuomintang]. These
> triumphs were won at a heavy cost
> which probably influenced Chinese pol-
> icy ever since. . . . Thus not all
> of Peking's objectives in the summer
> of 1950 were achieved by intervention
> in Korea. Moreover, further Chinese
> Communist adventures in Southeast
> Asia have been deterred by the impla-
> cable enmity of the United States.[39]

One observer of the Eisenhower administration noted
that Washington was cast into gloom, shame, and
disillusion over what many saw as that "unmention-
able victory." He goes on to say:

> History will cite Korea as the prov-
> ing ground of collective security, up
> to this time no more than a plausible
> theory. It will cite it as the turn-
> ing point of the world struggle
> against Communism and as the scene of
> a great victory for American Arms, one
> the future will celebrate even though
> the present does not.[40]

In terms of the initially stated U.N. objective of restoring the status quo ante bellum it
can be argued that the U.N. forces "won" the Korean
War. On the other hand, however, in terms of the
more ambitious objective of unification of all of
Korea a U.N. "defeat" can be argued equally strongly. The basic question remains, however, if the
United Nations' interests in general and the United
States' national interest in particular were served
by avoiding total war in 1952-53 at the expense of
accepting the more limited objective. The Korean
War experience taught the American people that in
limited war there was a "substitute for victory" at
least for traditional military victory. One of the

most profound effects of this excursion into limited war was the frustration that was experienced
and the "never again" attitude which was very
strong after the war.

Of the Korean War, Irving Kristol said:

> The Korean War was unpopular to a de-
> gree that makes it inconceivable for
> any future Administration to contem-
> plate that kind of limited rigorously
> defensive military action. The schol-
> ars and the diplomats can continue to
> devise ingenious gradients of warfare,
> countering each enemy action with just
> so much (and no more) reaction. But
> they are indulging in a paper game.
> The American people cannot provide
> the kind of mercenary, professional
> soldiers such plans require.[41]

This is strong language indeed but the author is of
the opinion that it rather well reflects what many
Americans were thinking after the Korean War. It
is interesting to note the relationship between the
above view and the "flexible response" philosophy
developed in the early months of the Kennedy administration.*

Although possibly not completely within the
scope of this chapter, because it was not a limited
war by definition, the Cuban missile crisis of 1962
offers some excellent examples of flexible objectives and fixed levels of conflict and will be commented on very briefly. This U.S.-Soviet confrontation provides an example of both participants

---

*The author is of the opinion that had the
Korean War not been brought to a conclusion in 1953
many of the frustrations and divisions that exist
in the United States in the early 1970's would have
manifested themselves in the mid-1950's.

trying very hard to prevent armed conflict that
might lead to total war. The desire to keep the
level of conflict limited was the fixed factor. In
the final analysis, both sides altered their initially announced objectives to achieve this. When
the crisis was over the Soviet government told its
people that they had achieved a victory in that a
promise not to invade Cuba had been extracted from
the United States. The United States, on the other
hand, claimed a victory in that the Soviet Union
agreed to remove the missiles from Cuba. This, of
course, at the expense of no on-site inspection.
The point to be emphasized here is that neither
side was willing to risk total war, so in the final analysis neither side achieved anything resembling total victory. The level of confrontation
was kept limited by mutual agreement and both sides
settled for a sort of limited victory.[42]

This chapter would, of course, not be complete
without reference to the limited war in which the
United States has been engaged in Southeast Asia,
in varying degrees, for over a decade. The eventual outcome of that conflict is yet to be determined but the confrontation can nonetheless be
examined conceptually. For practical purposes the
Vietnam War is the war the "never again" advocates
hoped so desperately to avoid. It commenced as
yet another East-West confrontation within the
overall framework of the cold war. One of the
great powers has been directly, and very deeply,
involved while the two Communist giants have been
involved by proxy only. One American historian
has commented that

> though American opinion understood
> limited war better than in 1950-53
> [the Korean War], it did not accept
> such war easily; and altogether the
> Vietnamese conflict raised political
> issues that appeared infinitely more
> complex and disturbing than those of
> Korea. The outcome of the Army's
> effort [in Vietnam] would finally

turn on the resolution of those
largely nonmilitary issues.[43]

What is now a limited war, in the fullest
sense of the word, started out several years ago at
the "incident" level and rather steadily escalated
to its peak in 1968 and has subsequently experienced a de-escalatory trend. There were and continue to be a great many overt and covert actions
taken by all concerned to keep the war limited.
From the U.S. point of view there has been firm
evidence that the level of conflict is the fixed
factor and objectives are altered to keep the level
of conflict fixed.* In a sense, the Vietnam War
presents the same sort of basic problems to the
leadership in the United States as did the war in
Korea. There are, however, several fundamental
differences that make it a much more difficult
situation from the point of view of the concept of
victory.

A major factor to be considered is that in
Vietnam the United States has not had the nuclear
monopoly it had at the time of the Korean War.
This makes it all the more desirable for the United
States to keep the level of conflict within the
"limited" bounds. Another major difference is the
so-called war within a war, or the "other war" as
it is sometimes called. This is in addition to the
"military war" and when the objectives of both
these wars are combined they somehow or other constitute the national objective of the United States
in Vietnam.

The avowed purpose of the "military war" has
been to commit enough military power to cause the

---

*The Cambodian incursion in the spring of 1970,
the brief resumption of the bombing of North Vietnam, as well as the raid on the suspected POW camp
near Hanoi in the fall did not apparently represent
a policy change in the desire to keep the war limited.

Viet Cong and the North Vietnamese to come to the
realization that it is entirely too expensive to
attempt to achieve their goals through armed force.
The purpose of the "other war" seemed to be to
create the necessary socio-political environment to
root out the Viet Cong infrastructure which inhab-
its the social, economic, and political life of
much of South Vietnam. Viewed in the abstract, the
objectives of these two wars are clear and not too
complex. The military war had a military objective
and the other war had an essentially nonmilitary
objective. What then is the problem? Why haven't
the military professionals been able to go about
winning the military war and the nation builders
been able to go about winning the other war? It
seems more probable that there have not been two
wars going on in Vietnam but that there has been
only one war with one set of objectives. Those objectives, however, have been replete with military,
political, economic, social, and other connotations
and at times contradictions.

The limited war in Vietnam has been further
complicated by the strong division of opinion and
frustration in the United States, which can, at
least in part, be attributed to the unsatisfactory
experience with total war and total victory of
World War II and also dissatisfaction with the limited war experience of the Korean conflict. World
War II was undeniably won militarily but the desired postwar political stability was not achieved.
In Korea, the political objective that was finally
settled upon--restoration of the status quo ante
bellum--was achieved but the war was not won in the
previously accepted sense. Clearly, the frustrations that seem to accompany the concept of limited
war in the United States are not original with the
conflict in Vietnam. Essentially, it would seem
that the Vietnam experience simply raises many of
the same questions that were left unsettled after
the Korean War. The basic question of whether the
United States, or any democracy, can conduct a
limited war and see it through, is yet to be answered.[44] The question is not one of whether or

not the nation has the physical means of doing it
but whether it is psychologically prepared to accept the concept of limited war and limited victory
along with its many inherent frustrations.

The author is reluctant to leave the war in
Vietnam on this rather inconclusive note. There
has been much written on that involvement to date
and much more can be expected from the pens of
critics and apologists in the years to come. From
the point of view of limited war and limited victory, however, the issue appears to be identified
and understanding would not be enhanced by a detailed review of that involvement.

Certainly, in any examination of the concept
of victory there must be some recognition of what
it is the nation is trying to achieve as a meaningful measure of how successful it has been. The
following section relates the concept of victory
with the concept of the objective.

THE VICTORY-OBJECTIVE RELATIONSHIP

In the preceding sections the concepts of victory in total war and limited war were examined.
In both instances the word _objective_ was used rather freely, but no attempt was made to define it or
place it in a meaningful perspective. In these
paragraphs the objective will be investigated conceptually and related to the concepts of total and
limited victory previously examined. The task will
be approached initially by way of the principles of
war as used by the United States Army.

The army recognizes nine principles of war
that are defined as

> fundamental truths governing the
> prosecution of war. Their proper
> application is essential to the
> exercise of command and to success-
> ful conduct of _military_ operations.

These principles are interrelated and
dependent on the circumstances, may
tend to reinforce one another or to
be in conflict. Consequently, the
degree of application of any specific
principle will vary with the situation.[45] [Emphasis added.]

From the definition it is clear that the principles are not taught as hard and fast rules that
are to be followed blindly and applied equally in
all situations. There can be little argument that
the proper mix and emphasis on the several principles in a total war environment such as World
War II would be quite different from that of a limited confrontation. There is no question in the
author's mind that the military profession as a
whole accepts this difference fully. It must also
be emphasized that the principles relate to the
conduct of military operations. However, conceptually at least, there may be a lesson to be learned
that is applicable in the broader sense of politico-
military affairs. This is especially true of the
principle of the objective, so the subsequent discussion will be limited to that principle.

The principle of the objective is identified
as the "overriding" principle. The specific statement of the principle is: "The ultimate military
objective of war is the destruction of the enemy's
armed forces and his will to fight"[46] [emphasis
added]. The British sometimes call it the "selection and maintenance of sin." In more contemporary
language the thought might be simply expressed as
deciding where it is one wants to go, then limiting
courses of action to ones that will get one there.
Put in still another way, the principle of the objective tells the military professional to achieve
his objective, accomplish his mission, win his battle above all else. He is further taught that the
successful accomplishment of his particular mission, while in itself perhaps innocuous, is critical to the overall effort.

It is by no means unusual for a military commander to be assigned an objective that requires
him to conduct an operation, such as a retrograde,
demonstration, or feint*--to mention a few--that is
itself not intended to produce a victory but is designed to contribute materially to the accomplishment of some broader objective elsewhere. It does
not seem unreasonable that the same philosophy
might be transferred from the principle of the
military objective to the advancement of the "national objective." In the past, Americans have
often taken the somewhat uncompromising view that
in time of war, hot or cold, military victory in
the classical sense is coincident with achievement
of the national objective. This is a dangerous notion shared by military and civilian leaders and by
liberal and conservative thinkers alike. It must
not go unchallenged.

The national objective must of necessity be
broad, and normally this means vague. An excellent
example of the broad terms in which an overall national objective must be stated is found in a book
called Goals for Americans prepared by the American
Assembly in 1960. Part II of the book is entitled
"Goals Abroad" and it defines the basic foreign
policy of the United States as one that must see to

> the preservation of its own indepen-
> dence and free institutions. Our
> position before the world should be

---

*A retrograde is any movement of a command to
the rear, or away from the enemy. It may be forced
by the enemy or made voluntarily. A demonstration
and a feint are both operations designed specifically to draw the enemy's attention from the point
of principal operation or to cause him to expend
resources unproductively. They are both, as is the
retrograde, conducted at a point where a decision
is not sought. The methodology of the latter two
differ only slightly.

neither defensive nor belligerent.
We should cooperate with nations
whose ideals and interests are in
harmony with ours. We should seek
to mitigate tensions, and search
for acceptable areas of accommoda-
tions with opponents. The safeguard reduction of armaments is an
essential goal.[47]

There must, however, be subordinate, or more de-
scriptively, supporting objectives that "support"
the overall national objective. For example, the
U.S. national objectives (or national interests) in
Europe would not necessarily be identical with
those for Latin America, but both should be within
the context of the overall national objective.
Charles Lerche and Abdul Said observed that

it is essential that a policy maker
formulate his objectives as precisely
as possible, not alone because it
gives him a means of concentrating
his attention and his effort on issues that to him are crucial, but
also because he can better appraise
degrees of success or failure if he
is quite clear about his aims.[48]

The nature of the international system is such that
the national objective is, and always must be, a
political objective. Diplomacy and military force
are but two means of pursuing that objective.

The Joint Chiefs of Staff define the national
objective as "the fundamental aims, goals, or purposes of a nation--as opposed to the means for
seeking these ends--toward which a policy is directed and efforts and resources of the nation are
applied."[49] And national strategy is defined as
"the art and science of developing and using the
political, economic, and psychological powers of a
nation, together with its armed forces, during
peace and war, to secure national objectives."[50]
[Emphasis added.]

The national objective then should identify
<u>what</u> it is the nation is striving to do and the
national strategy should outline, in very broad
terms, <u>how</u> the nation will go about achieving its
objectives. The nation's foreign and military policies are then constructed, along with economic,
social, and other policies, as subordinate parts of
the national strategy, to "secure the national objective." It appears to the author that the "principle" of the objective is completey relevant here
and that the overriding "principle" that must guide
the nation's political and military thinking is the
national objective.

To conduct any sort of reasonably relevant
planning it seems almost axiomatic that the politico-
military planner must constantly orient on the national objective. He must know what it is the
United States is trying to do in a given situation.
It is not in the least inconceivable that, in a
given confrontation, the national strategy may call
for a military policy that seeks a "stand-off" in
furtherance of the national objective. In another
situation the national strategy may require a military policy designed to destroy the armed forces
of the opponent to facilitate achievement of the
national objective. It is emphasized that in each
of the above two hypothetical examples the military
objectives had relevance only in that they supported eventual achievement of the national objective.
A military victory, a diplomatic victory, an economic victory, or any other victory is meaningless
in and of itself. It can have meaning only in its
relationship with the national objective, which in
the final analysis must be expressed in political
terms.

What is victory? What does it mean to win?
How can a nation tell when it has won? These are
questions that are being asked today as a direct
result of the situation in Southeast Asia, but
their relevance is by no means limited to that commitment. They lie at the center of the elusive
concept of victory. The word <u>victory</u> is defined by
Webster as "the overcoming of an enemy in battle,

or of an antagonist in any contest; . . . victory
implies the winning of any contest or struggle."
By the synonyms that Webster suggests it is apparent that victory can mean anything from the successful outcome of a struggle, to an overwhelming
conquest.

From the above it would appear that victory is
a rather barren word by itself. It has meaning
only in the context of the objective of the contest
--be it to score points, influence people, cross a
fighting line, occupy enemy territory, make money,
cause an enemy to surrender, to maintain the status
quo, or whatever it may be. Victory will have been
achieved only when the participant has done what he
has set out to do. Therefore, for the purpose of
this paper, victory at the national level is defined
simply as the achievement of the national objective
or objectives.

The earlier discussion on the principle of the
objective suggests that in support of any given national objective there are numerous supporting objectives assigned down through the many action
levels. The further down the chain of command one
goes the more likely he is to find something resembling a pure objective, be it purely military or
purely political, and the more likely he is to be
able to identify victory in terms of a particular
objective. In military operations, for example,
at the level of the individual in contact with the
enemy, the concept of the objective and the concept
of victory are quite basic. If an individual soldier becomes locked in mortal combat with an individual enemy soldier he either wins or le loses and
there is little room for polemics or philosophizing.
This sort of victory, as the political scientist
might say, can be measured empirically.

As the level of combat operations is raised
through the many levels of command, however, complicating factors are injected and the concept of
the objective is less precise and the concept of
victory is less tidy. At the national level it is

quite complex and a victory per se can have meaning
only with reference to the national objective it
was intended to facilitate. The United States had
established a rather remarkable record of losing
battles in the Revolutionary War and the War of
1812 but still eventually achieved the national objectives: independence and confirmation of independence respectively. In more recent times the
nation has perhaps been much more successful in
winning the military battles but less successful in
achieving the political goals of the wars and
thereby falling short of the national objectives.
It is indeed possible to win the battles but lose
the war and it is by no means impossible to lose
most of the battles but eventually win the war.

A recent article in the **Military Review** quotes
a contemporary German writer:

> Every war is waged for victory. But
> what constitutes a victory? Winning
> a battle? A campaign? The occupa-
> tion of a province or of the enemy's
> whole territory? The establishment
> of military superiority? The sup-
> pression of all organized resistance?
> The destruction of inhabitable places?
> The enslavement or decimation of the
> enemy population? The conversion to
> another faith of the survivors on the
> enemy side? The nature of war depends
> not only on its technology or on the
> economic resources of the belliger-
> ents but to a large extent upon the
> notion of victory which the belliger-
> ents entertain.[51] [Emphasis added.]

If, as suggested above, the nature of a war
depends "upon the notion of victory which the belligerents entertain," the "notion of victory" of
both sides in a war must be considered. Up to this
point most of the thinking has been directed toward
total and limited war objectives and victory as
viewed by only one contestant--the United States.

If one of the participants in a war unilaterally decides upon a total war seeking total victory it does not really make too much difference how the other sides views the situation. Unfortunately it only takes one participant to escalate to total war.

While it may take only one to make a total war it takes two to make a limited war and in order to keep the war limited it is essential that each side recognize the other's "notion of victory." The recognition of this is a political matter and it is imperative that there be some sort of political intercourse between the belligerents. This contact may, of course, be either direct or indirect.

If achievement of the national objectives in a given situation constitutes victory for the United States it would follow that the same thing could be said of any major contending power. In that the national objectives of major contending powers will infrequently coincide (otherwise there would be no point of contention), does it necessarily follow that one belligerent can win only at the expense of the other belligerent losing? Can a major power afford to lose a limited war, either directly or by proxy, without having used all its resources? Does it make sense for one major power to put another in the position of having only the alternative of obvious defeat or escalation to total war? Considering the objective-victory relationship it would appear that within the limited-war framework it is very possible to terminate a war with both sides claiming partial victory. The total war with its total objectives will demand total victory on the part of one side, provided total annihilation does not supersede victory. Limited war with its limited objectives permits limited victory, which can be shared by both participants.

VICTORY IN PERSPECTIVE

This portion of the chapter will bring together the concepts that have been examined in the

preceding pages and evaluate and relate them in
such a way as to point to some meaningful concept.
Every individual has some concept of victory in his
own mind and this is normally a product of his own
experience and education, but it still remains a
very individual thing. Not all diplomats, for example, have the same concept of victory nor do all
military professionals view victory in the same
light. Certainly in the United States, both in and
out of government, there are many diverse views of
the concept of victory.

     Earlier in the study it has been argued that
Americans have at long last come to accept the fact
that neither political nor military considerations
alone are adequate in the nation's national security
policy deliberations and, in the abstract sense at
least, it should not be difficult to obtain agreement as to the necessity for the closest possible
politico-military integration. It is only natural
that there is disagreement, sometimes bitter, as to
how the politico-military equation should be kept
in balance. The essential point, however, is that
there is in the United States a heritage, relatively young though it may be, of acceptance of the
fact that foreign policy and military policy are
both essential elements in the conduct of war, be
it cold, limited, or total.

     The American people have found it relatively
easy to understand total war. The section on "Total War and Total Victory" pointed out that the experience of the two great world wars had a profound
effect on the thinking of the American people.
Perhaps it may be said that while in theory it was
agreed that politics and war were not separate
functions but were inexorably intertwined, in practice it was much easier for the United States to
embark upon an ideologically based crusade than it
was to face the politico-military realities of the
day and accept the restrictions such realization
would place on the national concept of victory.

     In the post-World War II years it became ap-
parent that the United States had failed to take

some very basic political factors into consideration. The nation became reeducated to the requirement for integrating the political and military aspects of any future war and developed a certain
national sophistication in this area. The "confes-
sion of faith" was recited in many volumes of postwar literature but when the Korean War put the faith
to a test it was found to be shallow indeed. Americans did some remarkable backsliding into the comfortable conceptual surroundings of total war and
total victory and voted an administration out of
office over the frustrations of a limited war-
limited victory concept. The nation is now again
deeply involved in a limited war in Vietnam and the
national impatience and frustration are once more
apparent.

     In the "Limited War and Limited Victory" sec-
tion it was suggested that the fixed and limited
factors are not the same in total and limited war.
In total war the objective was identified as the
relatively fixed factor while the level of conflict
necessary to achieve the objective was the major
variable. In limited war, on the other hand, the
level of conflict was identified as the relatively
fixed factor, due primarily to the nuclear threat,
and the objective was the variable. Further, it
was pointed out that objectives are limited as a
means of keeping the conflict short of total war
and limitation of objectives is not an end in itself.

     It was pointed out in the "Victory-Objective
Relationship" section that there must be some meaningful relationship between the national objectives
and victory. An analogy was made to the army's
principle of the objective and it was suggested
that any actions taken, be they political or military, in the name of the national objectives can
have relevance only as they relate to those objectives.

     In the politico-military environment within
which a concept of victory must be constructed
there are a number of players, each with a somewhat

different role to perform. For the purpose of this
study they are the policy maker, the public, the
diplomat, and the military professional. In the
succeeding few pages the function of each of the
players in developing a meaningful concept of victory will be examined.

The group referred to here as the policy maker
is intended to include the president, his immediate
staff, and his principal advisors to include such
officials as the secretaries of state and defense,
plus others he may wish to consult. The first, and
possibly the most difficult, task of the policy
maker is the formulation of the national objectives
and the enunciation of those objectives to the national and international communities. Of course,
the policy maker arrives at the national objectives
only after thorough consideration of all the factors involved to include the recommendations of the
professional diplomats and soldiers. The public
attitude is also a most important consideration for
the policy maker.

After the objectives are decided upon they
must be translated into guidance to the diplomats
and the soldiers in the form of supporting political and military objectives. This guidance must
include, among other things, any restraints on
diplomatic or military activity that are applicable.
For example, in pursuit of a particular objective
the guidance may be that the objective will be approached exclusively through diplomatic channels
with the military in a purely passive role. On the
other hand it may be decided that direct military
pressure will be applied while the diplomat remains
on the periphery until certain conditions more conducive to diplomacy have been created.

The public, broadly used here to include the
Congress, has the responsibility of debating decisions taken by the policy maker and expressing its
opinions through constitutionally established channels. The diplomat and the soldier, of course,
have the responsibility of implementing actions to

achieve the national objectives. Finally, and
equal in importance to deciding upon the national
objectives, the policy maker must make the determination of when the objectives have been achieved,
that is to say, when the nation has achieved victory.

The responsibilities suggested above represent
an admittedly overly simplified view of how a concept of victory might be developed, yet with little
imagination one can identify American World War II
thinking in it. The administration, as the policy
maker, identified military defeat of the enemy as
the national objective of the war. The major portion of the responsibility of accomplishing this
was assigned to the military professional who pro-
ceeded, in a truly magnificent manner, to defeat
the enemy while the diplomat played a very secondary role waiting in the wings to be called on
stage. The public understood the war (with a great
assist from the Japanese attack on Pearl Harbor)
and supported the policy maker virtually without
exception. The military objective of defeating the
enemy was eventually achieved and, inasmuch as this
was also the national objective, the administration
had no trouble in convincing the public that victory had, in fact, been achieved. There was absolutely nothing elusive about the concept of victory.
It was all quite clear.

In the less-than-total-war environment, however, it is not quite so simple. It is, for example,
much more difficult for the policy maker to state
clearly the national objectives because the whole
environment is filled with anomalies and contradictions. Furthermore, as suggested earlier, the objectives are the variable and therefore subject to
constant modification, thus making it even more
difficult for the administration to state clearly
the national objectives. All this, of course,
makes it more difficult for the diplomat and the
soldier to perform their assigned functions, and in
combination the above factors make it virtually impossible for the public to understand what the

policy maker is doing. Closing the circuit, it
might also be said that these same complicating
factors make it more difficult for the policy maker
to recognize when victory has been achieved.

Turning again briefly to the U.S. commitment
in Southeast Asia, the concept of victory in that
confrontation will be considered. The war in Vietnam serves as an excellent example of dynamic objectives. Initially, the stated U.S. objective was
couched in rather ideologically oriented idealistic
terms centering on this nation's desire to aid a
small defenseless nation to choose its own way of
life. This all had a flavor of the crusade for
which Americans had gone to war before, but a crusade with a limited objective that did not have
staying power. More recently American policy makers have been prone to state the national objectives for Vietnam in less idealistic and more realistic terms.

There is nothing sinister or evil in changing
national objectives, but rather it demonstrates a
realization on the part of the policy maker of the
facts of limited-war life. It is not the purpose
of this study to argue for or against any decisions
taken by any of the policy makers in the war in
Vietnam, but to emphasize that objectives will not
remain fixed in such wars and that it is one of the
tasks of the policy maker to bring the national objectives into accord with the ever-changing international environment and to maintain public support.

While one may sympathize with the policy maker's problem in enunciating meaningful objectives
in a dynamic situation and with the frustrations of
the diplomat and the soldier in attempting to
achieve the national objectives, one must sympathize equally with the public in trying to understand it all. In a book written just before the
major U.S. commitment was made in Vietnam, Bradford
Westerfield had this to say about the American public and limited war:

> [The] limited-war means of effectuat-
> ing the containment policy might be
> so exasperating at home as to make
> the policy itself unacceptable to so
> many Americans that no Administration
> would be able to maintain it in the
> long run. Yet, only in the long run
> can it hope to succeed. There is no
> evident way out of this dilemma ex-
> cept education and courageous politi-
> cal leadership and a willingness to
> experiment with limited war again (if
> ever, apart from the domestic politi-
> cal reaction, it comes to be desirable)
> to see whether by then the American
> people will have finally become recon-
> ciled to the costly responsibilities
> of world power in this regard as they
> have in others. The Kennedy Adminis-
> tration seemed to be moving toward
> such an experiment in South Vietnam
> in early 1962.[52]

American policy makers were well aware of this and
there was a noticeable emphasis in statements by
responsible officials in the late 1960's on the
need for patience by the American public.

Limited war has placed additional burdens on
the diplomat. Even if he would be so inclined, as
Secretary Hull apparently was in World War II, it
is impossible for him to step aside until the war
is over and then resume diplomatic activity. The
diplomat is as much, or more, a combatant in limited war as is the military professional.

The military professional learned in Korea,
and this learning is being constantly reinforced in
Vietnam, that a limited war is a much more difficult operation than a total war. There are a number of reasons for this, but they all center on the
word limited. As was suggested earlier, the closer
a given confrontation is to the limited-war end of
the scale the more heavily the political side of

the politico-military equation is weighted. In
limited war in general and in Vietnam in particular
this means real "limitations" on military action.
It means restraints on bombing targets and on
ground actions relating to Cambodia and Laos. It
means not crossing the DMZ (demilitarized zone)
even though it might be "militarily" sound to do so.
It means recognition of the fact that the national
objective and military victory are not necessarily
synonymous, and it means centralized control of
military operations--often from the highest political level.

In his book on foreign policy in the Kennedy
administration, Roger Hilsman has, in that part of
the book that deals with Vietnam, a chapter entitled, "And How Do You Know if You're Winning?"[53]
This is a most profound question and one that the
public, the diplomat, the soldier, and others can
expound upon, but in the final analysis it is the
national policy maker who must tie the question to
the national objectives.

Certainly some, although the author believes
very few, in the United States would hope to see a
U.S. victory over North Vietnam in the World War II
pattern. Possibly they envision a delegation of
North Vietnamese officials coming aboard a U.S.
battleship (the New Jersey might have served the
purpose while it was in commission) to formally
sign a document that essentially says "the United
States wins and North Vietnam loses." Others would
prefer to see the United States simply withdraw
from the area with the admission that it was all a
bad mistake and accept a "defeat" gracefully if not
formally. It is most unlikely that any U.S. policy
maker will adopt either of the above alternatives
but will settle on some sort of an "honorable" settlement that will satisfy U.S. national objectives
as well as the national objectives of the opposing
nations. Limited war will end in limited victory.
A nation that demands total victory--unconditional
surrender of a de facto as well as a proxy enemy--
must be willing to wage total war to achieve it.

Total victory will be elusive forever when pursued
through limited war.

RESPONSIBILITIES

No matter how desirable it may be, the possibility of an international community without conflict in the foreseeable future is not promising.
While every effort must be made to eliminate force
as a means of settling international disputes, nations must be realistic in seeing to their own national security. For the great powers, national
security is a major problem that demands much of
the nation's time and resources. There are three
basic courses of action a great power at war can
elect in pursuit of its national objectives. The
two extremes of total war or acquiescence to the
demands of an opponent are generally seen as unrealistic and reliance is usually placed on the
ability of the nation to conduct some sort of limited effort between the two extremes.

To survive in this environment between the two
extremes, Americans must come to accept several
rather basic yet somehow elusive responsibilities.
First, the nation's policy makers must make a con-
certed effort to select national objectives that
are truly relevant in the environment in which they
are to be sought. Further, the policy makers have
the very great responsibility of enunciating the
national objectives so that they are understood in
the international and the national arenas. Recognizing the dynamic nature of the contemporary international environment, the policy makers have the
heavy responsibility of keeping the national objectives relevant.

In a democracy such as the United States, the
public carries a responsibility not shared by its
counterpart in many nations. The public has the
responsibility of expressing its views through constitutional channels and influencing the policy
makers in that manner. An informed and responsible

public is the strength of a democracy, but irresponsibility may well prove the major weakness of
democratic government. Recent violent dissent over
the nation's commitment in Southeast Asia may well
border on irresponsibility.

The diplomat must face up to his responsibility
of carrying a heavy share of the politico-military
burden in limited war and resist the temptation to
abdicate in favor of the soldier in other than
purely technical military matters. The diplomat
must assert himself to be certain that the political implications of even predominantly military operations are fully explored. Finally, the diplomat
must familiarize himself sufficiently with military
affairs so that he can participate intelligently in
politico-military deliberations.

The military professional must come to accept
the fact that in limited war there are "limitations"
within which he will be required to conduct his
operations and that those limitations are a necessary constraint in pursuit of the national objective. The military professional must recognize
that in limited war military victory and the national objective are not necessarily synonymous,
that the political side of the politico-military
equation may well be the most heavily weighted side,
and that the diplomat and not he may be playing the
leading role. The soldier must also familiarize
himself sufficiently with international political
affairs so that he can participate intelligently in
politico-military deliberations. Lastly, the military professional must come to realize that, while
technical proficiency continues to be a necessary
attribute of the military professional, the "ordered application of force in resolution of a social problem," in the less-than-total-war environment, will require an unprecedented degree of true
military professionalism.

It is difficult at best for a nation like the
United States to fight a limited war. While there
is a certain amount of skill required to lead a

nation on a "crusade," it requires infinitely
greater skill and leadership to lead a nation in
the contemporary, less-than-total-war environment.
The national policy makers must deal with more diverse factors and react in a shorter time than ever
before in the nation's history. The diplomat and
the soldier must maintain their own professional
skills at the highest level ever expected of them
and still develop a deep appreciation for their mutual relationships within the politico-military
equation and to the overall national objective.
The public, through education and maturity, must
develop techniques for carrying out constructive
debate on major national policy matters and must
further develop a type of patience that will come
only from a true understanding of the politico-
military realities of today's world.

    Admitting that the above thoughts are perhaps
more than a bit idealistic and esoteric, it would
seem that the United States must develop a relevant
concept of victory if the nation is to remain a
great power in the world today. The alternatives
are total war with untold destruction or voluntary
abdication of great power status, neither of which
are acceptable. Within the framework of the elusive concept of victory, the British poet Robert
Southy, in "After Blenheim," articulated a thought
that may well be pondered by the American political
scientist, diplomat, and soldier:

            And everybody praised the Duke
              Who this great fight did win.
            "But what good came of it at last?"
              Quoth little Peterkin.
            "Why that I cannot tell," said he,
              "But 'twas a famous victory."

NOTES

1. Quincy Wright, A Study of War, abridged
ed. (Chicago: University of Chicago Press, 1964),
p. 18.

2. Douglas MacArthur, A Soldier Speaks (New
York: Frederick A. Praeger, 1965), p. 251.

3. Mendel L Rivers, Address to the Navy
League, San Diego, Calif., September 26, 1966, Congressional Record, October 3, 1966, p. A5088.

4. U.S., Congress, Senate, Committee on Foreign Relations, Conflicts Between United States
Capabilities and Foreign Commitments, Statement by
Lt. General James M. Gavin (Washington: U.S. Government Printing Office, 1967), pp. 2-9.

5. Nathan F. Twining, Neither Liberty nor
Safety (New York: Holt, Rinehart and Winston,
1966), p. 104.

6. Harold K. Johnson, "Vietnam Revisited."
Speech delivered to the Economics Club of New York
on April 27, 1966.

7. E. P. Demetracopoulos, "Admiral Burke:
How to Win the War," San Diego Union, September 4,
1966.

8. John K. Waters, "A General Tells How U.S.
Can Win in Vietnam," U.S. News and World Report,
December 19, 1966, p. 56.

9. Norde Wilson, "Another Pilot's Report from
Vietnam," Aviation Week and Space Technology, October 24, 1966, p. 22.

10. "Dispatch From Saigon: A Fresh Look at
the Vietnam War," U.S. News and World Report, September 25, 1967, p. 62.

11. "Dirksen Notes Need for Vietnam Solution," The Washington Post, November 8, 1967, p. A20.

12. A. E. Jolis, "Victory or Submission," The New Leader, December 1, 1952, p. 7.

13. Richard Hofstadter, "Uncle Sam Has Cried 'Uncle' Before," The New York Times Magazine, May 19, 1968.

14. U.S., Department of Defense, Joint Chiefs of Staff Publication No. 1; Dictionary of United States Military Terms for Joint Usage (Washington: U.S. Government Printing Office, December 1, 1966), p. 84.

15. A. J. P Taylor, The Origins of the Second World War (London: Hamish Hamilton, 1961), p. 26.

16. Richard W. Leopold, The Growth of American Foreign Policy (New York: Alfred A. Knopf, 1962), pp. 552-56.

17. See pp. 28-33 of this book.

18. Sir Stephen King-Hall, Total Victory (New York: Harcourt, Brace and Company, 1942), p. 4.

19. Anne Armstrong, Unconditional Surrender: The Impact of the Casablanca Policy Upon World War II (New Brunswick, N.J.: Rutgers University Press, 1961), p. 249.

20. Ibid., p. 250.

21. Raymond Aron, Peace and War: A Theory of International Relations (Garden City, N.Y.: Doubleday and Company, Inc., 1966), p. 40.

22. John L. Chase, "Unconditional Surrender," Political Science Quarterly, June, 1955, p. 274.

23. Urs Schwarz, American Strategy: A New Perspective (Garden City, N.Y.: Doubleday and Company, 1966), p. 134.

24. Omar N. Bradley, <u>A Soldier's Story</u> (New York: Henry Holt and Company, 1951), p. xi.

25. <u>Ibid</u>., pp. 528 and 536.

26. J. C. Wylie, <u>Military Strategy; A General Theory of Power Control</u> (New Brunswick, N.J.: Rutgers University Press, 1967), p. 14.

27. See p. 48 of this book.

28. U.S., Department of Defense, <u>Joint Chiefs Staff Publication No. 1 . . .</u>, op. cit., p. 109.

29. Bernard Brodie, <u>Strategy in the Missile Age</u> (Princeton, N.J.: Princeton University Press, 1959), p. 309.

30. <u>Ibid</u>., p. 312.

31. <u>Ibid</u>., p. 313.

32. The Truman-MacArthur controversy is addressed in great detail in: John W. Spanier, <u>The Truman-MacArthur Controversy and the Korean War</u> (New York: W. W. Norton and Company, 1965); see also pp. 47-51 of this book.

33. Robert J. Donovan, <u>Eisenhower: The Inside Story</u> (New York: Harper and Brothers, 1956), p. 17.

34. Mark W. Clark, <u>From the Danube to the Yalu</u> (New York: Harper and Brothers, 1954), p. 233.

35. <u>Ibid</u>.

36. Sherman Adams, <u>Firsthand Report</u> (New York: Popular Library, 1962), p. 56.

37. David Rees, <u>Korea the Limited War</u> (New York: St. Martin's Press, 1964), p. 433.

38. <u>Ibid</u>.

39. Ibid., p. 442.

40. Richard Rovere, Affairs of State, The Eisenhower Years (New York: Farrar, Straus and Cudahy, 1956), p. 145. See also Clark, op. cit., p. 297, and T. R. Fehrenbach, This Kind of War (New York: The Macmillan Company, 1963), p. 657.

41. Irving Kristol, "A Matter of Fundamentals," Encounter, April, 1960, pp. 56-57.

42. See Roger Hilsman, To Move a Nation: The Politics of Foreign Policy in the Administration of John F. Kennedy (Garden City, N.Y.: Doubleday and Company, 1967), Chapter 13, pp. 159-229. See also Elie Abel, The Missile Crisis (New York: J. P. Lippincott Company, 1966).

43. Russell F. Weigley, History of the United States Army (New York: The Macmillan Company, 1967), p. 547.

44. For a work that asked the same question in a somewhat broader context nearly a decade ago, see Harry Howe Ransom, Can American Democracy Survive Cold War? (Garden City, N.Y.: Doubleday and Company, 1963).

45. United States Army Field Manual 100-5, Field Service Regulations; Operations, February, 1962, para. 110.

46. Ibid.

47. The American Assembly, Goals for Americans (Englewood Cliffs, N J.: Prentice-Hall, 1960), p. 15.

48. Charles O. Lerche, Jr. and Abdul A. Said, Concepts of International Politics (Englewood Cliffs, N.J.: Prentice-Hall, 1963), p. 9. See also Aron, op. cit., p. 30.

49. U.S., Department of Defense, Joint Chiefs of Staff Publication No. 1 . . ., op. cit., p. 129.

50. Ibid.

51. Quoted in William I. Gordon, "What Do We Mean by 'Win'?" Military Review, June, 1966, p. 3.

52. Bradford H. Westerfield, The Instruments of America's Foreign Policy (New York: Thomas Y. Crowell Company, 1963), p. 514.

53. Hilsman, op. cit., pp. 441-67.

8

YESTERDAY,
TODAY,
AND
TOMORROW

The purpose of this final chapter is threefold. First, it is intended to bring together, in summary form, the many factors that have been touched on in the preceding chapters and to put them all in some sort of meaningful perspective. Second, it ventures a glimpse into the future to identify the sort of politico-military environment that the military profession may expect to face. And finally, it forces the author out on the proverbial limb by coming up with some rather general recommendations for the profession in the next decade. In Chapter 1 the overall objective of the paper was

> to examine in detail the extent to
> which the requirements of this new
> dimension [military involvement in
> the foreign policy process] have im-
> pacted on the military profession in
> order to make a valid judgment . . .
> and to recommend courses of action.[1]

The methodology that will be used is to address the three basic areas suggested by the chapter title. "Yesterday" is put in perspective in a section entitled "What Have We Done?" The subsequent section, "Where Are We Going?" takes a look at contemporary thinking and identifies trends of "today." Recommendations for a direction for the profession to follow in order to meet the demands of "tomorrow" appear in the final section, "How Do We Get from Here to There?"

WHAT HAVE WE DONE?

Historically, the growth of the American military profession roughly parallels the development of the nation as a whole. In Chapter 2 it was argued that, while the nation was well served by many highly competent individual military officers over the years who possessed the requisite characteristics of a military professional, the nation could not claim a true military profession until about the turn of this century. Of more than passing historical interest is the eventuality that it was at about this same time that the United States came to be recognized by the international community as a world power and a force to be contended with in the international system. In the author's view there is more than a coincidental relationship between the emergence of the nation as a world power and the appearance of an American military profession. The casual relationship is from world power status to a military profession, not the other way around.

With the exception of some limited "quasi-colonial" type experiences following the Spanish-American War, the American military profession came of age in the era of total war and total victory encompassing World Wars I and II. The profession was next confronted with the limited war and limited victory era of the cold war and, not without some trauma, is still adjusting to it. Throughout the entire period of American history one can identify a thread, spun in the colonial period and woven throughout the fabric of American thinking to the present, that identifies a general distrust and reluctant acceptance of the "regular" military man

and an emotional preference for the "irregular" as
exemplified in the person of the rugged frontiers-
man of years past and the reluctant but heroic
draftee in Vietnam today. Neither of these ideal
warriors is associated with the "system" and both
are viewed as being somehow above it.

American literature, virtually without exception, makes the "irregulars" the hero who successfully defies and eventually prevails over the somewhat dense and unimaginative "professional." All
of this has a bearing on how the United States
tends to view its military profession and thinks
about things military. At the same time it bears
on how the military professional perceives his role
in the American system. One may like or dislike,
agree or disagree with the validity of the historical perspective suggested above. Deserved or un-
deserved, the perception is a fact of national life
and the American professional military officer had
best understand it.

In World War II, the American military profession became deeply involved in the formulation of
foreign policy as well as in its implementation.
Whether this came to pass as a result of civilian
abdication of responsibility or for some other reason is of little consequence in the effect it had
on the development of the American military profession. The fact is that it did come about and it
tended to shape both military and civilian thinking
as the nation moved out of World War II and into
the cold-war period. While, in the absolute sense,
professional military participation in the foreign
policy-making processes may have become less, military considerations in the making of foreign policy
remained dominant. The military point of view came
to be presented by civilians of the Departments of
State or Defense or by the White House staff itself. Relatively speaking, military considerations
continued to play a major role in the making of
foreign policy throughout the cold-war period.

Before the United States became directly involved in World War II, there came into existence

a number of organizational entities that were specifically designed to coordinate the impending war
effort and specifically to coordinate the military
and the international political aspects of the national effort. While World War II is, from the
American point of view, hardly a classic example of
the optimum integration of military and political
factors and the balancing of the politico-military
equation, the organizational structures to achieve
that integration had come into being and prolifer-
ated throughout the war and into the cold-war period. There was an organizational revolution. The
details of this phenomenon are discussed in Chapter 4.

     As a result of this "organizational revolu-
tion" there now exists a highly institutionalized
approach to politico-military coordination. For
the most part this has been a welcome and useful
development but it is not without a price. Institutionalized coordination of this sort tends to become mechanical unless great care is exercised to
prevent it. There is a great danger that a military officer participating in this coordination
will fall into the trap of arguing the military
case as an end in itself and lose sight of the national objective that the policy under development
is intended to accomplish. Unless he fully understands the politico-military implications of what
he is doing, the military officer will tend to argue for greater military weight in constructing
the politico-military equation as it pertains to
any given situation. The existence of the machinery is a device by which military factors can be
injected into national policy making but it also
provides a vehicle by which "excessive" military
emphasis can be brought to bear. The professional
military officer must clearly understand this.[2]

     Also as a direct result of the experiences of
World War II and the cold war that followed it, the
nation's military educational system has undergone
a number of modifications. From the point of view
of this study the insertion of politico-military

education into the system at various levels is the most significant development. The author is convinced that this educational experience, which has now been enjoyed by thousands of professional officers over a number of years, has done much to enhance the military professional's understanding of the political aspects of the politico-military equation. The results of the survey of The National War College are but one manifestation of this.[3]

The capabilities and limitations of the military educational system were pointed out in Chapter 5 and it was emphasized that it must not become the objective of that system to compete with that of the foreign service. The professional military officer must not be expected to duplicate the expertise of the professional foreign service officer. He certainly must remain the military expert possessed of a meaningful understanding of international political affairs. An extremely important aspect of the nation's contemporary politico-military educational philosophy is that it is most likely that the more senior military professional will find himself in the position where some sort of reasonable politico-military expertise will be required. The educational structure is so designed that the politico-military emphasis is at the top of the educational pyramid rather than at its base.

The proper balancing of the politico-military equation in any society depends to a great extent on the perception that society has of military affairs and the perception its military professionals have of the nation itself. This line of thinking was explored in Chapter 6 and the concepts of "militarism" and the "military mind" were examined. "Militarism" was generally defined as excessive emphasis on the military factors relating to the politico-military equation and it was suggested that "militarism" and "military professionalism" are not compatible.

In a democracy like the United States there are two underlying characteristics that contribute

to militarism. The first is inherent in the very
equalitarianism and liberalism that is an integral
part of any democratic system. A related factor is
the ideological fervor with which a democratic society takes on a military venture. When the military profession, which is a mirror of the society
it represents, allows itself to be caught up in
that same ideological fervor it loses its objectiv-
ity and consequently its professionalism. A military officer hopelessly caught up in ideological
emotionalism is incapable of placing the military
side of the politico-military profession in perspective and excessive emphasis, or militarism, is
the likely result. This admittedly is an extremely
complex concept but the author is convinced from
his own experience that ideological emotionalism
and professionalism are not compatible. It can be
argued, for example, that some of the "excesses" in
Vietnam (and other wars also) can be traced to ide-
ology taking precedence over professionalism.

The second factor is that the United States is
the most technically highly developed society in
the history of mankind. This means that the military profession is consequently technically oriented and has become dependent upon the American
industrial community to support its technology.
Through the years there has grown a mutual dependence between the military and industrial sectors
of American society and there is in fact a
"military-industrial complex" in the United States.
This complex can be looked upon as an evil development intentionally perpetuated by those involved or
it can be seen as a fact of life associated with a
technically oriented society. The author sees it
in the latter light. Regardless of how one perceives the military-industrial complex, it can
serve as a source of militarism if it is allowed by
the society to do so. Many military professionals
argue that there is no such thing as a military-
industrial complex and that its alleged existence
is a fabrication of antimilitary forces in the nation. It is the author's opinion, however, that a
positive approach that accepts the existence of the

phenomenon is the most productive way to deal with
it.

It is essential that the military professional
fully understands the two dangers mentioned above.
Only then can he intelligently participate in the
affairs of state, as he is called upon to do so,
and insure that the military aspects of foreign
policy deliberations do not receive excessive emphasis and result in militarism. The military mind
of the true professional military officer is the
nation's best defense against militarism.

The concept of the military mind was developed
to emphasize the requirement for the professional
military officer to understand the politico-military
equation so that he can in fact use his military
mind to insure that it is properly balanced. An
essential aspect of military professionalism is
that the professional be equally prepared to recommend the appropriate use of military force when it
is called for and to recommend the nonuse of force
when in his view it is not appropriate. Historically, when military professionals have recommended
against the use of military force it has been, with
some exceptions, for reasons of lack of military
preparedness rather than for more subtle reasons
of balancing the politico-military equation.

It is not the business of the professional
military officer to make political decisions, except in the most exceptional cases, or to make recommendations of an international political nature
in the planning processes. There is absolutely
nothing out of order, however, for the military
professional to ask the relevant questions if he
feels the political considerations are not being
given adequate weight.

The level at which the military professional
might logically be required to exercise a certain
amount of politico-military expertise was also discussed in Chapter 6. It was suggested that a concept of "levels of professionalism" might serve as

a guide for determining the level of politico-
military expertise expected of professional military officers. The point was made that the general
or flag officer who fails to understand the implications of the politico-military equation is not a
professional as the word is defined in this study.
He is, rather, a liability and not an asset to his
profession and his country.

From the viewpoint of the politico-military
equation, one of the most significant changes that
has come about in the move from the total war-total
victory to the limited war-limited victory concept
has been the perception of what it means to "win"
in the contemporary international milieu. In Chapter 7, where this concept is developed, it is suggested that there has evolved a rather profound
philosophical difference in the concept of victory
between the two environments. In the total war-
total victory environment the essentially fixed factor was the objective, "unconditional surrender,"
and the primary variable factor was the amount of
military force that would be brought to bear to
achieve that objective. In the limited war-limited
victory milieu the fixed factor has come to be the
amount of military force that could be brought to
bear, that vague concept called the nuclear thresh-
old being the primary restraining factor, and it
has become the objective that is the variable.

One might agree or disagree with the specifics
of the above formulation but there can be no doubt
that the concept of victory has indeed become elusive and that it has taken on a new dimension in
the contemporary environment. The always existent,
but at times forgotten, relationship between the
national objective and the concept of victory was
developed in the same chapter. Of primary importance is the fact that, in the limited war-limited
victory environment, clear enunciation of the national objective is an absolute necessity. The
dynamic nature of the objective makes its precise
enunciation an extremely challenging vocation. The
objective must be the key to the political side of

the politico-military equation. If it is not, military considerations will, by sheer weight, tend to take up the slack and an unbalanced equation will likely result.

It was argued earlier in the study that the concept "in war there can be no substitute for victory" was anachronistic as it was used at the time of the Korean War. It might be just as strongly argued that in today's highly dynamic international milieu, whenever military force is committed, "there can be no substitute for a clearly enunciated national objective." Without it, military victory tends to become the objective and an end in itself. The professional military officer must understand this victory-objective relationship and he must constantly press his civilian superiors for a political objective if one does not exist or is not clear.

The United States has created a military profession in the image of the nation itself. The profession has evolved from a small and rudimentary one at the turn of the century to the highly sophisticated one of today. Concomitant with this growth have been developed the concepts, organizations, and educational structures to support it. The American military profession has mastered the technology of warfare to an unprecedented degree and it constantly strives to come to grips with the politico-military implications as well. The United States is still possessed, however, of a military profession that is prepared to fight the last war.

WHERE ARE WE GOING?

Predicting the future, which is essentially what this section of the chapter strives to do, is a hazardous occupation even under the most ideal conditions. The gamble is rendered all the more speculative by attempting to include in the prognostication a glimpse of what the American military profession may well be faced with in the years to come.

The distance one can logically look into the
future with any degree of certainty of course
varies with the subject matter. In something as
dynamic as international politics a decade seems to
be a reasonable projection. To reach much further
into the future would necessitate a level of abstraction at which only the broadest generalities
could be drawn. To address a time frame of less
than a decade would be too short a period to have a
meaningful impact on the military profession. This
profession is essentially conservative by nature.
It took nearly three decades, including two world
wars and a cold war, to bring about the growth suggested in the preceding section. Next year the
American military profession will not be much different than it is today. Ten years from now, however, it could be drastically revised.

In the past it has been all too true that the
American military profession has been prepared to
fight the last war and the diplomatic profession
has been prepared to prevent it. In the decade to
come the diplomat and the soldier must together be
prepared to prevent the next war and, if that fails,
to fight it together. What sort of military professionalism does a great power like the United
States need to accomplish this end? This is not a
question of force structure--that is to say the
number of divisions, aircraft carriers, or bomber
wings--it has to do with the quality of the individuals who make up the military profession.

Of course, the question can be answered at various levels of abstraction. At the more abstract
levels the standard can be expressed in very broad
philosophical terms and general agreement can be
attained. At the lower levels one tends to become
totally immersed in specifics and bogged down in
detail to the point that no meaningful standard can
be identified. For the purpose of this argument
the revised definition of a military professional
cited earlier in the study will be used. The military professional is defined as "a commissioned officer on active duty who possesses the requisite

level of training, education, experience, and intellect to perform the duties that he might logically be assigned."[4] The fact that professionalism
is a subjective rather than a simple objective determination is important.

The imprecision of this definition is recognized and that part of it that refers to "the
duties that he might logically be assigned" clearly
raises many more questions than it provides answers.
The strength of this definition lies in the fact
that the military professional must be "trained,"
"educated," and to the extent possible, "experienced" in the direction of a broad range of functions that had in the past been on the very periphery of military concern. What the nation may be
expected to call upon its military professionals to
do is a function of the international and domestic
environments of the future and is again quite imprecise.

There seems to be general agreement that the
nation has come to the end of an era in the international arena. In his 1970 "Report to the Congress" President Nixon spoke of "a new era," when
he said:

> The postwar period in international
> relations has ended.
>   Then, we were the only great
> power whose society and economy had
> escaped World War II's massive de-
> struction. Today, the ravages of
> that war have been overcome. Western
> Europe and Japan have recovered their
> economic strength, their political
> vitality, and their national self-
> confidence. Once the recipients of
> American aid, they have now begun to
> share their growing resources with
> the developing world. Once almost
> totally dependent on American mili-
> tary power, our European allies now
> play a greater role in our common

policies, commensurate with their growing strength.

Then, new nations were being born, often in turmoil and uncertainty. Today, these nations have a new spirit and a growing strength of independence. Once, many feared that they would become simply a battleground of cold war rivalry and fertile ground for Communist penetration. But this fear misjudged their determination to preserve their newly won sovereignty.

Then, we were confronted with a monolithic Communist world. Today, the nature of that world has changed --the power of individual Communist nations has grown, but international Communist unity has been shattered. Once a unified bloc, its solidarity has been broken by the powerful forces of nationalism. The Soviet Union and Communist China, once bound by an alliance of friendship, had become bitter adversaries by the mid-1960's. The only times the Soviet Union has used the Red Army since World War II has been against its own allies--in East Germany in 1953, in Hungary in 1956, and in Czechoslovakia in 1968. The Marxist dream of international Communist unity has disintegrated.

Then, the United States had a monopoly or overwhelming superiority of nuclear weapons. Today, a revolution in the technology of war has altered the nature of the military balance of power. New types of weapons present new dangers. Communist China has acquired thermonuclear weapons. Both the Soviet Union and the United States have acquired the ability to inflict unacceptable

damage on the other, no matter which
strikes first. There can be no gain
and certainly no victory for the
power that provokes a thermonuclear
exchange. Thus, both sides have
recognized a vital mutual interest
in halting dangerous momentum of the
nuclear arms race.

Then, the slogans formed in the
past century were the ideological ac-
cessories of the intellectual debate.
Today, the "isms" have lost their
vitality--indeed the restlessness of
youth on both sides of the dividing
line testifies to the need for a new
idealism and deeper purposes.[5]

This rather lengthy quotation is used in full because it quite clearly identifies, in conceptual
terms, how the U.S. government perceives the future.
The quotation also, by use of the "then" and "today"
technique, makes it quite clear what the administration sees as the significant differences between
the old and new environments.

In the same document the president announced a
strategic military policy emphasizing strategic
rather than general-purpose forces. In a sense this
is a tendency back toward the "massive retaliation"
concept of the 1950's and essentially it gives the
policy makers fewer options for balancing the
politico-military equation. This can have two general effects. First, it can have the positive effect of limiting military involvement to those
cases that are so clearly in the vital national interest that the decision makers would be willing to
risk nuclear war. If the nation does not have the
forces to do so, the possibility of "another Vietnam" would certainly be reduced. Second, it can
have quite the reverse effect of so inhibiting
American flexibility of action at the limited-war
level that the only remaining options would be total nuclear war or total submission. This is not a
critique of the strategy but only a statement of

the extreme possibilities so that it can be placed
in perspectivein its relationship to the politico-
military equation.[6]

If the postwar era has indeed come to an end
and we are in "an era of negotiations," it would
seem, as one writer suggested, that the guiding
principles of U.S. foreign policy will shift from
the concept of "no more Munichs" to one of "no more
Vietnams."[7] The impact of such a shift in philosophical orientation will have a profound effect on
the politico-military equation in the United States.
A case has been made for the argument that military
factors have played an extremely important part in
construction of the politico-military since 1940.
There is a real difference, from the point of view
of military professionalism, between military factors and military men having a strong hand in balancing the equation. It follows, however, that if
military factors are heavily weighted, the influence
of the military professionals will likewise be felt
either directly or indirectly. Extending this line
of thinking into the next decade, it appears that
there is a good chance that military factors will
command less weight than has been the case. It
would seem to follow that the role of the military
professional in the foreign policy-making process
will likewise be reduced.

Someday and somehow the war in Vietnam will
come to an end. Regardless of how this comes about
the American military professional can expect to
receive little of the credit for whatever positive
results may come from it. The profession can, on
the other hand, expect to be the recipient of most
of the blame when the post-Vietnam finger pointing
starts in earnest, if in fact it has not already
started. This blame will be directed from the political left and right for quite different reasons,
but it will come and it will tend to weaken rather
than strengthen the American military profession.

The political right will point the accusing
finger at the military professional who tried to
understand the delicate politico-military balance

and who sought something less than total victory
from limited war. This group will forever believe
that the enemy should have been "bombed back to the
stone age" and will defend the military man who argued for a "military victory" without regard for
the political implications. The political left can
be expected to continue to speak in terms of a military monolith and will condemn anybody and anything connected with the military profession. The
fact that the nation's foreign policy, which brought
on the Vietnam involvement, was made for the most
part by "Cambridge professors" will soon be forgotten by both camps because it is not a clear image
of the nation's perception of itself.

Another aspect of contemporary American life
that will have a significant impact on the direction
in which the nation is heading is a new generation
of young men and women who will be influencing foreign policy to an ever-increasing degree. Regardless of one's personal views of the practicality or
impracticality of their thinking, it cannot be de-
nied that it is essentially different from that of
the policy makers of the last three decades. A
great deal has been written on "youth" in the United
States and doubtless there is a great deal more to
come. There are, however, several aspects of this
line of investigation that are relevant here.

With some exceptions it is generally agreed
that the younger generation today sees the cold war
as a tragic folly, foolishly entered into by the
policy makers of the late 1940's, and even more
foolishly perpetuated by the leadership of the
1950's and 1960's. In an exceptionally thought-
provoking article,* a recent graduate of the United

_____

*This article is significant not only because
of the youth and views of the author but because it
is representative of a type of article that has been
appearing more and more in the service journals in
the last few years. This is a healthy development
in which officers of all ranks, including the very
junior, are looking at the military profession from
within.

States Naval Academy explained it as follows: "In short, the young American of today looks at the military endeavors of the past century and sees a Don Quixote at work, not a Sir Launcelot."[8] Some may argue that this sort of thinking is not representative of American young people today. The fact that the young author received his education at the Naval Academy and not on a more liberal campus certainly lends weight to his point of view. He went on to point out that young people today, in and out of the service, are not motivated by the same forces that influenced their seniors.

The same basic thought is expressed in the Graham Allison article cited earlier. In commenting on attitudes of young Americans as he perceives them, Allison said:

> Forced to give a short answer, I would offer two propositions. First, the current preoccupations of our youth are predominantly, pervasively and indeed almost entirely not issues of foreign policy. . . .
>   A second proposition modifies the first. To the extent that foreign policy is currently important to most young Americans, their posture expresses a generalized desire to "cool" foreign affairs.[9]

It is not particularly comforting for those who have fought World War II and especially the cold war to be accused of tilting at windmills for the past twenty or thirty years while all the time they thought they were rescuing fair maidens in distress. Windmills or fair maidens, it is essential that today's policy makers and military professionals understand this view.

Another factor that will in all probability have a bearing on the weighting of the politico-military equation in the future is the personal military experience of today's youth. The author

is not prepared to present great stores of empirical evidence to support a suspicion, so the following thought is suggested as a hypothesis only. A
significant element of the nation's most capable
young men have actively sought means of avoiding
military service in the decade of the 1960's. The
most intellectually endowed and the most financial-
ly solvent have done this by continuing their education in pursuit of graduate degrees and then
moved into the field of education or other voca-
tions that promised draft exemptions. Allison comments on this point:

> Not that many of the young Americans
> with whom we are concerned actually
> fought in Vietnam. Most of them
> watched it unfold on television, wor-
> rying about how to escape it by grad-
> uate school or other draft deferments.
> What is more important, many of them
> made the long march from belief in,
> or silent approval of the war, through
> doubt about what the government was
> doing, to active opposition.[10]

From this proposition two subordinate, but
highly consequential, factors evolve. First, a
significant number of the younger teachers at both
the secondary and college levels have drifted into
the teaching profession essentially as a device for
avoiding military service. The impact these young
men have had and will continue to have on the
younger people whome they teach cannot be overlooked. Secondly, this group of young men will
quite likely come to constitute a great segment of
the intellectual elite in the country and may well
be the "whiz kids" of subsequent administrations.*

----

*The possible effect of these teachers on sec-
ondary school students was brought to the author's
attention in a recent conversation with an educator
employed by the Pennsylvania school system.

Without wishing to detract in any way from the motivation, morality, or intellectual capacity of this group, it is simply pointed out that they are human with human strengths and weaknesses. Psychologically, it would seem, they would be prone to rationalize their way around decisions that would commit still another generation of young men to a military confrontation, which they themselves succeeded in avoiding, no matter how much such a commitment might be called for in the national interest. The concern is not that too much emphasis will be given to the political side of the politico-military equation. The nation has experienced too many situations when political factors received inadequate emphasis and knows full well the unhappy consequences. The concern is that military considerations will be rejected out of hand, probably unintentionally and for the psychological reasons suggested above, with equally unhappy results for the future of American democracy. The professional military officer must understand, fully understand, the possibility of this phenomenon developing and must be prepared to work with it intelligently.

The preceding paragraphs on the orientation of young Americans have dealt essentially with the non-military community. But what about the young man who becomes a military officer whether on a temporary basis or with the intent of becoming a professional? He too is part of the younger generation and he brings with him to the military profession a different orientation from that of his seniors. It seems only logical to assume that there is a "generation gap" in the military officer corps just as there is in American society as a whole.

The thought that there is a generation gap of sorts is supported by a study done by a young naval officer at the Naval War College in 1970. In the study, the "older" group of officers was represented by the Naval War College students and the "younger" group by students of the Naval Officer Candidate School. Some of the conclusions follow:

On most questions more of the younger
officers are liberals. They tend to
be more concerned with domestic issues than international issues, more
worried about issues of social justice, less worried about issues of
social justice, less worried about
issues of national security, somewhat
more often are likely isolationists,
and in any given circumstances less
often favor the use of military force,
all compared with the group of more
senior officers. . . . The typical
officer candidate as sketched in the
survey is no more a wild-eyed radical
than is the typical War College student a militarist--though there may
be an example or two of each in each
group.[11]

Professional officers who entered the service
during World War II served as junior officers in
that war but really learned their professionalism
in the cold war milieu. Generally speaking, most
flag and general officers on active duty today adjusted to the cold war environment better than did
their seniors who were the flag and general officers in the total-war environment. By the same
token, the young officer on active duty today will,
in all probability, find it easier to adjust to the
"new era," whatever that may eventually be, than
will today's senior officers. If, however, there
is any validity to the process of politico-military
sophistication for the military professional suggested in earlier chapters, the transition into
whatever is to come should be somewhat less trau-
matic at all levels than it had been in the past.

In Chapter 3 it was stated that the Korean War
was probably the most professionally fought war in
the nation's history. The reason was that the
Korean War was the first war since the profession
came of age in which the nation did not become

fully immersed both physically and ideologically.
It was, in fact, the first limited war the American
military profession was called upon to fight. From
the viewpoint of tactical operations the Korean War
was not unlike World War II. While the professional military officer found it necessary to adjust
his strategic concepts and his politico-military
thinking to conform to the limited war-limited victory concepts he was at least still on familiar
ground tactically. The military professional had
the requisite training, education, and experience
to do what he could logically be called upon to do.
At both levels of professionalism identified in
Chapter 6 (technical military expertise and politico-
military expertise), the Korean War was reasonably
well done.

The professionalism displayed in the Vietnam
War was intentionally not commented on in Chapter 3.
The logical progression would have been to recognize the high level of professionalism in Korea and
then go on to say that the war in Vietnam placed
even greater demands on the profession, that the
profession rose to the challenge, and that it displayed the highest level of professionalism in its
history in that conflict. Unfortunately, in the
author's view, the record does not support what
logic dictates.

The American military profession is going to
have to "live down" Vietnam--but only partly--for
reasons of overall unpopularity suggested above.
The military profession as a whole has done a su-
perb job in Vietnam at the first level of professionalism, that which emphasizes military technology. The techniques that were developed for tactical operations were, for example, without prece-
dent in American military history. Technically the
war has been well done. The weakness has been at
the second level of professionalism, that which
deals with politico-military expertise. This weakness was manifested primarily by those officers at
and beyond mid-career, serving on the spot, in
Vietnam.

The criticisms that are most apparent are leveled primarily at the army, because forces of that
service have been present on the ground in the vil-
lages and hamlets throughout the countryside. The
air force and navy cannot escape a share of the
criticism, but the nature of their operations was
rather more at the first level of professionalism
and in that sense less professionally demanding.
Standing offshore and providing naval gunfire support in response to onshore requests is one thing.
Being onshore among the population and in contact
with the enemy and having to weigh the consequences
of the requested fire support is quite another
matter.

Essentially the failure of American military
professionalism in Vietnam centers on the fact that
the techniques that were used to bring force to
bear, well done though they were, were frequently
inconsistent with the political objective. The
"ordered application of force in resolution of a
social problem" was not all that "ordered." The
reason for the application of force was often perceived in World War II and Korean War terms, and at
least initially the political objective was perceived in something resembling Korean terms. The
war in Vietnam was none of these and the American
military profession did not really come to fully
understand the war until about mid-1968. The fall
of 1968 saw the initiation of the "Accelerated
Pacification Campaign" which, in the view of many
observers, was the first truly politico-military
step toward bringing the war to a conclusion.

Henry Kissinger, shortly before he himself became an academician turned full-time White House
policy maker, criticized the military strategy as
being essentially irrelevant to the problem at hand.
He argued that "by opting for military victory
through attrition, the American strategy produced
what came to be the characteristic gesture of the
Vietnamese war: military success that could not be
translated into permanent political advantage."[12]
Townsend Hoopes, a ranking member of the Defense

Department during the time this strategy was initiated, observed that "it remained a miracle, and
in the last analysis a major failure of leadership
that . . . Washington did not seriously question or
modify the . . . strategy of attrition."[13]

   In retrospect, it is argued that a basic mis-
perception of the politico-military realities of
the war manifested itself in the strategy of attrition that was embarked upon at the time U.S. combat
units were committed. It must be clearly noted
that, as stated by Mr. Hoopes, there was no massive
outcry from the administration, the Congress, or
the public at the time. That was to come later
when the strategy proved to be costly and unpopular.
However, it was the execution of the strategy, not
the strategy itself, that raised some hard questions about military professionalism. For practical purposes, attrition became the guiding principle and from it evolved such reporting techniques
as "body count" and "kill ratio." Soon those techniques became ends in themselves and the political
reasoning behind it all became even more obscure.

   Professional reputations were made or lost on
the basis of those reporting techniques and the
relationship of it all to the politico-military
equation was seldom considered. The war in Vietnam
has produced many colonels and generals (and navy
captains and admirals) who earned their rank as
"technicians" not "professionals" and whose definition of the military professional would be quite
different from that used in this study. Many of
those officers have moved to key command and staff
positions in the several services and their perceptions of professionalism now carry great weight.
Of equal concern are the thousands of junior officers who saw their seniors succeed or fail on a
"technical" rather than a "professional" basis.
Their perceptions of military professionalism must
certainly be distorted accordingly. The nation,
probably through indifference, was satisfied with
the technical approach and it was not until revelations of the incidences at places like My Lai came

to light that a now "righteously indignant" public began to ask what had happened to the professionals. The major responsibility, however, rests with the American profession of arms. The profession was faced with a new and unprecedented challenge and it failed to meet that challenge fully. What had been taught in the educational system about politico-military affairs was not carried over to the battle-field. In many respects, this conclusion does not seem to be consistent with the findings of The National War College survey referred to previously in this study. The author is at a loss to explain this phenomenon and can suggest only that the "system" prevailed over what many individual officers may have disagreed with.

If one were to construct a graph depicting the increased demands on the American military profession from 1940 to the present, it would show a relatively steady and clearly perceptible upward movement with the sharpest upward turn in the mid-1960's, coincident with the commitment of major combat forces in Vietnam. If one were to portray the growth of American military professionalism on the same graph, it would generally parallel the "demand" line until it reached the point where it turns abruptly upward. At that point the "military technology" segment of the professionalism line would follow the demand line but the "politico-military expertise" portion of it would continue on as something of a straight line projection. A gap between what was demanded of the military profession and what the profession was able to deliver, at the second level of professionalism, is the result. For practical purposes this represents a "relative" decline in military professionalism.

This does not suggest "backsliding" on the part of the military profession but it does connote a failure of the profession to adjust to the dramatically changed demands. How long these lines will remain separate is conjecture. It can be argued that reflection on the Vietnam experience by the nation will precipitate action that will eventually bring the lines together. It is possible this will come about by a modification of the demands as well as by an increase in second-level military professionalism. It is argued persuasively by many that the demands were unrealistic and unattainable. Others would argue equally persuasively that the demands were realistic but the profession was reluctant or unable to accept the challenge.

There is abroad in the military profession today a deep conviction that it is the victim of poor civilian policies. In certain other segments of American society, there are equally strong feelings that the military professionals misled the civilian leadership into the morass that is Vietnam--either intentionally or through incompetence. The so-called Pentagon Papers that appeared in the American press in the early summer of 1971 provided ample ammunition for proponents of both schools of thought and served essentially to harden already preconceived prejudices.

The two perceptions suggested in the preceding paragraph combine to adversely affect military professionalism in the United States. The soldier's feeling of being "victimized" can lead only to unproductive self-pity and further isolation from the very society in which he is already something of an outsider. Irresponsible attacks by antimilitary factions will do nothing to enhance military professionalism in the United States but will only serve to turn it further inward. Both the American military and civilian leadership must recognize these dangers and take action to alleviate them. Considering the diverse and otherwise unmanageable nature of the American body politic, the problem of the civilian leadership is apparent. Considering the relatively cohesive nature of the American military profession it would appear that the segment of American society that cites "duty, honor, country" as the cornerstone of its professional ethic must show the way.

Returning then to the essential question that introduced this section, "Where Are We Going?" the following brief is suggested. The United States is moving toward an era of a more cautious foreign policy with noninvolvement, supported by the "no-more-Vietnams" philosophy serving as the guiding principle. The trend toward a military force structure that places more reliance on a "massive retaliation" concept rather than "flexible response" can be expected to continue as can the exceedingly low esteem in which the American military profession is now held by the nation as a whole. All of this in combination seems to demand highly imaginative and sophisticated military policies that incorporate the subtleties of a balanced politico-military equation for the future. This in turn requires a highly competent and truly professional military officer corps. The requirement of the next decade will be for more professionalism in the armed forces--the current trend is toward relatively less. If current trends continue, a balanced politico-military equation for the next decade is questionable.

HOW DO WE GET FROM HERE TO THERE?

This final section addresses the means by which the nation might go about reversing the trend of military professionalism and closing the gap between the requirements of the next decade and the ability of the profession to meet those requirements.

As has been suggested several times in this study, the American military profession is a reflection of the nation it serves. If the nation wants a military establishment that is professional at the first (technical) level and possesses a "body count" mentality as a substitute for the second (politico-military) level of professionalism, that is what it will get. If, on the other hand, the United States wants its armed forces to be possessed of meaningful professionalism at both levels, that

is what it will get.[14] In a democracy the military
profession does not and should not make the determination of what its role in that society should be.
This is, and must always be, a domestic political
decision made by the elected civilian leadership.
From the preceding chapters it is obvious that the
author feels the United States needs the second,
more inclusive and at the same time more demanding,
sort of military professionalism. The succeeding
paragraphs are based on the assumption that the nation will support reasonable efforts on the part of
the military profession to achieve that goal.

The first and by far the most important step
for the military profession is to recognize the
problem. Borrowing a concept from the preceding
chapter, it is a matter of identifying the objective. The problem is that there have been drastic
changes in the international and domestic political
and socio-psychological environments that present
the profession with the most demanding challenge in
its history. The military profession must accept
the fact that the postwar period is over and that
something different, but not yet clearly defined,
is taking its place. The objective is to maintain
a high standard of professionalism in the new environment.

Accepting the fact that the world has changed,
there are three broad courses of action that the
American military profession might adopt. One possible approach is to accept it all philosophically
and withdraw into some sort of social isolation as
was somewhat the case between World Wars I and II.
One of the most obvious factors mitigating against
this course of action is, of course, that because
the contemporary international environment is far
different from that of the 1920's and 1930's, the
speed with which the nation's security can be
threatened allows no such luxury on the part of the
military profession. Fortunately, there are very
few military officers who would recommend this
course of action. At times, one must admit, the
thought of withdrawing into some sort of a

professional ivory tower in the face of growing
criticism from nearly all quarters is not without
appeal. However, such conduct would be completely
inconsistent with the definition of the military
professional as used in this study.

In an article examining "The American Soldier
in an Equivocal Age," the vice chief of staff of
the army, after identifying "the temper of these
times," commented that "we need to put the role of
the military in our society into perspective."[15]
This is indeed sound advice, but the military profession cannot expect to identify this perspective
if it withdraws from the very society with which it
needs to relate. There would be no more positive
way for the profession to give credence to those
who take pleasure in emphasizing the negative aspects of the military profession than to turn inward as this course of action suggests.

A second approach is for the military professional simply to dismiss the existence of any sort
of a problem or to pass it off as a problem for the
civilian authorities and not the military. This,
of course, is the easy way out in that it does not
require any thought on the part of the military man.
If the problem suggested above proves to be unfounded nothing will have been lost. If, on the other
hand, the problem does exist and the military professional has not done his part to resolve it, he
will be guilty of gross negligence.

Even though any professional worthy of the
name would immediately reject this course of action
as a conscious approach, it may not be as unlikely
as it might appear on first examination. The possibility cannot be dismissed that the military man,
in his enthusiasm to get on with the more apparent
aspects of his professional business may fail to
recognize the problem at all. Whether the problem
is dismissed intentionally or unintentionally will
count for little. The consequences will be as
grave in either case.

The remaining broad alternative, and the only feasible one in the author's judgment, is for the military profession to remain clearly a part of the American society and to face the problems of the new era squarely. At the 1968 graduation exercises of The National War College, the secretary of defense emphasized the need for "brain power" in the military profession and the defense establishment. The profession seems to have no alternative than to apply some of that brain power to serious consideration of the professional problems that have been identified. At the outset, then, it is essential that the military profession understand the politico-military problem, face it, and consciously keep it separate from the problems of military technology.

By way of more specific actions, the military profession must constantly examine its vast educational system to ensure that it is responsive to contemporary requirements. The author is of the opinion that the trends in politico-military education are sound and must continue with increased emphasis. Closely related to its own educational system is the relationship between the American military profession and the nation's academic community. In the context of the particular problem under discussion, the military professional must come to understand the role of the political scientist in the academic community and his function in society as a "critic." The military profession has much to learn both directly and indirectly from the academic segment of American society. There must, in the same vein, be some rethinking by the services on the role of the "intellectual" within the military profession itself.[16]

Organizationally, the emphasis on institutionalized politico-military coordination must continue but it too must be constantly under study to insure relevance. Politico-military relationships are no more immune from the bureaucratic proclivity to proliferate unnecessarily than any other activity. The requirement for close and continuous coordination grows daily. The possibility exists that this

coordination might be more effectively carried out
by some completely different organizational concept.
The structure must be dynamic, receptive to improvement, and constantly under review.

Each of the military services, in its own way,
must do some professional soul searching with reference to its traditional personnel policies. The
historic preference for generalization over specialization as the route to high rank and responsibility must be carefully reviewed. It was suggested in an earlier chapter that the military profession tends toward more and more generalization
while most other professions in the United States,
in the face of advancing technology, have tended
toward specialization. Does the American military
profession ask too much of its individual members
by expecting them to be expert in the techniques of
"the management of violence" and at the same time
to be equally expert at participating in the intri-
cate balancing of the politico-military equation?

The profession cannot renege on its responsibilities that are constantly more demanding. The
profession can, however, meet its responsibilities
without expecting that each of its senior members
be equally expert in all things. In a hierarchical
organization such as the armed forces one achieves
positions of high responsibility concomitant with
high rank. High responsibility with few exceptions,
requires understanding of sophisticated politico-
military relationships. The rank that leads to
those responsibilities, however, is normally
achieved by a "balanced" career that includes a
certain amount of time spent between command, staff,
and other duties, most of which are oriented more
toward the first level of professionalism.

Clearly, the basic mission of the armed forces
is to fight when called upon to do so. It is sometimes added, but usually in small print, that the
fighting must be done in a manner consistent with
the political objectives the nation pursues. This
is the "ordered application of force" mentioned

previously. Using the army as an example, other
things being reasonably equal, in today's environment the colonel who has a distinguished combat
command record in Vietnam but has little appreciation for the politico-military equation has a significantly better chance of becoming a general officer than does his colleague who has a distinguished
record in politico-military affairs but has little
or no command--particularly combat command in Viet-
nam--on his record.

This is a fact of life and it is certainly
applicable to the other services to an equal if not
a greater degree. The fact that a military officer
has demonstrated his ability to "fight" cannot be
dismissed as a matter of little consequence. The
question in today's highly complex environment,
however, is whether that is in itself the only, or
even the most important, qualification for higher
rank and responsibility. There is no easy answer
to this complex question. The author suggests that
acceptance of the "levels of professionalism" as a
conceptual approach is an essential starting point.
If this concept is accepted by the profession as a
whole and its civilian leadership, the necessary
personnel management procedures to implement it in
the several services will logically follow.

In the final analysis, the American military
profession must understand that military force cannot be viewed as an end in itself but only as a
means to an end. That end is achievement of a
given national objective and that objective is a
political one. Both the military professional and
his civilian colleague in government must understand that today's world is not the same as that of
twenty, ten, five, or even one year ago. Only then
will the American military profession be in a position to serve the American people in a positive way
and contribute meaningfully to a balanced politico-
military equation attuned to the decade ahead.

NOTES

1. See pp. 8-9 of this book.

2. See Adam Yarmolinsky, "The Military Establishment (or How Political Problems Become Military
Problems)," _Foreign Policy_, Winter, 1970-71, pp.
78-97.

3. See the Appendix. For a discussion of the
survey see p. 293 of this book.

4. See p. 165 of this book.

5. Richard Nixon, _U.S. Foreign Policy For the
1970's: A New Strategy for Peace_ (A Report to the
Congress by the President of the United States,
February 18, 1970) (Washington: U.S. Government
Printing Office, 1970), pp. 2-3.

6. _Ibid_., pp. 111-27. For a more complete
development of this line of thinking see Paul C.
Warnke and Leslie H. Gelb, "Security or Confrontation: The Case For a Defense Policy," _Foreign Pol-
icy_, Winter, 1970-71, pp. 6-30.

7. Graham Allison, "Cool It: The Foreign
Policy of Young America," _Foreign Policy_, Winter,
1970-71, p. 160.

8. David G. Deininger, "The Career Officer as
Existential Hero," _United States Naval Institute
Proceedings_, November, 1970, p. 20.

9. Allison, op. cit., p. 148.

10. _Ibid_., p. 157.

11. James A. Barber, Jr., "Is There A Generation Gap in The Naval Officer Corps?" _Naval War
College Review_, May, 1970, pp. 31-32.

12. Henry Kissinger, "The Vietnam Negotiations,"
Foreign Affairs, January, 1961, p. 212.

13. Townsend Hoopes, <u>The Limits of Interven-</u><u>tion</u> (New York: David McKay Company, 1969), p. 63.

14. Adam Yarmolinsky, <u>The Military Establish-</u><u>ment</u> (New York: Harper and Row, 1971), p. 419.

15. Bruce Palmer, Jr., "The American Soldier in an Equivocal Age," <u>Army: 1969 Green Book</u>, October, 1969, p. 29.

16. See Ward Just, "Soldiers" (Part II), <u>The Atlantic Monthly</u>, November, 1970, p. 70.

APPENDIX

May 4, 1970

NWC Faculty and Students:

I am in the process of preparing a doctoral dissertation with the tentative title of "Military Professionalism and the Politico-Military Equation in the United States." The thought of seeing you leave Fort McNair without taking advantage of all this assembled talent is too much--so I will impose on you by asking you to take a few minutes with the questionnaire I have attached. The questionnaire is very basic and may appear innocuous but I assure you that your views, coupled with other sources I am exploring will be most helpful to me. The NWC Class of 1968 replied to the questionnaire and your answers will serve as a basis of comparison.* The next few paragraphs explain what I am attempting to do in the study and some specific directions for answering the questions are on the questionnaire itself.

The dissertation will be based on the hypothesis that U.S. national security interests will be best served in the foreseeable future by increasing emphasis on the thorough integration of political and military considerations at the national level. It is further hypothesized that there will be a continuing and ever-increasing requirement placed on the professional military officer to become intimately associated with the formulation as well as the implementation of the nation's foreign policy.

The requirement suggested above has placed, and will continue to place, demands on the military professional that tend to conflict with his more technically oriented role of the application of armed force. The possibility exists that some

---

*The letter addressed to the faculty and students of The National War College in 1968 was identical to this one with the exception of the underlined sentence.

adjustments within the military profession in particular and in the national security environment in general may be called for to deal with the dilemma posed by these conflicting demands.

It is one of the purposes of the dissertation to examine the extent to which the conflicting demands have impacted on the professional military officer, either adversely or favorably, so that a value judgment may be made on the extent to which national interest is being served.

There is no intentional "loading" of any of the questions but semantics may well present a problem in some cases. Please read the questions and give your answers based on your impressions. If you wish to qualify your answer, please do so in the space provided for comments.*

Many thanks.

Donald F. Bletz
Colonel, United States Army

---

*In the space following each question the combined 1968 and 1970 responses are reported. When the respondents did not answer the question that fact is entered under "other." There were no significant differences in the responses between the several services and the civilian members of the college or between the 1968 and 1970 groups except where indicated. The comments that follow several of the questions are the author's and are used to amplify the figures where it is deemed necessary.

QUESTIONNAIRE

Directions: Most of the questions are designed for a short "yes" or "no" answer with an invitation to add any explanatory comments you may feel the urge to make. Please return the questionnaire to the Mail Room when you have completed it. Sign your name or be anonymous as you wish.

Please check appropriate box:
         Student _____   Faculty _____
         Civilian _____   Rank   _____   Agency _____
         Military _____   Rank   _____   Service _____

1. Do you basically agree with the hypothesis set forth in the covering letter?
Yes 96%   No 3%   Other 1%
Comment:*

2. In your view does adequate governmental machinery exist for the integration of the nation's foreign and military policies?
Yes 70%   No 29%   Other 1%

3. Do you feel the average civilian official who is involved in politico-military affairs has an adequate appreciation of the military side of the politico-military equation?
Yes 22%   No 72%   Other 6%
Comment: There was a tendency here for the military
         officers to express the feeling that their
         civilian colleagues did not fully understand
         the military problem.

4. Do you feel the average military officer who is involved in politico-military affairs has an adequate appreciation of the political side of the politico-military equation?
Yes 22%   No 71%   Other 7%

_____

*The space for comments appeared with each question in the original questionnaire. It is eliminated here to avoid needless repetition.

Question 4 (continued)
Comment: Quite the opposite from question 3, the
     tendency here was for the civilian respondents
     to feel that the military officer did not un-
     derstand the civilian aspects of policy making.

     5. Concerning questions 3 and 4 above, are you
aware of any trends in the last five years:
Toward more mutual understanding?   88%
Toward less mutual understanding?   3%   Other   9%

     6. Do you feel that the military point of view
is being <u>heard</u> at the highest decision-making level
in our country?
Yes   87%   No   11%   Other   2%

     7. Assuming the military view is being <u>heard</u>,
do you feel it is being given adequate weight at
the highest decision-making level in our country?
Yes   75%   No   20%   Other   5%
Comment: There was an increase of about 10% in the
     "yes" responses in 1970 over 1968 and mostly
     from the military officers. The comments by
     many of 1970 respondents indicated that the
     Cambodian decision prompted them to answer as
     they did.

     8. In your view is there such a thing as a
"military mind"?
Yes   53%   No   46%   Other   1%
     If you answered "Yes" above, what connotation
do you attach to the term <u>military mind</u>?
Generally detrimental to the national interest   43%
Generally contributory to the national interest 48%
                                        Other   _____
Comment: If you would care to try a definition of
     <u>military mind</u> it would be appreciated.

     9. Do you believe continued emphasis on
politico-military factors will dilute or strengthen
the professionalism of individual military officers?
Dilute   6%   Strengthen   88%   Other   6%

10.   Is there a place for a politico-military specialist in the military profession in somewhat the same sense that there are logistics specialists, etc.?
Yes _40%_   No _58%_   Other _2%_

11.   Is there a place for a politico-military specialist in the foreign service in somewhat the same sense there are area specialists, etc.?
Yes _53%_   No _43%_   Other _4%_

12.   In a war such as that in Korea and Vietnam, do you see the U.S. national objective as primarily a military or a political objective?
Military _3%_   Political _85%_   Other _12%_
Comment: There was a slight increase in "political" responses in 1970 over 1968.

13.   In your view is the "unconditional surrender" concept of World War II valid in the contemporary international environment?
Yes _5%_   No _91%_   Other _4%_
Comment: There was about the same increase in "No" responses in 1970 over 1968 as there was in question 12.

14.   The thought has been expressed that following Vietnam there will be a strong "isolationist" reaction in the United States. Do you agree?
Yes _75%_   No _20%_   Other _5%_
      If you answered "Yes" do you consider this to be in the best interest of the United States?
Yes _4%_   No _96%_

15.   A distinguished military figure recently said, "In the old days, war was war and peace was peace. Our nation did not ask its political leaders for a definition, 'Is this a "limited war" or a "general war" or a "total war"? When the nation was at war, Americans were at war, and Americans did what was necessary to win." Assuming the above was valid in "the old days" do you believe it is valid today?

Question 15 (continued)
Yes __9%__   No __88%__   Other __3%__
Comment: There was a slight increase in "No" re-
    sponses in 1970 over 1968.

    16. If you had answered this questionnaire
last September do you believe you would have answered
it any differently?
Yes __38%__   No __60%__   Other __2%__
Please explain your answer briefly: The purpose of
this question was to evaluate the effect of The
National War College course on the student's
politico-military thinking. Among those answering
"No," a great many commented that they had politico-
military assignments before reporting to the college
and their views were reinforced--not changed. In
1970 there were more who answered "No" for the reason given above.

                    _____
                    Name (optional)

SELECTED BIBLIOGRAPHY

Government Publications

Nixon, Richard. U.S. Foreign Policy for the 1970's:
A New Strategy for Peace. (A Report to the
Congress by the President of the United States,
February 18, 1970). Washington: U.S. Govern-
ment Printing Office, 1970.

_____. U.S. Foreign Policy for the 1970's: Build-
ing for Peace. (A Report to the Congress by
the President of the United States, February
25, 1971). Washington: U.S. Government Printing Office, 1971.

U.S., Congress, Senate, Committee on Foreign Relations. Developments in Military Technology
and Their Impact on United States Strategy and
Foreign Policy. Compilation of Studies 1-8,
Vol. I, December, 1959, 86th Cong., 1st sess.
Washington: U.S. Government Printing Office,
1959.

_____. The Formulation and Administration of United
States Foreign Policy. Compilation of Studies
9-13, Vol. II, September, 1960, 86th Cong., 2d
sess. Washington: U.S. Government Printing
Office, 1960.

_____, Committee on Government Operations. The Am-
bassador and the Problem of Coordination.
Study by the Subcommittee on National Security
Staffing and Operations, 88th Cong., 1st sess.
Document No. 36. Washington: U.S. Government
Printing Office, 1963.

_____. <u>Basic Issues</u>. Study by the Subcommittee on National Security Staffing and Operations, 88th Cong., 1st sess. Washington: U.S. Government Printing Office, 1963.

_____. <u>Final Statement of Senator Henry M. Jackson</u>. Submitted by the Subcommittee on National Policy Machinery, 87th Cong., 1st sess. Washington: U.S. Government Printing Office, 1961.

_____. Hearings Before the Subcommittee on National Security Staffing and Operations, Part 1, March 11, 22, and 25, 1963. 88th Cong., 1st sess. Washington: U.S. Government Printing Office, 1963.

_____. Hearings Before the Subcommittee on National Security Staffing and Operations, Part 2, June 14 and 17, 1963. 88th Cong., 1st sess. Washington, U.S. Government Printing Office, 1963.

_____. Hearings Before the Subcommittee on National Security Staffing and Operations, Part 6, <u>Memorandum on the Department of State's Politico-Military Organization and Staffing</u>. December 11, 1963, 88th Cong., 1st sess. Washington: U.S. Government Printing Office, 1963.

_____. Hearings Before the Subcommittee on National Security Staffing and Operations, Part 9, June 25, 1964. 88th Cong., 2d sess. Washington: U.S. Government Printing Office, 1964.

_____. <u>The National Security Council</u>. Study by the Subcommittee on National Policy Machinery, 86th Cong., 2d sess. Washington: U.S. Government Printing Office, 1960.

_____. <u>Super-Cabinet Officers and Superstaffs</u>. Study by the Subcommittee on National Policy Machinery, 86th Cong., 2d sess. Washington: U.S. Government Printing Office, 1960.

U.S., Department of Defense. The Armed Forces
    Officer. Washington: U.S. Government Print-
    ing Office, 1950.

Upton, Emory. The Military Policy of the United
    States. Washington: U.S. Government Printing
    Office, 1917.

                        Books

Abshire, David M. and Allen, Richard V., eds.
    National Security. New York: Frederick A.
    Praeger, 1963.

Andrzejewski, Stanislaw. Military Organization and
    Society. London: Routledge & Kegan Paul, 1954.

Armbruster, Frank E. et al. Can We Win in Vietnam?
    New York: Frederick A. Praeger, 1968.

Armstrong, Anne. Unconditional Surrender: The Im-
    pact of the Casablanca Policy Upon World War II.
    New Brunswick, N.J.: Rutgers University Press,
    1961.

Aron, Raymond. The Great Debate: Theories of
    Nuclear Strategy. Translated from the French
    by Ernst Pawel. Garden City, N.Y.: Doubleday
    & Company, 1965. (Originally published by
    Calmann-Levy in 1963.)

_____. Peace and War: A Theory of International
    Relations. Garden City, N.Y.: Doubleday &
    Company, 1966.

Beard, Charles A. American Foreign Policy in the
    Making: 1932-1940. New Haven, Conn.: Yale
    University Press, 1946.

Bernardo, Joseph C., and Bacon, Eugene H. American
    Military Policy. 2d ed. Harrisburg, Pa.:
    The Telegraph Press, 1961.

Bradley, Omar N. A Soldier's Story. New York: Henry Holt and Company, 1951.

Bramson, Leon and Goethals, George W., eds. War: Studies from Psychology, Sociology, Anthropology, rev. ed. New York: Basic Books, 1968.

Brodie, Bernard. Strategy in the Missile Age. Princeton, N.J.: Princeton University Press, 1959.

Buchan, Alastair. War in Modern Society. London: C. A. Watts & Co. Ltd., 1966.

Clark, Harold F. and Sloan, Harold S. Classrooms in the Military. New York: Teachers College, Columbia University, 1964.

Clark, Mark W. From the Danube to the Yalu. New York: Harper and Brothers, 1954.

Coats, Wendell J. Armed Forces as Power. New York: Exposition Books, 1969.

Coffin, Tristram. The Passion of the Hawks. New York: The Macmillan Company, 1964.

Collins, J. Lawton. War in Peacetime: The History and Lessons of Korea. Boston: Houghton Mifflin Company, 1969.

Cook, Fred J. The Warfare State. New York: The Macmillan Company, 1962.

Cooper, Chester L. The Lost Crusade: American in Vietnam. New York: Dodd, Mead & Company, 1970.

Donovan, J. A. Militarism USA. New York: Charles Scribner's Sons, 1970.

Eccles, Henry E. Military Concepts and Philosophy. New Brunswick, N.J.: Rutgers University Press, 1965.

Eisenhower, Dwight D. Crusade in Europe. Garden
    City, N.Y.: Doubleday and Company, 1948.

Ekirch, Arthur A., Jr. The Civilian and the Mili-
    tary. New York: Oxford University Press, 1956.

Eliot, George Fielding. The Ramparts We Watch. New
    York: Reynal, Hitchcock & Company, 1938.

Feis, Herbert. Churchill, Roosevelt, Stalin: The
    War They Waged and the Peace They Sought.
    Princeton, N.J.: Princeton University Press,
    1957.

Finer, S. E. The Man on Horseback. New York:
    Frederick A. Praeger, 1962.

Fulbright, J. William. Old Myths and New Realities.
    New York: Random House, 1964.

Fuller, J. F. C. The Conduct of War. New Brunswick,
    N.J.: Rutgers University Press, 1961.

Furniss, Edgar S., Jr. American Military Policy.
    New York: Rinehard & Company, 1957.

Galbraith, John Kenneth. How to Control the Mili-
    tary. New York: The New American Library,
    1969.

Gavin, James M. War and Peace in the Space Age.
    New York: Harper and Brothers, 1958.

Ginsberg, Robert, ed. The Critique of War; Con-
    temporary Philosophical Explorations. Chicago:
    Henry Regnery Company, 1970.

Ginsburgh, Robert N. U.S. Military Strategy in the
    Sixties. New York: W. W. Norton & Company,
    1965.

Graebner, Norman D. The Cold War, Ideological Con-
    flict or Power Struggle? Boston: D. C. Heath
    and Company, 1963.

Hackett, Sir John. The Profession of Arms. London:
     Times Publishing Company, 1962.

Halle, Louis J. The Cold War as History. New York:
     Harper and Row, 1967.

Hallgren, Mauritz A. The Tragic Fallacy. New York:
     Alfred A. Knopf, 1937.

Halperin, Morton H. Contemporary Military Strategy.
     Boston: Little, Brown and Company, 1967.

Hilsman, Roger. To Move a Nation: The Politics of
     Foreign Policy in the Administration of John
     F. Kennedy. Garden City, N.Y.: Doubleday &
     Company, 1967.

Hoffmann, Stanley. The State of War: Essays on
     the Theory and Practice of International Poli-
     tics. New York: Frederick A. Praeger, 1965.

Howard, Michael. Soldiers and Governments. Bloom-
     ington: Indiana University Press, 1959.

_____. Studies in War and Peace. New York:
     Viking Press, 1971.

Huidekoper, Fredrick Louis. The Military Unpre-
     paredness of the United States. New York:
     The Macmillan Company, 1916.

Huntington, Samuel P., ed. Changing Patterns of
     Military Politics. New York: The Free Press
     of Glencoe, 1962.

_____. The Common Defense. New York: The Columbia
     University Press, 1961.

_____. The Soldier and the State. Cambridge, Mass.:
     The Belknap Press, 1959.

Jackson, Henry M., ed. The National Security Coun-
     cil. New York: Frederick A. Praeger, 1965.

Janowitz, Morris, ed. The New Military. New York: Russell Sage Foundation, 1964.

_____. The Professional Soldier. New York: The Free Press of Glencoe, 1960.

_____. Sociology and the Military Establishment. New York: Russell Sage Foundation, 1959.

Kauffmann, William W. The McNamara Strategy. New York: Harper & Row, 1964.

_____. Military Policy and National Security. Princeton, N.J.: Princeton University Press, 1956.

Kecskemeti, Paul. Strategic Surrender: The Politics of Victory and Defeat. Stanford, Calif.: Stanford University Press, 1958.

King-Hall, Sir Stephen. Total Victory. New York: Harcourt, Brace and Company, 1942.

Kissinger, Henry A. American Foreign Policy. New York: W. W. Norton & Company, 1969.

_____. The Necessity for Choice: Prospects of American Foreign Policy. Garden City, N.Y.: Doubleday & Company, 1962.

Lasswell, Harold D. and Kaplin, Abraham. Power and Society. New Haven, Conn.: Yale University Press, 1950.

LeMay, Curtis E. and Smith, Dale O. America in Danger. New York: Funk & Wagnalls, 1968.

Liddell Hart, B. H. Strategy, 2d rev. ed. New York: Frederick A. Praeger, 1967.

Lyons, Gene M. Education and Military Leadership; A Study of the ROTC. Princeton, N.J.: Princeton University Press, 1959.

_____ and Morton, Louis. Schools for Strategy: Education and Research in National Security Affairs. New York: Frederick A. Praeger, 1965.

MacArthur, Douglas. A Soldier Speaks. New York: Frederick A. Praeger, 1965.

March, Peyton C. The Nation at War. Garden City, N.Y.: Doubleday, Doran & Company, 1932.

Masland, John W. and Radway, Laurence I. Soldiers and Scholars. Princeton, N.J.: Princeton University Press, 1957.

Meade, Edward Earle, ed. Makers of Modern Strategy: Military Thought from Machiavelli to Hitler. New York: Atheneum, 1966.

Millis, Walter, ed. American Military Thought. New York: The Bobbs-Merrill Company, 1966.

_____. Arms and Men. New York: G. P. Putnam's Sons, 1956.

_____, Mansfield, Harvey C., and Stein, Harold. Arms and the State. New York: The Twentieth Century Fund, 1958.

Morgenstern, Oskar. The Question of National Defense. New York: Random House, 1959.

Moskos, Charles C., Jr., ed. Public Opinion and the Military Establishment. Beverly Hills, Calif.: Sage Publication, 1971.

Murphy, Robert. Diplomat Among Warriors. Garden City, N.Y.: Doubleday and Company, 1964.

Neustadt, Richard E. Presidential Power: The Politics of Leadership. New York: John Wiley & Sons, 1960.

Osgood, Robert E. Limited War: The Challenge to American Strategy. Chicago: University of Chicago Press, 1957.

Pogue, Forrest C. George C. Marshall: Education of a General. New York: The Viking Press, 1963.

Ransom, Harry Howe. Can American Democracy Survive Cold War. Garden City, N.Y.: Doubleday & Company, 1963.

Rees, David. Korea: The Limited War. New York: St. Martin's Press, 1964.

Ridgeway, Matthew B. The Korean War. Garden City, N.Y.: Doubleday and Company, 1967.

Sapin, Burton M. and Snyder, Richard C. The Role of the Military in American Foreign Policy. Garden City, N.Y.: Doubleday and Company, 1954.

Schelling, Thomas C. Arms and Influence. New Haven, Conn.: Yale University Press, 1966.

Schwarz, Urs. American Strategy: A New Perspective. Garden City, N.Y.: Doubleday & Company, 1966.

Stanley, Timothy W. American Defense and National Security. Washington: Public Affairs Press, 1956.

Stein, Harold, ed. American Civil-Military Decisions: A Book of Case Studies. Birmingham: University of Alabama Press, 1963.

Swomley, John M., Jr. The Military Establishment. Boston: Beacon Press, 1964.

Taylor, Maxwell D. The Uncertain Trumpet. New York: Harper and Brothers, 1960.

Thompson, Sir Robert. No Exit from Vietnam. New York: David McKay Company, 1969.

310   THE ROLE OF THE MILITARY PROFESSIONAL

Twining, Nathan F. Neither Liberty nor Safety.
     New York: Holt, Rinehart and Winston, 1966.

U.S., Department of the Army, Office of the Chief
     of Military History. Command Decisions. New
     York: Harcourt, Brace and Company, 1959.

Vagts, Alfred. A History of Militarism: Civilian
     and Military, rev. ed. New York: The Free
     Press of Glencoe, 1967.

Weigley, Russell F., ed. The American Military:
     Readings in the History of the Military in
     American Society. Reading, Mass.: Addison-
     Wesley Publishing Company, 1969.

Wright, Quincy. A Study of War, abridged by Louise
     Leonard Wright. Chicago: The University of
     Chicago Press, 1964.

Wylie, J. C. Military Strategy: A General Theory
     of Power Control. New Brunswick, N.J.: Rutgers
     University Press, 1967.

Yarmolinski, Adam. The Military Establishment.
     New York: Harper and Row, 1971.

Articles

Allison, Graham. "Cool It: The Foreign Policy of
     Young America," Foreign Policy, Winter, 1970-71.

Barber, James A., Jr. "Is There a Generation Gap in
     the Naval Officer Corps?" Naval War College Re-
     view, May, 1970.

Beard, Charles A. "Our Confusion Over National De-
     fense," Harpers Magazine, February, 1932.

Bletz, Donald F. "Military Professionalism: A
     Conceptual Approach," Military Review, May,
     1971.

Blumenson, Martin. "Some Thoughts on Professional-
     ism," Military Review, September, 1964.

Bundy, McGeorge. "The End of Either/Or," Foreign
     Affairs, January, 1967.

Chase, John L. "Unconditional Surrender," Political
     Science Quarterly, June, 1955.

Church, Frank. "The Korean Paralysis," The Nation,
     April 6, 1964.

Deininger, David G. "The Career Officer as Exis-
     tential Hero," United States Naval Institute
     Proceedings, November, 1970.

Doble, Frank J. "Samples of the Army Mind," Harpers
     Magazine, December, 1946.

Douglas, William O. "We Have Become Victims of the
     Military Mind," Look, March 11, 1952.

Fergusson, Charles M., Jr. "Strategic Thinking and
     Studies," Military Review, April, 1964.

Fleischman, Gordon K. "The Myth of the Military
     Mind," Military Review, November, 1964.

Flynn, John T. "The War Boom Begins," Harpers Maga-
     zine, July, 1937.

Fox, William T. R. "Civilians, Soldiers and Ameri-
     can Foreign Policy," World Politics, April,
     1955.

Ginsburgh, Robert N. "Challenge to Military Pro-
     fessionalism," Foreign Affairs, January, 1964.

Hauser, William L. "Professionalism and the Junior
     Officer Drain," Army, September, 1970.

Hofstadter, Richard. "Uncle Sam Has Cried 'Uncle'
     Before," The New York Times Magazine, May 19,
     1968.

Huntington, Samuel P. "Interstate Competition and the Political Roles of the Armed Services," American Political Science Review, March, 1961.

Janowitz, Morris. "Military Elites and the Study of War," Journal of Conflict Resolution, March 1, 1957.

Jordan, Amos A., Jr. and Schless, William A. "Social Sciences and the Military Profession," Military Review, December, 1963.

Joulwan, George A., Jr. "ROTC: An Academic Focus," Military Review, January, 1971.

Just, Ward. "Soldiers." (a two-part article appearing in successive issues), The Atlantic Monthly, October and November, 1970.

Katzenbach, Edward L., Jr. "The Demotion of Professionalism at the War Colleges," United States Naval Institute Proceedings, March, 1965.

Lane, Thomas A. "The Peace Talks Are Immoral," Human Events, July 6, 1968.

Lerche, Charles O., Jr. "The Professional Officer and Foreign Policy," United States Naval Institute Proceedings, July, 1964.

Lyons, Gene M. "The Military Mind," Bulletin of the Atomic Scientists, November, 1963.

Masland, John W. "The National War College and the Administration of Public Affairs," Public Administration Review, December, 1952.

McCloy, John J. "In Defense of the Army Mind," Harpers Magazine, April, 1947.

McConnell, John P. "USAF 1968: Real World Professionalism," Air Force and Space Digest, September, 1968.

Middleton, Drew. "The Enigma Called 'The Military mind,'" <u>The New York Times Magazine</u>, April 18, 1968.

Nitze, Paul H. Address to the Joint Session of the National War College and Industrial College of the Armed Forces, March 19, 1964, Washington, D.C. <u>United States Naval Institute Proceedings</u>, July, 1964.

Norman, Lloyd. "Top Brass vs. 'Whiz Kids,'" <u>Newsweek</u>, May 29, 1961.

Norris, John G. "New Call for Joint Defense Staff Stirs Fear of 'Man on Horseback,'" <u>The Washington Post</u>, February 3, 1965.

Palmer, Bruce, Jr. "The American Soldier in an Equivocal Age," <u>Army: 1969 Green Book</u>, October, 1969.

Paone, Rocco. "Foreign Policy and Military Power," <u>Military Review</u>, November, 1964.

Pearson, Drew. "Last of the Heroes," <u>The Washington Post</u>, February 7, 1965.

Reese, Thomas H. "Divided Loyalty for the Military Officer," <u>Military Review</u>, October, 1964.

Rehm, Thomas A. "Ethics and the Military Establishment," <u>Military Review</u>, September, 1970.

Selton, Robert W. "Rational Victory," <u>United States Naval Institute Proceedings</u>, February, 1968.

Senter, Raymond D. "The Dilemma of the Military," <u>Bulletin of Atomic Scientists</u>, December, 1963.

Sevareid, Eric. "American Militarism: What is it Doing to Us?" <u>Look</u>, August 12, 1969.

Shoup, David M. and Donovan, J. A. "The New American Militarism," <u>The Atlantic Monthly</u>, April, 1969.

Simmons, William E. "The Liberal Challenge in the
    Military Profession," Air University Review,
    July-August, 1966.

Taylor, Maxwell D. "Military Advice--Its Use in
    Government," Vital Speeches, March 15, 1964.

Truscott, Lucian P. "Body Count: The Degrading
    Illusion," The Nation, November 16, 1970.

Tyler, John P. "Decision Making and the Military
    Mind," Army, November, 1963.

Wallace, Henry A. "Militarism in the United States,"
    The New Republic, January 26, 1948.

White, Thomas D. "Strategy and the Defense Intel-
    lectuals," Saturday Evening Post, May 4, 1963.

Wolk, Herman S. "The New American Military," Air
    Force, April, 1966.

Yarmolinsky, Adam. "The Military Establishment (or
    How Political Problems Become Military Prob-
    lems)," Foreign Policy, Winter, 1970-71.

Unpublished Document

Hanks, Robert J. "The Role of the American Military
    Officer in U.S. Foreign Policy" (paper prepared
    at the Center for International Affairs, Har-
    vard University), Cambridge, Mass., April, 1971.

Colonel Donald F. Bletz, currently on the faculty of the Army War College at Carlisle Barracks, Pennsylvania, entered the United States Army as a private soldier in the summer of 1943 and served in combat in Europe as an infantry noncommissioned officer. He was commissioned from the infantry Officer Candidate School in 1946 and integrated into the Regular Army in 1947.

In the late 1940's and early 1950's Colonel Bletz performed company grade duties in the Free Territory of Trieste. Other foreign service tours include Korea in 1957-58 and Vietnam in 1968-69. In Vietnam he was Chief, International Affairs Division, Headquarters, MACV and later Deputy Commander, 173d Airborne Brigade. He has had several previous faculty assignments to include the Army's Command and General Staff College and the National War College.

Formal military education includes the Army Command and General Staff College, the Armed Forces Staff College, and The National War College. Colonel Bletz received a B.G.E. degree from the University of Omaha in 1963, an M.A. in International Relations from The American University in 1965, and is currently completing the requirements for a Ph.D. in International Studies at The American University. In the 1970-71 academic year he was a Fellow at the Harvard University Center for International Affairs.